THE
CHURCH
EMERGING

The CHURCH EMERGING

A U.S. Lutheran Case Study

edited by
John Reumann

with contributions by

James A. Bergquist Donald G. Luck
Philip Hefner Lee E. Snook

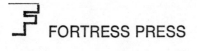 FORTRESS PRESS Philadelphia

COPYRIGHT © 1977 BY FORTRESS PRESS

Library of Congress Catalog Card Number 76–62618

ISBN 0–8006–1259–0

6182B77   Printed in U.S.A.   1–1259

In memory of
KENT S. KNUTSON (1923–73),
Pastor, Seminary Professor,
President of The American Lutheran Church, 1971–73,
and Chairman of the LWF Commission
which developed this study on ecclesiology:

He spoke for his church
He spoke to the churches,
He spoke of the Church.

CONTENTS

INTRODUCTION:
IDENTIFYING THE CHURCH
OF JESUS CHRIST
IN A TIME OF CHANGE

At times of crisis and maturing, the question of "identity" comes to the fore. "Who am I?" a young person asks while growing up, especially at crisis times in the early teens. Adults go through identity-crises, for example, when they turn forty or reach retirement age. Nations, too, can pause to ask about their identity; witness all the soul-searching in the U.S.A. when the nation turned two hundred in 1976.

The same thing is true of churches. There are times when internal questionings and events outside make even the Church of Jesus Christ ask about identity—Who are we? On the heels of the tumultuous events of the 1960s, the last part of the decade of the seventies is such a time.

This is so for theology in general, as Gordon K. Kaufman has observed in a recent review:

> About fifteen years ago the consensus about the meaning of Christian faith and about the methods of Christian theology, which had developed during the period of neo-orthodoxy, . . . —the authority of "the Christian revelation," the authority of the Bible and of tradition, the authority of pompous theological pronouncements made with dogmatic finality—began to break down. And throughout the sixties and early seventies a wide range of theological opinions were proposed or proclaimed. A new spirit of experimentation and excitement infused the theological scene as every new social movement or cultural crisis seemed to open up new theological insights, perspectives, and possibilities. This changed climate was exhilarating for many, but it soon became clear that what had supplemented the previous authoritarian

1

order was largely anarchy: almost anything that anyone wished to say might be called "theology."

The time has arrived for some careful attempts to reassess and define what theology is all about and how it is to carry on its works.[1]

Kaufman's remarks apply particularly to that sector of theology which deals with "the doctrine of the church"—its missions, aims, and purposes, its structures or order, its daily life and raison d'être, its underlying faith and rapprochement with the world.

"Ecclesiology" has always had its ups and downs. The late 1960s saw the topic peak and then fade and disintegrate. The Second Vatican Council, for example, brought the Roman Catholic Church new prominence and aroused great hopes; yet (probably in spite of the Council's reforms, not because of them, as some conservatives contend) that Church has suffered from defections by clergy, religious and average believers, and from worldwide loss of influence in the last ten years. This same period saw great hopes arise ecumenically for the union of at least many Protestant churches; yet such proposals as those involving Anglicans and Methodists in Great Britain have failed, and in the United States COCU (the Consultation on Church Union, or Church of Christ Uniting) remains an unfulfilled prospect.

Nor did society treat the churches very well in this period of great change. From the fifties, when the surge of World War II piety drove U.S. church membership to record heights, a steady decline set in during the late sixties and early seventies which meant a drop in attendance and adherence. In this period institutions generally came under attack, and like education, religion did not fare too well. "Big church" felt repercussions, just as did big business, big labor, and big government. A lack of trust developed between local congregations and national church headquarters in many denominations, and local or regional judicatories expressed their feelings by holding back funds from the national church. Often this caused staff cutbacks and program curtailments, particularly in social action or political involvement activities—the frequent target of irate lay people in the pews. Yet local congregations often did not know how to cope with changing neighborhoods, shifts in society and social values, or the remaking of the world politically, scientifically, and economically. In many cases the neighborhood church went into eclipse or closed its doors. Couple all

1. Notes appear at the end of the Introduction.

this with a decline in vocations, the number of people offering themselves for full-time church service, and a kind of "failure of nerve" in faith itself—this was the period when secularism and "God-is-dead" theology began to have often unrecognized effects, and the breakup of neoorthodoxy and the demise of "biblical theology" affected the Christian enterprise—and you have a crisis for "the church" of epic proportions.

To this list of factors helping to explain the questioning of older ecclesiologies in the last decade must be added also the following phenomena. The charismatic or neopentecostal movement had the effect of moving some of the most dedicated believers in Jesus Christ outside the framework of traditional church structures. At the least this movement, as it emerged in mainline Protestant and Roman Catholic circles, challenged assumptions of the past about church, ministry, and denominational identity. A bumper sticker proclaiming I Found It, a reference to conversion to the new life in Christ, does not follow party lines! At precisely this time too, many denominations were going through a phase of influence from the "organizational development" movement, and were spending vast amounts of time, dollars, and energy to restructure and computerize, in the name of greater efficiency. It was inevitable that these two trends, toward local freewheeling cells of lively believers and toward managerial efficiency (often created from the top down) would be seen by some as conflicting: the Holy Ghost or the program-planning-budgeting system?

We have said little thus far of developments within Christian theology itself, but one may recall the concerns with new social-ethical issues during the period (from Selma, Alabama, to Namibia; the debate over how just was the Vietnam war; American obligations in the Middle East; the abortion debate); the death of theological giants of the past generation (Barth, Tillich, Bultmann); and the emergence of new ways of "thinking theologically" (as in a more "secular" Christianity, or "process theology")—add one's own examples to the list of changes.

The same holds true for Christian life and piety, whether in the lessons read and hymns sung Sundays in the local church or the prayer patterns (or lack of them) weekdays. "Change" was the order of the day. Even in so traditional a thing as lectionaries for Sunday services in the liturgical churches, Vatican II wrought greater change for Roman Catholics, and U.S. Episcopalians, Lutherans, and others who have followed the structure of the Ordo Lectionum Missae, than any event in fifteen hundred years of lectionary making. The songs sung at Mass, Morning Prayer, and the Lutheran Service—and the instruments to accompany them—shifted from chorales and organ to folk ditties and guitars in a way that would have surprised our grandfathers and made some of them remark, "The more things change, the more they are the same!" Worship changed, for better or for worse, in this period.

Finally, one cannot stress too strongly the lengthy agenda of concerns emerging from a changing world which impinged upon the church in the exciting sixties and seventies: black power and the call for reparations, not to mention the quest of other minorities for justice; the women's liberation movement; liberation theology generally in the Third World; world hunger, the oil crisis, and the panic or ennui over ecology. Then too, there was resurgence of other world-religions, not only in their native lands but also—with a new fervor—in the United States, so that "Hare Krishna" or "Allah" might be heard more often than "Jesus Christ" (except as profanity) in Times Square or on countless Main Streets. Inevitably, therefore, came a recognition that in "foreign missions" the church has moved in the United States from a role of "sending" missionaries to awaken "benighted heathen" in a Rudyard-Kipling world to a period, plainly visible after World War II, of daughter churches overseas rapidly becoming independent, to a new stage (where we have the wisdom to discern it) of "interdependent churches" laboring together in a concept of mission which includes far more than saving souls.[2]

Given all this ferment and unfinished business of the recent past and the uncertainties on the horizon ahead, one needs little imagination to predict that a major question for the final quarter of this century among Christians will be "ecclesiology"—What is the church, where is it going? What is emerging ecclesiologically, as we approach the nineteen-hundred-fiftieth anniversary of the beginnings of the church?

This book, a collection of four essays and some reactions, has been produced to make a small contribution to this topic, about (and for) the church which is developing out of these questionings, ferment, and change.

At the least, these chapters provide some case studies concerning two Lutheran churches in the United States. On a larger scale, they are part of a worldwide Lutheran study on the identity of the church amid its service to the peoples of the world. But since ecclesiology by its very nature cuts across denominational lines, it is hoped that these essays have something to say which will also be useful to many others than Lutherans ecumenically who struggle with similar questions. Finally, because of the way the questions are posed—by the world today in which we live, and deliberately from the manner in which the study process leading to these chapters has been set up—there is a desire to treat the topic in an interdisciplinary way, beyond the usual bounds of biblical studies, systematic theology, and "church language."

For some, the approaches and findings which follow are anything but traditional. There are those who may even take offense at the ways of doing ecclesiology pursued in these essays, ways which reflect the exciting sixties and the dilemmas of the seventies. Readers will find the pages less a road map of previously well-chartered paths we have come, and more an analysis of where we are and whither (it may be ventured) we as a church may be going—as we are dragged kicking and screaming, or march with banners flying, into an ever-changing world.

CONTEXT AND TERMS

On the pages which follow, the terms *identity, church,* and *world* or *humanity* or *the whole human being* appear frequently. They arise out of the background of an even longer study, as will be explained below.

Discovering "identity" seems everyone's concern in the sixties and seventies—blacks, women, new nations, even age-old institutions; so rapid and upsetting has been modern social change, so disrupted and discontinuous our links from the past. Indeed, one man in Philadelphia, a survivor of the Nazi death camps during the Holocaust, has started a museum in his home because he fears his fellow-Jews have already forgotten the events of the 1930s and 1940s and have lost their "Jewish identity"—just thirty-some years afterwards!

World, humanity, and *the whole person* have been set as referents in our essays because such is the context in which people take their identity nowadays. A deliberate attempt has been made to identify the church, not by traditional landmarks, but in the face of change and the data from the world.

For all this, even though the concern is with the church generally (catholic or universal), our focus, in order to provide specificity, will be on two U.S. Lutheran churches in particular—the Lutheran Church in America (LCA), and The American Lutheran Church (ALC). These pages will clearly show they were written at latitude 40° north and longitude 75° west of the Greenwich meridian (in the case of Philadelphia; or wherever the author's location happens to be in Ohio, Illinois, or Minnesota), and not "in Long. 30° W." (somewhere southeast of Greenland), as Lord Acton instructed contributors to the *Cambridge Modern History.* But this U.S. specificity—which makes each essay a case study on one facet of church identity viewed from factors in the world in which we live—is meant to be part of a larger whole, concerning the One, Holy, Catholic Church.

Perhaps a U.S. Lutheran willingness to examine itself, in light of a quest for larger identity, may be especially enlightening at precisely this time. It is no secret that, as Professor Robert H. Fischer has observed, "For many reasons North American Lutheranism is confronted with an identity crisis. In its larger dimensions this is a crisis in understanding both our churchly mission in the world and our Lutheran identity within the Christian ecumenical scene."[3] The most painful example of the present crisis, he suggested, is the cleavage developing within the Lutheran Church—Missouri Synod (LC-MS), particularly over the efforts to let *A Statement of Scriptural and Confessional Principles* by that denomination's president, J. A. O. Preus, function as a guide for scriptural interpretation (or more accurately, in order to reject "the historical-critical method" from any real role in understanding the Bible). For "solid Missourianism" *A Statement* looms as a new confession of faith. The LCA and ALC, the bodies reflected in the essays below, have rejected such a stance, but the current discussions and battles within the Missouri Synod cannot help but be reflected in what is written theologically and in the ecclesiology which is to emerge, at least among U.S. Lutherans. (One suspects the same issues lurk in other denominations and in other parts of the world also, however.)

The following pages will not deal with or be influenced by the new confessionalism of the Missouri Synod, for that body is not a party to the current Lutheran World Federation study process. But the very specificity of our case studies demands we note that one of the three major Lutheran bodies in the United States is going its own way ecclesiologically.[4] Part of the price for that direction in "official Missouri" is schism in the LC-MS, as congregations leave its membership to form the "Association of Evangelical Lutheran Churches" (AELC), beginning in 1977, the significance of which—for new configurations among Lutherans and ecumenically—remains to be seen.   Lutheran ecclesiology in the next few years is likely to be lively, and developments in Missouri are a part of the change which will contribute to the church, or more likely the churches, emerging.

THE LWF STUDY INTERNATIONALLY: THE IDENTITY OF THE CHURCH AND ITS SERVICE TO THE WHOLE HUMAN BEING

For its sixth world Assembly in Dar es Salaam, Tanzania, June 13–25, 1977, the LWF set as a general theme, "In Christ—A New Community."   But already in 1973 its Department of Studies in Geneva began a major study to culminate in a report at the Tanzania meeting on "The Identity of the Church and Its Service to the Whole Human Being."   This study effort, which ties together many interests and embraces activities in over forty member churches on six continents, has usually been referred to more briefly as "the ecclesiology study."   The essays which follow are a part of the U.S. contribution to the worldwide study process.

Such thematic theological studies are not unprecedented in connection with the assemblies of the LWF, which occur every seven years. Thus, for example, the theme of the 1957 Lutheran World Assembly in Minneapolis, Minnesota, "Christ Frees and Unites," was addressed by Martin J. Heinecken in a lecture series that year.[5]   From the 1963 meeting at Helsinki, Finland, a number of papers and reports were published on the topic, "Justification Today."[6]   For the 1970 meeting (scheduled for Porto Alegre, Brazil, but shifted at the last minute to Evian les Baines, France, because of political difficulties) preparations were even more extensive.   From 1963 on, the LWF Commission on Theology directed its attention to "The Quest for True Humanity and the Lordship of Christ."[7]   In English there were published documents and reports from three national study groups (in Sweden, the United States, and the German Democratic Republic),[8] as well as a three-volume set of essays produced by American churchmen meeting for a two-year period in Philadelphia, Chicago, and San Francisco.[9]   While the efforts for 1970 engaged a larger number of theologians in the

United States and Canada than the present studies have—about fifty compared to forty this time—and over a slightly longer period of time, the 1976 essays probably have benefited from insights by persons in a greater variety of disciplines and areas of human expertise, and the worldwide study efforts for 1977 are far more impressive than ever before.

In part the breadth of involvement in the years from 1970 to 1976 stems from deliberate changes undertaken in those years and a new method of working adopted by the Geneva staff. Like many organizations in this period, the LWF restructured itself following the Evian Assembly. Nowhere was the change more striking than in what had been the Commission and Department of Theology. What had been assigned to separate departments or commissions—Evangelism, Stewardship, Worship, Education, and Theology—was now pulled together in a single area called "Studies." (It was symptomatic of the times—and of grave concern to some—that "theology" per se was no longer a separate unit but was expected to inform and interact work in a host of areas.) In addition to these inherited tasks and the assignment of existing and future ecumenical dialogues, the new Studies Commission and Department was asked by the 1970 Assembly to develop strategies for peace and human rights and to dig into the encounter of member churches with other cultures and ideologies. After 1970 the Commission changed from a kind of "high court" of theologians (eight in number, mostly systematicians, chiefly from Europe and the United States) to a group of nine persons reflecting much more the Third World and a variety of disciplines.

Change was heightened by the fact that the new Executive Director, Dr. Ulrich Duchrow, with his staff and the commission, sought after a methodology which would be both interdisciplinary and decentralized. That is, theologians would still play their part in studies, but along with sociologists, psychologists, experts in politics and economics, lawers, educators, and other specialists whose skills were needed to tackle new problems; and case studies, pertinent to each country or church, reflecting its situation, would be encouraged. No more "international ukases" from dogmaticians, or "perennial truths" to be exported for direct use elsewhere; theology is to fit and express the regional or local situations and traditions. Thus, for example, a 1971 letter to all member churches and national committees (which coordinate in a country like the United States where LWF has two member churches) asked for study groups which would focus on local manifestations of certain broad topics, employing "many different scientific and scholarly disciplines and practical professions." Underlying a great deal of the thinking in this methodology was a model which (to borrow terms from H. Richard Niebuhr) seeks neither to impose Christ over culture or let culture stand over Christ; nor to set Christ in opposition to culture; nor even to hope for Christ permeating culture, but rather to have a constant interplay, back and forth, between Christ and cultures. It is a model which rests, at bottom, on the classic Lutheran idea of "two kingdoms," as that has come to be more dynamically understood since World War II.[10]

The Commission and Department of Studies, from 1970 to 1977, under the chairmanship of Americans (first, Dr. Kent S. Knutson, President of the ALC from 1970 until his premature death in 1973; Dr. Fred Meuser, President of the Lutheran Theological Seminary, Columbus, Ohio, and the Vice-President of the ALC; and later Professor Karl H. Hertz, of the LCA's Hamma School of Theology faculty in Springfield, Ohio) eventually developed a four-pronged approach to its many tasks. Its project areas for the septennium included:

1. *The life and work of the church faced with new challenges.* Ongoing tasks such as lectionary systems used in worship (a question brought to the fore by Roman Catholic changes after Vatican II); the roles of women in the church; stewardship; theological education; scholarships for study in another land; Christian education in congregations; and communications—all were placed here, as was eventually the "ecclesiological study" with which we are concerned.

2. *Interconfessional dialogues, especially with Roman Catholics, Reformed-Presbyterian churches, the Anglicans, and the Orthodox.* Many concerns here are handled by the LWF-related Institute for Ecumenical Research, Strasbourg, France (the role of which in the study of church identity will be noted below).

3. *Peace, justice, and human rights* (a 1970 concern). The concentration has been on such topics as "A Multi-dimensional Strategy for Peace"; such practical concerns as education for social responsibility; and, with others, such places as Namibia and South Africa.

4. *The encounter of the church with religions and ideologies.* Under this project area an early decision was made to concentrate on Marx-

ism and in particular on the "New China" on the Asiatic mainland. A fortuitous choice in light of the thaw between China and the United States under Richard Nixon, this program has led both to independent studies and cooperative involvement with others, as for example in conferences sponsored with the Catholic Pro Mundi Vita organization.[11]

It is no confidential matter, however, that the new staff of nine persons in Geneva and its international Studies Commission had a difficult time putting together these many tasks and implementing its difficult methodology. Inheriting a mandate from Evian which may have reflected "a high tide in the concern with questions of social justice and human rights," the Commission had to struggle to show not only how theology was implicit in all it did but also that there was much theology involved at all, and "only with the initiation of the ecclesiology study" and "the fundamental theological question of the identity of the church"[12] did theology become really explicit in its work. As Karl Hertz put it in 1974:

> We are wrestling with the basic question: How do ecclesiology and humanity relate? It is the genius of the Confessions not to prescribe an organizational norm; organizational diversity has always been a Lutheran fact of life. But the Confessions remind us that organization exists to serve the gospel; we must ask whether it enables the gospel to do its proper work and how that work can find expression in the priesthood of believers and in Christian freedom. For example, in questions of peace and human rights, we must ask for the identification of the proper Lutheran accent, distinguishing tasks proper for governments from those of the churches, those which citizens should undertake through secular organizations from those where the churches must bear witness. The ecclesiology study should illuminate these questions as well as those asked in other project areas.[13]

How, then, did this all-encompassing ecclesiology study arise?

Initially the themes in Project Area I did not talk about ecclesiology as a subject, but a 1971 circular letter from the staff warned, "The churches must ask whether their concrete forms of life and work are structured in such a way that they can meet" challenges in "strategies for peace" and "encounter with other ideologies." Given concerns carried over from the theme of the 1970 Assembly, "The Quest for True Humanity, . . ." the currents moving in the World Council of Churches in the early 1970s, and the priority given in many parts of the world to liberation and even revolution in a time of change, it is not surprising that the efforts of LWF/Studies, Geneva, to "listen" to member churches resulted in a list of problem areas which sound almost exclusively "world-oriented." The response tallied in Geneva to a questionnaire about urgent "burning issues" in the spring of 1973 listed conflicts: (a) concerning development and the use of natural resources; (b) between male and female, and between generations; (c) in the political realm; and (d) involving church and culture, or "secular pluralism."

It seemed as if the focus for any kind of "umbrella" to cover these matters would reasonably be "The Service of the Church to the Entire Human Being." But three factors intervened to create a counter-focus, so that the topic eventually became an ellipse with two foci, "the Identity of the Church" being the other point involved. One factor, of course, involved the need to find an umbrella big enough for all the items raised by member churches in a survey of their "urgent issues." It became apparent that many of the issues themselves raised questions about what *church* means and how its service is to be understood in a changing world. Secondly, the Institute for Ecumenical Research in Strasbourg had in 1972 addressed itself to the question of "Unity in the Context of Theological Pluralism." The pluralism of contemporary theology and the existence of a certain diversity in material propria (or distinctive elements) in Lutheranism itself pointed to the question of identity as an important one, as did interconfessional dialogues. The ecumenical challenges and theological pluralism of the day cause one to reconsider Lutheran identity.[14]

Thirdly, and most important, was the catalytic effect of the now famous letter of the Evangelical Church Mekane Yesus in Ethiopia "On the Interrelation between Proclamation of the Gospel and Human Development." In January, 1971, that church's General Assembly passed a resolution asking LWF to approach churches and agencies in Germany and elsewhere "with a view to reconsidering criteria for aid" so that more funds would become available for supporting congregational work, training leaders, and providing for church buildings. Too often, the implication was, money had flowed in for social development projects, but not enough for the "obligation to proclaim the gospel to the ever-growing crowds expecting more than bread." A fuller statement followed from Addis Ababa in May, 1972.[15] The ensuing discussion, worldwide, was known as the Proclamation/Development

debate. It is worth recalling that the impetus for the Ethiopian resolution was a desire for help in coping with a growth rate in church
membership that was twenty-seven per cent in 1970; the plea was not
for "witness" and *against* "service," but in favor of a better balance, to
meet local needs, in light of the priority to "proclaim Christ" in "evangelical outreach." Thus the Mekane Yesus Church posed the question
of church identity, in mission, alongside the norm of "service" to people in the entirety of their needs.

In this way the overall theme for the LWF Studies Department
emerged. It was approached first by taking the four areas of conflict,
noted above, and trying to enlist participating churches on special
questions. Thus, Ethiopia, India, Indonesia, and the United States,
among others, were to deal with "development and the use of resources." (At times, in the LWF project, an attempt has been made to
pair participants on a "north-south" basis, thus breaking the stereotype
of "east-west" impasses.) It would be perhaps more accurate to say
that member churches, in the spirit of decentralization, directed efforts
to studies of greatest concern to them individually, and Geneva,
through a series of consultations, sought to share findings and work-in-
process and suggest some overall methodologies. An initial consultation in Addis Ababa in 1974 sought to define problems and develop
working hypotheses. Four areas of crucial concern were identified, as
noted above, and sharpened: resources; relations among men, women,
and youth; political crises; and pluralistic cultures. The second consultation at Bossey, near Geneva, in the fall of 1975, and the third in
Arusha, Tanzania, in October, 1976, carried the project forward from
the descriptive phase to the analytical and strategic. The goal is a report and evaluation for the Dar es Salaam Assembly in June, 1977.[16]

As a step from the descriptive to strategies for change, particular attention has been paid to analysis of theological criteria for defining
church. (This element is important to emphasize, in an approach
which has often been heavy on the social sciences.) The Augsburg
Confession, in a notoriously open and ecumenical statement about the
"marks of the church" (*notae ecclesiae*) lists only two, "that the gospel be preached in conformity with a pure understanding of it and that
the sacraments be administered in accordance with the divine Word."
But on the grounds that the "signs" of the true church are not limited
to these, and that both these activities are limited to the ordained

clergy—with the attendant dangers of institutionalism—the 1974 consultation directed attention to other signs of the church noted in Luther's treatise, "On the Councils and the Church" (1539), such as the "power of the keys"; functions and offices; prayer; suffering; and fulfillment of the Ten Commandments which concern the neighbor. Particularly when read and applied under conditions facing Lutheran Christians (black and white) in South Africa, the living transmission of the word of God points to a church that must be marked by identification with those dispossessed and by suffering—the "theology of the cross" transposed into an ecclesiological key.[17]

The variety and magnitude of the Geneva-inspired studies are amazing. The first two consultations included papers by a Mexican sociologist, Ethiopian "identity studies"; reports on women and youth from Tanzania and West Germany, and on pluralistic cultural contexts from Sweden and East Germany; plus a meditation on the Suffering Servant by Bishop Helmut Frenz—exiled from Chile for his work with refugees—and an address entitled "Wholeness Includes *Women*." It's a bit like attending an annual meeting of the American Academy of Religion or strolling the midway of a world's fair of religions, only here all is under the overarching umbrella of Lutheran ecclesiology and the world today!

It is worth reporting that two of the hypotheses developed in the course of the study have, in the opinion of the Geneva staff, become increasingly compelling: that (1) churches reflect the interests of their particular society or groups within it, and (2) specific theological elements in Lutheranism have been used to jeopardize "the identity and service of the churches through deliberate or unwitting toleration of negative elements in the environment." The "strategic phase" accordingly must go on to ask critical questions about "the shaping or reshaping of ecclesial organization" and "possibilities for change" and how a church can "extricate itself from its class interests and . . . take its place solidly with people in suffering social strata."[18]

The report to the 1977 Assembly thus results from one of the most extensive study processes undertaken by an international organization, at least by a Protestant church group. Over forty Lutheran churches engaged in some three years of self-studies. The findings put together by a team in Geneva amplify the earlier hypotheses. The conclusion was drawn that just as in business, so in religion, the Third World has been made dependent on the West. Hence the LWF was asked to "engage in self-criticism" so as to avoid "being used by some churches to dominate other churches"; to study the "effect of relative wealth" of Lutheran churches on ecumenical relations; to "redress any imbalances" on "the ratio of representatives between the northern and southern churches in the LWF decision-making bodies"; and to provide "Christian introduction to and an interpretation of Marxism."

North European and North American churches are asked to examine how they may be involved in "American and European exploitation and domination," and further to review development aid projects lest these "reinforce dependency." European "folk churches" are even asked to reassess baptismal and confirmation practices; ties with the state; the notion the "Herr Pastor" stands over against, rather than within, the local community; and indeed the whole concept of a dominant "institutionalized, professional full-time ministry."

Churches in Asia, Africa, and Latin America receive recommendations to ponder too: they have, all too often, adapted to their cultural contexts at the expense of the gospel, or failed to take into consideration the ethnic heritage of members. Native-born pastors are needed. Black and white churches in South Africa should be open to merger.

So wide the net of ecclesiology extends!

The four essays which follow are a U.S. contribution to this worldwide LWF study. The way of approaching ecclesiology in them may seem less strange to traditionalists when the broad study of which they are a part is taken into consideration. They reflect some of the burning issues prioritized in 1974. What they omit or include may seem more logical also when we look at other studies under way elsewhere and the approach which the U.S.A. National Committee decided upon when it became a part of the LWF project.

SOME RELATED STUDIES

It would be irresponsible for Lutherans (or any other group) to talk about ecclesiology without careful attention to often parallel discussions going on elsewhere in Christendom, ecumenical efforts in which Lutheran churches are themselves usually involved. First to be mentioned must be the work of the World Council of Churches, particularly in its Faith and Order Commission. Secondly, the extensive and often fruitful bilateral dialogues, between Lutherans and other churches, like the Roman Catholic and Anglican, are an influence. Thirdly, in the economy of theological labors, the research efforts of the Ecumenical Institute of the LWF in Strasbourg have a particular role.

There has regularly been an intertwining of sorts between LWF and the World Council of Churches. Both are located in Geneva, at the same address (150 route de Ferney), and LWF is obligated by its constitution to give priority to the existence and growth of the WCC. Granted, world confessional families have been a burr in the saddle of some ecumenists, and Strasbourg is not Bossey (the location in Switzerland of the WCC's Ecumenical Institute) or, vice versa, Bossey has had a totally different type of program than the research thrust at Strasbourg by the Lutheran staff, but the point remains: LWF study themes have reflected WCC topics, and there have been fruitful connections in both directions.

Surely the emphases from the WCC-sponsored World Conference on Church and Society (Geneva, 1966) and the Fourth Assembly of the World Council at Uppsala, Sweden, 1968, had impact on the LWF Study Commission's work concerning "The Quest for True Humanity and the Lordship of Christ."[19] Indeed, the "youth protest" movement at Uppsala and the Third World orientation toward "revolutions of our time"[20] at Geneva in 1966 both symbolize and set the stage for the mood of change in ecclesiology in the last decade. Likewise there was a sense of the déjà vu in the WCC's choice of theme for its Fifth Assembly in Nairobi, Kenya, November 23 to December 10, 1975: "Jesus Christ Frees and Unites." LWF had used that theme eighteen years earlier at its Minneapolis Assembly. But as the Lutheran Bishop of Holstein, Friedrich Hübner—a member of the WCC Central Committee—has remarked, "Lutherans too would speak differently today than they did in 1957 about the Minneapolis theme, because the global context has changed for them as well."[21]

The Nairobi meeting of the WCC, in an African setting like the LWF's 1977 Assembly, has been on the minds of those in Geneva and elsewhere who developed the Lutheran ecclesiology study, particularly the work of Nairobi's Section II, which dealt with "What Unity Requires." Attention has been directed to the fact that Nairobi reflected something of a shift from models of church *union*, as in South India, to the possibility of "conciliar fellowship" as having greater viability, and further that the role of confessional world families, like LWF, was frequently faced, with some desire expressed "to clarify the unique Christian 'identity' within given church traditions."[22]   Indeed, *identity* as "shorthand for the way mission conceives its goals," was one of the key words to surface at Nairobi.[23]

Given the ecclesiological situation in Kenya itself—where only nineteen per cent *of the Christians* are members of churches which belong to the WCC: twenty-three per cent are Roman Catholic, and fifty-eight per cent or 4.7 million are adherents of groups not in the WCC, often conservative-evangelical or native-indigenous or syncretistic in outlook—there was attention to the polarization which had developed since Uppsala between Evangelicals (Bible-oriented, evangelistic, and "fundamentalist" in the vocabulary of some) and those who advocate political action for liberation, even in "non 'nonviolent' ways."   While Nairobi did not deal with ecclesiology directly and centrally, it touched on the churches and their identity while serving in the world in many ways.   To quote a Lutheran participant:

> If Uppsala let the emphasis fall on action for Christian world service rendered in a sociopolitical manner, it did so at a time when the basic understanding of theology was in a state of crisis, and, when, correspondingly, the understanding of the church's task in mission was in a state of uncertainty.   Nairobi, for its part, signified a determined summons to a resumption of work on the basic understanding of theology and to obedience to the task in mission which Jesus Christ has given his church.   Only when set in this context can service in the world— from which Christians are not permitted to withdraw—express the freedom and unity which Christ has brought into the world.[24]

The concern for ecclesiology and all aspects of the doctrine of the church in interconfessional dialogues is so well-known as to need no comment.   What deserves note here is the fact that dialogue with other Christian churches has led to reopening, for Lutherans, of old questions about identity ecclesiologically, and facing of new ones, sometimes not previously ventured in the Lutheran tradition but now faced together with other confessional groups who are likewise groping in unexplored areas of the mystery of the church.   Space does not allow this to be the place for any sort of report, or even a full listing, on results in Lutheran dialogues, since 1963 with Reformed-Presbyterian churches, the Roman Catholic Church, the Anglican communion and the Protestant Episcopal Church in the U.S.A., and the Eastern Orthodox, among others.[25] Candor demands the assertion, however, that one dialogue usually feeds another, and since many of those involved in LWF's ecclesiology study are also participants in ecumenical dialogues, or at least keep abreast of results, what is said ecumenically with partners from other churches shapes thinking about one's own church.

As dialogues have proliferated, from twenty-six bilaterals in 1970 to forty-seven in late 1974 (and one suspects the progression must be geometric, the last few years, curbed only by tightened budgets), interest has risen among Lutherans, as in other groups, to examine the methods being used and then compare the results in one dialogue with those in the others; to check that a reasonably consistent stance was being taken all around, lest a church become "all things to all churches." Accompanying this was also a kind of futurist orientation which wanted to see which way(s) bilaterals might be going and to test the possibilities of a universal council involving all interested churches.[26] To meet some of these needs, LWF/Studies, Geneva, instituted a study on "Ecumenical Methodology" from 1973 onwards, which encouraged groups engaged regionally or nationally in ecumenical activities to evaluate their processes and forward results for consideration, eventually on an international scale.[27] Report on the project is to be completed for the 1977 Tanzania Assembly.

As part of the U.S. input to this LWF project, and because of American interest in the topic, the LWF/USA National Committee, Office of Studies, and the Lutheran Council in the U.S.A., Division of Theological Studies (where the Missouri Synod is involved), convened a task force of eight theologians who met in 1975–76 and produced a detailed report on "Ecumenical Methodology" in the U.S. Lutheran bilaterals with the Reformed, Roman Catholic, Episcopal, and Orthodox churches up to early 1976.[28]

Out of the findings in this study on bilaterals, which concluded that "positions taken by Lutherans in various dialogues do not in any overt way contradict one another," we note the following observations as pertinent for church identity: (1) developments in historical and biblical scholarship and changes in the situations of the churches help account for a common experience of progress in most dialogues; (2) participants, almost always trained-theologians, report the dialogues have contributed to changes in their own attitudes, and these changed attitudes are often reflected in their teaching of students who will be future leaders in the church; (3) impact of the bilaterals on the local level has been limited, except for a few cases (like Wyandach, New York, involving an LCA congregation and a Roman Catholic parish), but there are signs of desire to implement findings ecclesiologically; (4) there has been "a shift in attitude in the churches toward ecumenical relationships evidenced by openness and cooperation at many levels of their life and work," and if the bilateral dialogues are not direct cause, they serve at least as "a legitimation and ratification of the attitudinal shift." Influences from interconfessional dialogue in the 1960s and increasingly in the seventies cannot be left out of any picture of emerging ecclesiology.

A third related study which feeds into the international picture of efforts to examine the doctrine of the church in the mid-seventies stems from the Institute for Ecumenical Research in Strasbourg, France. Already noted above several times, this Institute is the center for the Lutheran Foundation for Inter-Confessional Research, incorporated in 1963. Its initial professor, Dr. Vilmos Vajta, has been in Strasbourg since 1964, and its library-study facilities were opened in 1965. Its staff of five, plus research assistants, is international and seeks to function as a team, specializing in historical, confessional, ecumenical problems. In many ways its chief focus has been Roman Catholic relations, but the Leuenberg Agreement between continental Lutheran and Reformed churches, and "secular ecumenism," have also been interests. There is heavy emphasis on publication (33 volumes, including translations, to date), among which have been a yearbook, *Oecumenica* (1966–72), *The Gospel Encounters History* series, and seven volumes thus far in *Ökumenische Perspektiven* and three in *Ökumenische Dokumentation*. There is far less of a teaching-classroom emphasis than at Bossey, though there is an annual seminar at Strasbourg (that in 1976 dealt with Christian identity, confessional identity, and Christian unity). Some 600 persons have attended seminars through 1976. In recent years there has been a far greater effort to share programs outside Strasbourg with member churches of the LWF or ecumenically, in Spain, Mexico, Madagascar, and elsewhere.[29] The Institute works closely with the LWF Studies Department in Geneva in the latter's Project Area II.

Already in 1972, during its study of "Unity in the Context of Theological Pluralism," the staff of the Institute began to see the question of Lutheran identity emerging as a fresh topic. The old characteristics no longer sufficed in a changing world. Bilateral dialogues had raised the question for some of whether the Lutheran side exhibits enough coherence to be a "trustworthy" ecumenical partner, and for others the fear that the traditional Lutheran confessional identity might be lost and fellowship already existing between Lutheran churches might be made more difficult or broken down. Furthermore, experiences with churches in different parts of the world and with Christians of many sorts who took part in Strasbourg seminars made clear the pluralism which exists theologically and the varying trends even among Lutherans. The Lutheran state churches in Europe found themselves faced with a need to examine an identity ingrained in the society and culture of their lands. Those in the socialist countries of Eastern Europe were having to come to grips with completely new situations. In Asia and Africa, churches planted by Lutheran missionaries were seeking to "indigenize." In Latin America immigrant churches had become more native and faced new challenges, as did Lutherans in Canada and the United States in their own ways. "Identity," it was observed, is a question being asked about in secular realms as well, involving racial, ethnic, national, and sexual consciousness and consciousness-building activities. Finally it became apparent that Christian thinking, after the social-action phase, had once again begun to ask "centripetal" questions: What is Christianity (Lutheranism)? What makes one's religious identity?

In 1974 the Strasbourg staff and Kuratorium (Board) began to formulate specific plans for what became known as "the Lutheran identity study." Its full title is "The Identity of the Lutheran Churches in the Context of the Challenges of Our Time." Envisioned were a series of papers on "identity"; "Christian identity and Christian identities" (the relationship between Christian confession of faith and various confessional documents); a similar one on Lutheran identity and self-understanding at various periods of history; Lutheran identity in light of bilaterals, and on efforts to define identity by Lutherans. A key item, to be produced by the Strasbourg staff, would be a working paper describing basic elements of Lutheran identity—to be tested to see how its hypotheses work out in various parts of the world, through consultations in Africa, Asia, and North America as well as Europe. Parallel and related studies in Strasbourg (see below), Geneva (as described above), and elsewhere, would be examined as part of the working relations with others, before the Institute staff would put together a report for the Dar es Salaam Assembly in 1977 and for possible publication. As part of the documentation on Lutheran self-understanding in the past, the Strasbourg staff accepted responsibility for editing a volume in a series "Churches of the World" to be entitled "The Evangelical Lutheran Church: Past and Present."[30]

Most significant in the process is a working paper on "Basic Elements of Lutheran Identity." In the 1972 colloquium at St. Paul, Minnesota, sponsored by the Institute in cooperation with United States Lutheran agencies, the Summary Report suggested, apropos of Lutheran identity:

> Lutheranism is a movement within the church catholic which continues to propose to the whole church, in continually contemporary language, those essential features (*propria* and parameters) of the church's theological understanding of the gospel which were especially set forth in the Lutheran confessional writings. Such are, in traditional formulation: a) justification by grace alone for Christ's sake through faith; b) the christological capacity of the finite for the infinite; and c) the way of identifying the church enunciated in Article VII of the Augsburg Confession. It will be noted that we have a diversity of material *propria* within Lutheranism itself.

The document went on to speak also of Scripture, which is "treasured by all Christians," so that the particulars of the Lutheran understanding are listed as:

a) the centrality of the word of God—Jesus Christ the living word and the proclaimed gospel;

b) the dialectic of law and gospel as a key for interpretation;

c) use of historical methods to discern the meaning of Scripture; and, in addition, "gospel and social justice" as an identifying concern.[31]

The draft on "Identity" by the Strasbourg staff has gone through a number of stages: the first "in-house" version examined by some fifteen Lutheran theologians in Europe and the United States and the Kuratorium; a second version reworked in 1975, and the document then tested in consultations in Bukoba, Tanzania, 1975; and in 1976 in Madison, Wisconsin; Edmonton, Alberta, Canada; and Gurukul, Madras, India; as well as in Europe. The several drafts have listed identifying Lutheran propria in the following ways:

(Earlier draft)	(Revised draft, summarized)
1. Witness to the meaning of Justification	1. God's condescension (cf. 2)
2. Confession of God's condescension (kenotic love which stoops to serve)	2. Justification (1)
3. Word of God and Scripture	3. Law/Gospel (4)
4. Law and Gospel	4. Word/sacraments (5)
5. Word and sacraments as means by which Christ creates and maintains his church	5. Priesthood of all believers (6)
6. Priesthood of all believers	6. Responsibility in the world (added)
7. Commitment to Christian confessions as means of preserving right proclamation of the gospel and church fellowship	7. Word/Scriptures (3)
8. Theological-critical quest for the truth of proclamation here and now	8. Confessions (7)
	9. Theological quest (8)

Of course there were more changes in the revision's contents than just adding a new sixth point and changing the order here and there. Final recasting may produce a different document entirely.

Criticisms are easy enough to make. The document is "too traditional," a kind of mini-systematic theology; or, it mixes "modern language" with traditional expressions and thereby "loses what Lutherans have always held." Or again: "Many of these points are shared with numerous other Christians, there's nothing particularly 'Lutheran' about them." The Tanzanian consultation wanted to add references to "the reality of evil and even the demonic powers," not just allude to "the unredeemed situation of humankind"; and something about church discipline, and greater stress on the Spirit and sanctification. In the U.S. discussion, Missouri-Synod voices questioned the stance on Scripture as "a mere collection of texts, . . . by itself not the active Word of God," while "only the Word of God as gospel . . . is the liberating message of salvation." Other Americans were critical that the "identity document" paid no attention to "the challenges of our time," as announced in the theme.

Here it needs to be noted that the document outlined above is really entitled "Basic *Theological* Elements as Essential Components of Lutheran Identity," and is only a *part* of the overall Strasbourg project on "The Identity of the Lutheran Churches in the Challenges of our Time." If it is asked where these challenges which help define current identity are dealt with, the answer for the Strasbourg Institute is that each church in its local situation must appraise these. But further, the Institute has had another project concerning "New Transdenominational Movements." These are among the challenges and include: (1) the Evangelicals, who stress Bible, conversion, an individualistic understanding of the Christian faith, and frequently a conservative attitude toward society; (2) action-centered movements, which want to immerse Christianity in the social-political problems of the world, stressing Jesus, liberation, and God's saving activity in political developments; and (3) the charismatics or neopentecostals.[32] It may be objected that these movements, which frequently transcend usual denominational lines and form church groupings of their own, are only a part of the spectrum of challenge, but they are significant ones—in Kenya and elsewhere. Nineteen hundred and seventy-six has been dubbed by American journalism as "the Year of the Evangelicals" in the United States, with the election of Jimmy Carter as President merely the tip of the iceberg; charismatics are a movement *within* Lutheran churches, raising identity questions, as well as a potent force outside; and the concern for social involvement carries over from the sixties and is a legitimate part of Christian and Lutheran identity.

The importance of the Strasbourg project is that it brings to the fore traditional Lutheran propria, while examining them within the context of specific church situations in different parts of the world, and being open to contemporary challenges.

THE WORK OF THE U.S.A. COMMITTEE

Given all these projects and studies in recent years, how did the two U.S. churches which belong to the LWF decide to go about participating in Geneva's "ecclesiology study" in such a way which led to the four essays in this book? The answer, in brief, frankly, is at first *hesi-*

tatingly; then, in light of *past experience*; and, finally, with allowance for some *creativity*, and toward *publication* in such a way that a larger audience might see how the parts come together in a global consideration of ecclesiology.

1. *Hesitatingly*. The Advisory Committee on Studies at the outset hoped to avoid yet another study! The two U.S. churches, ALC and LCA, it should be explained, relate to LWF not only directly but also through a "U.S.A. National Committee of the LWF." (In 1977 this cumbersome title has been replaced by "Lutheran World Ministries," but with the old descriptive phrase retained as subtitle.) The small staff of the National Committee, located in New York City, included one person, the Rev. Virgil R. Westlund, Ph.D., who handles Studies as well as International Exchange, the bulk of his time going into overseeing LWF-scholarship students coming to the United States and going abroad. An Advisory Committee of some nine persons[33] from the two member churches shapes program in studies, subject to the National Committee and its officers and in liaison with Geneva. In the late sixties the USA National Committee, especially in its studies role, was seemingly becoming vestigial, as more and more programs, including bilateral dialogues, were transferred from LWF/USA National Committee to the Lutheran Council in the U.S.A. (especially its Division of Theological Studies) where the Missouri Synod is a full partner. Besides, both ALC and LCA had numerous study/action programs and projects of their own going on. The one dark cloud which could overshadow inter-Lutheran cooperation in LCUSA and give a new reason for being to Studies in LWF/USA National Committee (where only two churches were members) was the impending conflict in the Missouri Synod.

Even so, when the Advisory Committee of LWF/USA National Committee first responded in 1973 to Ulrich Duchrow's invitation to take part in the then-emerging ecclesiology study, its expectation was that simply to list the studies then in process by U.S. Lutheran churches would be more than sufficient. In early 1974, when materials were sent to Geneva reflecting all the facets of the four areas of "conflict" noted in the ecclesiology study, some seventy documents were included, among them LCA Social Statements on "Sex, Marriage, and Family," ecology, and "Reform of the Criminal Justice Systems"; "Racism in the Church" (ALC); and Missouri Synod reports on the charismatic movement, women's suffrage in the church, and abortion, not to mention *A Statement of Scriptural and Confessional Principles.* Later, other major items, like the LCA "Theological Affirmations" and ALC bicentennial study "Toward the Third Century" could be included too.

To answer questions posed by Geneva of each national situation in its first "circular letter" of July, 1973, the U.S. Advisory Committee enlisted three churchmen active in social ministry[34] to frame responses. To the question of what "concrete, burning issue" serves as "starting point" for study in the United States of America, they answered, "Our burning issue is that we do not have a burning issue." (There was no willingness to elevate the Missouri Synod controversy over the historical-critical study of Scripture into a major issue for the rest of U.S. Lutherans.) How to relate salvation and service, or Sunday and Monday, was seen as a critical issue, though, as was the identity of the church in its cultural captivity. No particular aspects of the biblical message or the Lutheran tradition could be said to be currently divisive, but there is "confusion about how best to relate Christian faith to the uncertain world of the 1970s." Need was seen to amplify "the Christ-centered gospel" Lutherans accept, into "all of its trinitarian glory," to stress all three articles of the creed, and not just offer "sixteenth-century answers to twentieth-century questions." Social-ethical involvements were given high priority, and Namibia was flagged as a particular international concern. The statement closed with a warning, however, that "no universally Lutheran answer" should be expected from the ecclesiology study; that would smack of a "theology of glory."

2. *Past experience.* As the Geneva program began to take shape, the U.S. Advisory Committee, while continuing to forward study documents from the U.S. churches, decided in late 1974 to make its particular contribution in the form of a book. This followed past experience, particularly the study process and publications for the 1970 Assembly.[35] A subcommittee[36] was appointed to draw up plans for a volume on "the identity of the church in light of current issues." Careful consideration was given to the possibility of regional study groups, as many as six, on such concerns as mission; identity-consciousness among women, Blacks, Hispanics, Indians, and other minority groups; pluralism in society; natural resources; and problems of youth, the aging,

and the family. But, for reasons of budget and problems of coordination, the Advisory Committee in February, 1975, opted for a model of four essays developed topically around the following broad outline:

in
The Identity   light
of the Church   of
 	
The Church coming to self-
consciousness
 	
Questions to be asked in all
five topic areas:
  "What is the Church?"
  "What is the Church for?"
	I. The Struggle for Human Identity,
	  by women,
	    youth,
	    minority groups,
	    people in cultural captivity,
	    the aging;
	
	II. Developing Ideas of Mission
	  internationally ("Mission on Six Continents," the "moratorium issue," proclamation/service, independence/interdependence).
	  nationally,
	  in the local congregation;

III. Development and Use of Resources
  (Quality of Life Today), including human potential (leadership), natural resources (ecology, stewardship of the earth);

IV. Accelerating Change, and

V. Pluralism
  in Bible and traditions,
  in world religions and concepts of
    God ("process"),
  cultural pluralism.

Topics IV and V were later combined, for the total of four essays. The Advisory Committee committed itself to theological discussion of these essays as part of a timetable leading to publication for the 1977 Assembly. So that essayists would not labor alone, and to pick up a positive feature of past experience, regional study groups in the form of discussion and consultation forums were to be developed to aid them.

3. *Creativity and publication.* For all this reflection of successful past experience in the 1970 publications, the Advisory Committee wanted to produce seminal essays which could pose questions and merit discussion. There was a desire to give writers considerable room for creativity. (For that reason, each topic included a number of possible lines of development, with the author given freedom to select which he wanted to follow, and in what way.) No rigid limits on length were imposed. The regional study group (or local support

group), to be chosen by staff, with possible inclusion of a member of the Advisory Committee, was to reflect the author's interests and needs for developing his topic. (Those who participated actively in this way are listed at the start of each essay. It is fair to say that these local groups operated differently in each case, some meeting several times to consider ideas and drafts with the author, others acting really as consultants, more individually.) The finished essay remains the author's responsibility.

A deliberate attempt was made to seek out younger theologians or at least essayists not yet as well-known through publication as some who might have written. For a look at "the church emerging" it was a calculated decision to enlist persons under fifty, on the cutting edge of things, who are likely to contribute to, as well as be a part of, the church of the future. If the four essayists are all ordained, white, male, and college or seminary teachers, it is not because no consideration was given, or attempts made in the spring of 1975 to approach, lay persons, women, and others. How creative and lively the four Lutherans were who undertook the task of drafting an essay by early 1976, is for readers to decide.

The four authors met together in Minneapolis on May 31, 1975, for a briefing and planning session with Dr. Westlund, two members of the Advisory Committee from the area, and Dr. Duchrow from Geneva. One essayist participated in the '75 and '76 Department of Studies consultations in Switzerland and Ethiopia. Dr. Westlund kept in touch with all four of them, on progress of the project.

4. In production of this book, plans for the Advisory Committee to discuss thoroughly all four essays, with a meeting of the essayists (and their local groups), early in 1976, were thwarted, even though the Advisory Committee delayed its meeting from February until April. All four essayists had developed written outlines by October, 1975. The paper by Dr. Snook was completed in January; that by Dr. Hefner arrived for the April meeting, but because of their schedules, Dean Bergquist and Professor Luck were able to submit only outline/resumés, albeit rather complete ones. Naturally this meant there were varying degrees to which the essayists could incorporate the comments and suggestions of the Advisory Committee. To a considerable degree, those still at work in the summer of 1976 were most able to benefit from such ideas. But all essays went through at least two drafts, and constant

attempts were made to strike a balance between the demands of academic theology (with its tendencies to be theoretical) and the empirical orientation of the Geneva project (with its tendencies toward social, political, and economic factors).

The Advisory Committee at its April meeting requested its chairman to provide an introduction, pointing up the major issues in the essays and indicating the genesis of the project. It has seemed useful to sketch in some detail the broad context for the ecclesiology study, of which this book is a part. He was also asked to reflect the reactions of committee members on a number of points. Specifically their resolution states, "The book does not necessarily speak for the U.S.A. National Committee, nor does it have official status of any kind. Its purpose is simply to get discussion started." That is how it should be with creative essays—each stands on its own merits. All this may be an inevitable comment on the situation today when we have, as one committee member suggested entitling the volume, "Traditions in Transition."

This Introduction, then, is the work of the Editor, as are the biographical notes at the start of each essay. At one point, because of the prominent use made of "process theology," it was felt helpful to add a bibliographical Editor's Note on what may be to many an unfamiliar, though well-established, development in philosophy and theology. The essays are as they came from the hand of each author, edited only for details of style and consistency. The Epilogue reflects judgments of the Advisory Committee, but the final formulation is the responsibility of the Editor. All these components are part of the church that is emerging for the future.

NOTES

1. *Religious Studies Review* 2, no. 4 (October 1976):7–8.

2. Well documented ecumenically in the essays in the series *Mission Trends* (New York: Paulist Press), and in U.S. Lutheran circles in the essay by David L. Vikner, Executive Director of the Division for World Mission and Ecumenism, *Lutheran Church in America*, "The Era of Interdependence," *Missiology: An International Review* (October 1974, reprinted by LCA/DWME).

3. "Hermeneutics of the Lutheran Confessions," a paper read Oct. 22, 1976, for the Hermeneutics Project of the Division of Theological Studies, Lutheran Council in the U.S.A. *Crisis* and *identity* are terms frequently used in recent years by *Lutheran Forum*; e.g., Martin E. Marty, "Scenarios for a Lutheran future: A case of Identity," 9, no. 2 (May, 1975):6–10; or "The Search for Identity" as an

overall heading for articles on church-related colleges, Scandinavian Lutheran churches, and political developments, 10, no. 4 (November 1976).

4. In *A Statement,* adopted officially at the 1973 LC-MS convention, the largest number of paragraphs is devoted to "Holy Scripture." In addition there are sections on "Christ as Savior and Lord," "Law and Gospel," "Original Sin," and "Confessional Subscription." There is one on the "Mission of the Church," which is the only section which can be said to treat *ecclesiology.* It reads,

> We believe, teach, and confess that the primary mission of the church is to make disciples of every nation by bearing witness to Jesus Christ through the preaching of the Gospel and the administration of the sacraments. Other necessary activities of the church, such as ministering to men's physical needs, are to serve the church's primary mission and its goal that men will believe and confess Jesus Christ as their Lord and Savior.
>
> We therefore reject any views of the mission of the church which imply: That an adequate or complete witness to Jesus Christ can be made without proclaiming or verbalizing the Gospel.

The identity of the church is here seen in classic evangelistic terms. "Service in the world" is clearly and totally subordinate.

5. Martin J. Heinecken, *Christ Frees and Unites.* The Knubel-Miller Lectures, 12. Philadelphia: Board of Publication of the United Lutheran Church in America, 1957. Cf. also *The Unity of the Church: A Symposium* (Rock Island: Augustana Press, 1957).

6. *Justification Today: Studies and Reports,* Supplement to *Lutheran World* (Geneva; hereafter *LW*), vol. 12, no. 1 (1965).

7. Reports on the work of the Commission on Theology were published over the years in *LW/Lutherische Rundschau.*

8. *Christ and Humanity,* ed. Ivar Asheim (Philadelphia: Fortress, 1970). Asheim, Director of the Department of Theology, LWF, in Geneva, provided an essay on "Humanity and Christian Responsibility," based on the Commission's overall work. "The Scope of Christ's Lordship," by John Reumann, summarizes discussions by U.S. and Canadian theologians meeting 1966–68 in Philadelphia. Ethical norms in contemporary society, as treated by a group in Sweden, are analyzed by Ragnar Holte under the title "Humanity as a Criterion." The East German (DDR) study committee report takes up "The Christian in a Post-Christian Context." A fifth paper, "Humanity and the Religions of Men," by James Scherer, of Chicago, was originally read at a Department of Theology conference in 1969.

9. *Christian Hope and the Lordship of Christ,* ed. Martin J. Heinecken; *Christian Hope and the Future of Humanity,* ed. Franklin Sherman; *Christian Hope and the Secular,* ed. Daniel F. Martensen (Minneapolis: Augsburg Publishing House, 1969).

10. Compare especially Ulrich Duchrow, *Christenheit und Weltverantwortung* (Stuttgart: Klett Verlag, 1970); and the three volumes in the series "Texte zur Kirchen- und Theologiegeschichte," 17, 21, and 22 (Gütersloh: Gerd Mohn), Duchrow and Heiner Hoffmann, *Die Vorstellung von zwei Reichen und Regimenten bis Luther* (1972), Duchrow and W. Huber and L. Reith, *Umdeutungen der Zweireichelehre Luthers in 19. Jahrhundert* (1975), Duchrow and Huber, *Die Ambivalenz der Zweireichelehre in den lutherischen Kirchen des 20. Jahrhunderts* (1976). A selection of texts from those three volumes, and other selections, are available in Karl H. Hertz, ed., *Two Kingdoms and One World* (Minneapolis: Augsburg Publishing House, 1976).

11. A brief summary of the work of LWF/Studies appears in *LW* 22 (1975): 69–75. Lists of its publications (available from LWF, 150 route de Ferney, 1211

Geneva 20, Switzerland), appear from time to time in *LW* or can be obtained by writing the Department of Studies.

12. *LW* 21 (1974), pp. 45–46, from a report on the Studies Department/ Commission. Cf. also the brief remarks of Mikko E. Juva, LWF President, *LW* 19 (1972): 329.

13. *LW* 21 (1974):46.

14. Cf. *LW* 20, no. 1 (1973), "Identity—Pluralism—Oekumene," prepared by the Strasbourg Institute, featuring papers by Robert W. Bertram and Harding Meyer at a colloquium in St. Paul, Minnesota, June 19–23, 1972, and a report of discussions there, pp. 61–64. The volume, *The Gospel and the Ambiguity of the Church,* ed. Vilmos Vajta (Philadelphia: Fortress, 1974) in the Institute's series "The Gospel Encounters History," also gets into the ecclesiological question.

15. Text in *LW* 20 (1973):187–92, in an issue otherwise devoted to "Perspectives on Liberation and Development."

16. Compare the reports in *LW* 22 (1975):69–75; in more detail 23 (1976): 10–20, and 309–12 (a chart shows how all Studies' projects relate to "ecclesiology"). The reports of the 1974 and 1975 consultations are available from LWF/ Studies, Geneva, for $3.50 each, postage included (documents 1.01/3 and 1.01/4.) Encounter with Scripture was built in by including a series of "Bible meditations" at consultations. In addition, at the very outset of the program the staff took up "New Testament Ecclesiologies and their Significance for our present-day Understanding of the Church" as the theme for a seminar in November, 1973. To this extent, the New Testament witness is *presupposed,* rather than assumed to be able to give *answers* to all our modern questions in church and world.

The final report for Dar es Salaam, as well as the report on the 1976 consultation in Arusha, are contained in two volumes published by LWF/Geneva, Department of Studies, 1977, under the title of *The Identity of the Church and Its Service to the Whole Human Being. Final Reports and Final Volume II.* Included are the Commission's Final Report, descriptions of self-studies in each church, and reflections and interpretations by a special team, T. Bakkevig (Norway), J. Kiwovele (Tanzania), G. Scharffenorth (Federal Republic of Germany) and W. Everett and K. Hertz (U.S.A.).

17. *LW* 23 (1976):14–15, and "The Proclamation of the Gospel and Other Marks of the Church," by Wolfram Kistner (University of Pietermaritzburg) and Manas Buthelezi (Braamfontein, Transvaal). The report of the first ecclesiology seminar of the Commission on Studies in April, 1974, was entitled "The Christian Identity of the Lutheran Churches in Relation to Power and Suffering."

18. *LW* 23 (1976): the quotes are from pp. 13, 19, 15, and 19 respectively,

19. Ivar Asheim wrote in 1969, "In this period the approach to socioethical problems in an ecumenical context has *constantly* shifted. . . . When the Commission began its work the controversy between a lordship-of-Christ ethic and the traditional doctrine of the two kingdoms was very pertinent. The stages which we have since gone through in rapid succession are marked by the catchwords 'co-humanity,' 'rapid social change,' 'theology of development,' and 'theology of revolution.' The informed reader will note how all these steps in greater or lesser degree are reflected in the Commission's study document." *Christ and Humanity,* pp. xii–xiii. Those sentiments apply even more so to the period since 1970. One dare not read 1976 essays in ecclesiology without an awareness of the changes which began to take effect in the sixties.

20. The full title of the Church and Society Report is *Christians in the Technical and Social Revolutions of Our Time: World Conference on Church and Society, Geneva, July 12–26, 1966* (Geneva: World Council of Churches, 1967).

21. "Setting a New Course," *LW* 23 (1976):99.

22. The phrases are from "Some Reflections on Nairobi," by Daniel F. Martensen, LWF/Studies, Geneva, in *LW* 23 (1976): 97–98. The issue contains a series of articles about Nairobi, "A World Assembly Assessed."

23. Ibid., see Hübner, p. 101.

24. Ibid., see Hübner, pp. 100–101. Note should also be made of the presentation by the Associate General Secretary of the WCC, the Rev. Dr. Konrad Raiser, "The Identity of the Church in Ecumenical Perspective," at the LWF/Studies 1975 consultation, pp. 109–17 of the report (cited above, note 16), reprinted without the response and discussion in *LW* 23 (1976):46–49.

25. For a survey up to 1972, see Warren Quanbeck, *Search for Understanding: Lutheran Conversations with Reformed, Anglican, and Roman Catholic Churches* (Minneapolis: Augsburg Publishing House, 1972); the book deals with international (LWF) and national (LWF/USA National Committee and Lutheran Council in the U.S.A.) efforts. Since 1972 in the United States, dialogues have also been begun with the Reformed churches (second round, 1972–74), the Episcopal Church (second round, 1976–   ), Conservative-Evangelicals (1975), Methodists (1977), and Pentecostals (in planning), plus a Lutheran—Reformed—Orthodox "trialogue" (1973–75). For Jewish conversations—surely a significant element in shaping Christian identity, cf. *Speaking of God Today: Jews and Lutherans in Conversation*, ed. Paul D. Opsahl and Marc H. Tanenbaum, of the Lutheran Council and the American Jewish Committee respectively (Philadelphia: Fortress, 1974). While the papers there published come from four colloquia in the United States between 1969 and 1973, the volume also alludes to international contacts and includes the LWF document, "The Church and the Jewish People," Logumkloster, Denmark, 1964. A U.S. seminar is planned for 1978 with the Anti-Defamation League of B'nai Brith. Subsequent LWF discussions on "Christian Witness and the Jewish People" were held at Neuendettelsau, Germany, and Oslo, Norway, in 1973 and 1975 respectively, and are reported on in *LW* 23 (1976): 62–69. Papers from the 1975 consultation have been published by LWF/Studies, Geneva (1976, #1), under the title *Christian Witness and the Jewish People* (preparatory papers by C. Burchard, H. Ditmanson, M. Saebø, K. Stendahl, and J. Thurèn, plus consultation statement).

26. Compare Harding Meyer, "The Future of Bilaterals and the Bilaterals of the Future," *LW* 22 (1975):226–34, and the accompanying papers by Nils Ehrenstrom and Paul A. Crow, Jr., entitled "Unity Talks by Twos," pp. 216–26 and 235–37. "Conciliarism" has been an especial concern of the Strasbourg Institute; cf. Günther Gassmann, "The Future of Church Unity," ibid., pp. 212–16; and *LW* 20 (1973):64–65, for the Institute's "Statement."

27. Compare *LW* 22 (1975):73. The 1973 statement on "Ecumenical Methodology" is available from the Geneva office of LWF/Studies.

28. It is scheduled to be published in 1977 in the "Studies" series of the LCUSA/Division of Theological Studies, 360 Park Avenue South, New York, N.Y. 10010.

29. For a recent report, cf. B. [Theodore Bachmann], "Strasbourg: The Institute for Ecumenical Research," *LW* 23 (1976):57–62. A list of publications of the IER is printed in *LW* 21 (1974):410–12, and they are available from the Institute, 8 rue Gustave-Klotz, 67000 Strasbourg, or the several publishers.

30. *Die evangelische-lutherische Kirche: Vergangenheit und Gegenwart*, scheduled in the series "Kirchen der Welt," ed. Hans Heinrich Harms (Stuttgart: Evangelisches Verlagswerk in 1977). Eng. trans., Minneapolis: Augsburg Publishing House.

31. *LW* 20 (1973):63.

32. Cf. *Neue transkonfessionelle Bewegungen: Dokumente aus der evangelika-*

len, der aktionszentrierten und der charismatischen Bewegungen, "Ökumenische Dokumentationen," 3 (Frankfurt: Verlag Otto Lembeck, Verlag Josef Knecht, 1976); Gunnars J. Ansons, "The Charismatics and their Churches; Report on Two Conferences," *Dialog* 15 (Spring 1976):142–44.

33. During the period of this study, Committee members included (titles as of 1975–76):

the Rev. Dr. Gerhard L. Belgum, Director, Center for Theological Study, California Lutheran College, Thousand Oaks, Calif. (ALC);

the Rev. Dr. Eugene L. Brand, Project Director, Inter-Lutheran Commission on Worship, New York, N.Y. (LCA), secretary of the Committee;

the Rev. Dr. James Burtness, Professor, Systematic Theology and Ethics, Luther Seminary, St. Paul, Minn. (ALC);

the Rev. Dr. Kent Gilbert, Executive Director, Division for Parish Services, LCA, Philadelphia, Pa.;

the Rev. Dr. Harold Haas, Executive Director, Division of Mission and Ministry, Lutheran Council in the U.S.A., New York, N.Y. (LCA);

the Rev. Dr. Gerald K. Johnson, President, Illinois Synod, LCA (retired, 1975), Chicago, Ill. (deceased, Sept. 1, 1976);

the Rev. Dr. John Reumann, Professor, New Testament, Lutheran Theological Seminary, Philadelphia, Pa. (LCA), chairman;

Dr. Evelyn Streng, Professor, Science, Texas Lutheran College, Seguin, Texas (ALC);

the Rev. Wayne C. Stumme, Assistant Director, Division for Theological Education and Ministry, ALC, Minneapolis, Minn.;

the Rev. Dr. Walter Wietzke, Director, Division for Theological Education and Ministry, ALC, Minneapolis, Minn. (through 1974).

In addition, U.S. members of the LWF Studies Commission sometimes attended meetings.

34. Dr. Carl Reuss, Director, Office of Research and Analysis, ALC; Dr. William Lazareth, then Dean, Lutheran Theological Seminary, Philadelphia (LCA); and Dr. Cedric Tilberg, Secretary for Social Concerns, Department of Church and Society, LCA.

35. See above, notes 8 and 9.

36. Mrs. Streng, Drs. Brand, Burtness, and Reumann, with Dr. Haas attending some sessions as an alternate.

ONE

THE IDENTITY OF THE CHURCH
IN LIGHT OF THE
DEVELOPMENT AND USE OF RESOURCES

"Development and use of resources" emerged worldwide as one of the areas of conflict from 1973 on in the LWF/Studies survey of burning issues. It was a topic with which the Studies Department especially asked U.S. churches to deal. The U.S. response in 1974 to Geneva's questionnaire was written with full awareness of problems involving "global interdependence," "multinational structures," and the need to promote justice in the world. The reply of the Lutheran churchmen who answered the questions about a starting point in concrete problems of the day spoke of "the widespread sense of personal helplessness felt in the face of massive power structures" and the "apathy, indifference, and insensitivity to others . . . common among members of our congregations. How to move from faith, via reason and power, to justice in the structures of society and in the supporting value systems is an ongoing challenge." Specifically, "many Lutherans . . . frequently think and act in 'sacred vs. secular' contrasts that contradict their formal beliefs in the triune God who is alive and at work throughout all of life, and not merely church life."

In spite of the much that had already been said about "ecology," among Lutherans notably by Professor Joseph A. Sittler, Jr.—cf. also the LCA Board of Social Ministry Statement, *The Human Crisis in Ecology* (New York, 1972), or H. Paul Santmire, *Brother Earth* (New York: Thomas Nelson, 1970)—it was inevitable that the present study should look at the church in light of the ongoing ecology question. True, a kind of interlude or "calm" had set in during 1974–75 since the concerns early in the seventies, but use of natural resources is a challenge which breaks out anew every time the OPEC nations meet to set oil prices, supersonic jets threaten the ozone layer, or a tanker spills oil in the sea. The Advisory Committee was also aware some Lutherans felt the "ecology crisis" had been a ploy to divert attention from the issue of civil rights; yet one need not shut out one concern to do justice to the other. Therefore the committee set "Development and Use of Resources" as one of its areas for attention (see above, p. 25).

Dr. Lee E. Snook, the essayist on ecology and ecclesiology, was born in 1930 and educated in Pennsylvania schools (Gettysburg College, B.A., cum laude and Phi Beta Kappa, 1952; Gettysburg Seminary, 1956). He served as a parish pastor at Roaring Spring and then Harrisburg, Pennsylvania, 1955–59 and 1959–62, before becoming pastor of the Lutheran congregation at Cornell University, Ithaca, New York, 1962–70. He completed his S.T.M. in 1967 and the Ph.D. in 1970, the latter magna cum laude with a dissertation on "Luther's Doctrine of the Real Presence, A Critique and Reconstruction from the View of Process Theology," at Union Theological Seminary, New York. Since 1970 he has been on the faculty of Luther Seminary, St. Paul, Minnesota, teaching systematic theology, an Associate Professor since 1972. His courses include both ecclesiology and ethics interests. Raised in the LCA and for a decade and a half in its ministry, Dr. Snook is now a member of the ALC.

The author of articles, sermons, and reviews published in *Dialog, Lutheran Quarterly,* and *Theology Today,* Professor Snook has been active in various church and professional groups, and lists his interests theologically as centering on worship, social ethics, and the possible relationships and conflicts between the Lutheran tradition and American process theology. The Advisory Committee's listing of possible topics for this study included "process" among the elements of pluralism in present-day theology. A brief bibliographical survey on "process" appears in a note appended to this essay, defining further the methodology espoused by Dr. Snook, and a recent article by him on the "process" view of death and resurrection is treated in the Epilogue.

The regional discussion and support group with whom Dr. Snook conferred in developing the essay which follows included:

Mr. Donald G. Brauer, President, Brauer and Associates, Eden Prairie, Minnesota;

Dr. Richard A. Chilgren, Professor, Medical School, University of Minnesota;

Dr. Wallace H. Hustad, President, Hustad Development Corporation, Eden Prairie, Minnesota;

Mr. Charles P. Lutz, Director for Church in Community, ALC, Minneapolis;

the Rev. Dr. William A. Miller, Director, Department of Religion and Health, Fairview Hospital, Minneapolis;

Dr. Robert T. Moline, Professor, Gustavus Adolphus College, St. Peter, Minnesota;

the Rev. Kenneth H. Olson, Pastor, American Lutheran Church, Chinook, Montana;

Dr. Allen R. Utke, Professor of Chemistry, University of Wisconsin, Oshkosh, Wisconsin;

Dr. Bruce Wrightsman, Professor, History of Science and Philosophy, Luther College, Decorah, Iowa.

ECOLOGY AND ECCLESIOLOGY:
AN AMERICAN VIEW

Lee E. Snook

The church in the United States shows signs of schizo-phrenia. Its identity is a fractured one. Although the Christian com-munity has always identified itself as that people who live *in* but not *of* the world, the identity crisis referred to here stems as much from the confusion about how to assess the world situation as it does from the confession of the church's dialectical relationship to that world. In the 1960s there was, it could be said, a similar identity crisis within the American churches. But the internal crisis of that decade—civil rights, the Vietnam War, political assassinations—will probably prove to be minor in comparison to the crises now looming over all of humankind. In the 1960s American Christians were as divided as their non-Christian neighbors over the issues of race, war and political ideology. What kind of America did we want to be in the last quarter of the century? For all the importance of that question, it now seems to have been more narrowly and parochially understood than most Americans would have imagined at the time.

As the Christian church which is *in* the United States but not *of* the United States continues to clarify its own identity, the role of the United States in the world will be a major consideration in that quest for clarification. In much of the discussion about the American pres-ence around the earth the focus has been largely on the flow of Amer-ican money and American military power. Money and military might have seemed to be the key for understanding the realities of interna-tional politics. The consequence, in the popular mind, was to produce a certain consciousness, namely, that the United States, so richly en-dowed with human and natural resources could somehow, on its own, generate all that money and all that military power out of the riches of our technological know-how and our bountiful land. Even after the defeat in Vietnam this consciousness of real or potential, self-generated power was intact. The problem, it still seemed possible to say, was in our lack of will or in the lack of worldwide support from other nations or in the loss of patriotism. This consciousness of unlimited potential that needs only the willpower to make it actual, sometimes accompanied by religious or quasi-religious symbols, has made it difficult for many Americans to admit that United States is neither omnicompetent nor omnipotent.[1] Many of those who have accepted a limited role for United States as a military power or world benefactor have not been able to alter their consciousness and accept the fact that the United States is a very dependent, though highly developed, nation.

The ambiguity of being both highly developed and extremely dependent on the rest of the world is really a fact of life, it is a reality factor which has been symbolized more and more by the imagery of "space-ship earth" or of ecosystems. Global interdependence, in turn, is more accurately and empirically described by an analysis of resources—human and natural—than by attending exclusively to ideology or theology. We do not thereby dismiss theology but we cannot rush too quickly to offer a theological interpretation or analysis until the reality of global interdependence is quantitatively established. An adequate empirical description is impossible in this essay, in part because there are all the usual pitfalls of erroneous information or the pretension of value-free selection of data. Nevertheless it is becoming increasingly apparent that the *basis* of global interdependence is physical. We are interdependent as the people of this earth because we are all physically dependent on the measurable resources of the earth.

It is necessary to linger longer than we often do over the point that our interdependence with the whole of humankind has a physical base: namely, the resources of the earth. Christians confess the earth as the creation of God and confess that redemption has come through the incarnation and yet find it easy to move too quickly away from the physical base of all reality, that is, to move away from nature to a notion of grace and to a doctrine of the word that is cut loose from the physical dimensions of reality. The schizophrenic identity of the church can be traced to this flight to denatured grace, and to a nonphysical

1. Notes appear at the end of the essay.

word. It has been hard for Christians to *conceive* of nature as the bearer of grace. Therefore it has been easy for Christians to neglect the hard facts about the natural world, and easy to disconnect their identity as Christians from the realities of nature. The consequence has been the now familiar charge by Lynn White and others that Christians act toward nature with a certain arrogance.[2]

Later in this essay it will be argued that the schizophrenia of the church as related to nature does not flow so much from the Christian confession but from the difficulty of conceiving nature in ways which are implied by the confession, even though such conceptions are not explicit in either Scripture or Christian faith. The task of conceptualizing nature in ways which are compatible with (rather than schizophrenically contradictory to) Christian confession is a theological task of great importance today.[3] But faith need not wait upon such a reconceptualization, indeed Christian faith obliges the Christian church to pay attention to what is happening to the earth, to its resources and to its inhabitants. In faith the church accepts the testimony of Scripture that the earth is the Lord's. One cannot be truthful to that confession and be indifferent to the earth. To be indifferent to the earth is to be indifferent to the Lord of the earth. Professor Sittler quotes a paragraph from H. W. Robinson to the same effect:

> The Hebrew vocabulary includes no word equivalent to the word "nature." This is not surprising if by "nature" we mean "the creative and regulative physical world and as the immediate cause of all its phenomena." The only way to render this idea into Hebrew would be to say simply "God." We would have to describe a particular physical activity through anthropomorphic phrases such as the "voice" of God, heard in the thunder; the "hand" of God felt in the pestilence; the "breath" of God animating the body of man; the "wisdom" of God ultimately conceived as his instrument in Creation.[4]

Sittler goes on to observe how far our modern views of nature are from this biblical one. Christian schizophrenia, then, is really trying to hold together two contrasting identities in relation to nature: the biblical view which assumes that "nature comes from God, cannot be apart from God, is capable of bearing the 'glory' of God"[5] and a dominant contemporary view which assumes that nature and natural causes can, in principle at least, be exhaustively described without reference to God.

Thus, whatever reasons others may have for attending to the earth, Christians do so out of loyalty to the biblical vision of the earth as the

Lord's, and while the Christian message is a message of redemption, the scope of redemption is not less than the realm of creation, indeed it encompasses a new heaven and a new earth.

THE POLITICS OF RESOURCES AND DEVELOPMENT

An Emerging World Consciousness

Global interdependence is literally a fact of daily life for the inhabitants of the world. While people who live in the heartland of the United States may not have reflected very consciously upon this fact of their lives, it has become part of their experience. One story will suffice as an illustration.

> The winter 1971–72, with its prolonged low temperatures and strong icy winds all over Eastern Europe, effectively destroyed one third of the Russian winter wheat crop. Surprisingly, the government bureaucracy ignored the situation, and the spring wheat acreage allocation remained unchanged. Since the direct per-capita consumption of wheat in that region is rather high (three times higher than in North America), it was urgent that the deficit be eliminated. In July 1972 the U.S. government extended a $750 million credit to the Soviet Union for the purchase of grain over a three-year period. Actually, the value of the purchase increased significantly before the delivery got under way since food prices soared all over the world. The price of wheat doubled in North America—hitherto a bastion of cheap food supply. Public resentment arose because people felt that in effect they were being made to pay for a transaction that did not involve the ordinary citizen. More important, and much more unfortunately, the same year's late monsoon heavily damaged the crops on the Indian subcontinent, resulting in a disastrous loss in food supply, which came in the aftermath of a tragic war. Nowhere was wheat to be found, for most of the world's surplus had been sold. Then a drought hit China and Africa and while China was acquiring whatever foodstuffs were left on the market, hundreds of thousands of Africans faced starvation. In a similar situation several years earlier, millions of tons of wheat had been rushed from North America to avert disaster; but this time only two hundred thousand tons could be made available.
>
> *The most outstanding lesson which can be drawn from these events is a realization of how strong the bonds among nations have become.* A bureaucratic decision in one region, perhaps the action of just one individual—not to increase the spring wheat acreage—resulted in a housewives' strike against soaring food prices in another part of the world and in tragic suffering in yet another part of the world.[6]

An assortment of interdependencies can be noted in this particular incident. Everything which touches people's lives—government, agriculture, economics, climate, production and distribution of goods—also puts them in touch with people throughout the whole world. The world is not, then, an aggregate of one hundred and fifty separate nations together with a variety of economic or political groupings. The world must be viewed as a single worldwide system comprised of interdependent communities bound together by the common dependence on the earth. When the fact of interdependence is acknowledged as the worldwide background and the inescapable condition within which diverse people and nations are reaching for the necessities of life on this one earth, then the issue of development becomes singularly acute.

The first report to the Club of Rome, *The Limits of Growth,* was regarded by many as an effort to subvert all attempts by underdeveloped nations to gain sufficient economic stability to provide for the needs of their citizens.[7] The report stipulated what the limits to growth are and that clearly the earth could not sustain the expanding population of the world if everyone were to develop and achieve the same level of consumption as, for example, the average citizen of the United States. The resources would be almost immediately used up, the pollution would be deadly, the possibilities for life would be destroyed. This is now a familiar story to many, and yet most people probably still do not understand the peculiar mathematical properties of exponential growth. When the projections of exponential growth are applied to the rate of growth in the consumption of the limited resources of the earth (fuel, nonfuel minerals, water, oxygen) the prospects of international catastrophe though massive shortages, economic collapse, war, and starvation are ominous.

The second report to the Club of Rome, from which the preceding illustration was taken, has proposed a very important qualification to the dire warnings of the first. The authors of this second report offer a valuable distinction between types of growth, a distinction which, when applied to the analysis and resolution of global crises, can go far in avoiding sheer despair on the one hand or easy optimism on the other. Neither despair nor optimism can yield hope because each extreme attitude is a justification for doing nothing and letting nature take its course.

Growth can be thought of as *linear growth* (1, 2, 3, 4, 5, . . .) which is the way one's wealth would increase if one only added a fixed amount each year to the money under the mattress, or as *exponential growth* (1, 2, 4, 8, 16, 32, . . .) which is the way one's wealth would increase if invested at compound interest so that at a given percentage there would be periodic "doublings." There is also *organic growth.*

Linear and exponential growth are undifferentiated modes of growth. There is simply an addition (linear) or a multiplication (exponential) of the number of units over a given period of time. Undifferentiated exponential growth is the sort which is usually thought of when considering the limits of growth. The well-known French puzzle was cited in the first Club of Rome report to illustrate how distressingly fast the limits to growth can be reached, shortening the time available for corrective action even more alarmingly.

> Suppose you own a pond on which a water lily is growing. The lily plant doubles in size each day. If the lily were allowed to grow unchecked it would completely cover the pond in thirty days, choking off the other forms of life in the water. For a long time the lily plant seems small, and so you decide not to worry about cutting it back until it covers half the pond. On what day will that be? On the twentyninth day of course. You have one day to save your pond.[8]

The authors of the second Club of Rome report observe that such exponential growth is not the only way in which growth can be conceptualized. They offer an organic model of growth. One advantage of growth conceived organically is to allow planning for growth or development which will not only halt the dangerous consumption of nonrenewable resources but will still provide for development even so. In other words, an organic model of growth has the advantage of not simply calling for stop-action, freezing the human situation in its present state of unequal distribution while trying to scale down consumption so as to postpone the final doom. Another advantage is that this model of growth can guide planning and make use of the emerging techniques of systems analysis by which the various components of an interrelated system can receive from and feed back information to all other components thus achieving harmony. The organic model of growth, when applied to worldwide planning, assumes that cooperation not confrontation, diplomacy not war, and mutual helpfulness not animosity, offer some real hope for the future of the world. And, of course, the organic model of growth would be congenial to Christians who are familiar with Paul's use of the metaphor of the body or of Jesus' frequent reference to organic entities.

> The current discussion on the crisis in world development centers on growth as though it were necessarily the undifferentiated type. There is no reason, however, why parallels to organic growth should not be drawn upon; indeed, our analysis reported in this book, of the options available to mankind for dealing with the world crisis syndrome, points out the crucial importance of the organic growth concept for the future development of mankind.[9]

Growth for growth's sake, or development simply for the sake of development, is indefensible because it is dangerous to the rest of humankind when one component or several within the ecosystem are allowed to grow without consideration for the effect on the rest of humanity or of the earth. When such growth occurs in a human body we call it cancer. "The world has cancer and the cancer is man."[10] Of course, that cynical judgment is a correct one if one assumes that human population can grow unchecked on the face of the world without regard to the effect of that growth for the general health of the world. Growth for growth's sake and for none other is a form of evil, and the organic model helps us to conceptualize the relationship between desirable (good) and undesirable (evil) forms of development and to devise ways of planning realistically and hopefully.

With an organic model of growth or development it is possible, in principle at least, to promote growth where it is needed for the sake of the members of the whole, and to check growth where it is damaging for the development of the whole. In some parts of the world, undifferentiated growth at exponential rates has, indeed, assumed cancerous qualities which are dangerous for the whole world. Humankind is in danger because of that growth. On the other hand, humankind is in danger at other places because of lack of growth as in regional food production. "It is this pattern of *unbalanced* and *undifferentiated* growth which is at the heart of the most urgent problems facing humanity—and a path which leads to a solution is that of organic growth."[11]

In nature, of course, one finds organic growth following a distinctive path. Unlike undifferentiated growth that proceeds without restraint as in cancerous growth, organic growth proceeds by a process of differentiation. Groups of cells do not merely multiply endlessly but begin to differ in structure and function; they become organ-specific;

there will be multiplication but there comes a point of dynamic equilib-
rium in which the cells are constantly renovated, in a human body
approximately every seven years. Organic growth proceeds this way,
of course, because it is encoded in the genetic structure of each cell.
The total organism has what amounts to a blueprint or a master plan.
The function of each part is related to the whole and the whole is
dependent on the functioning of each part within the scope of the
genetic plan.

What, though, is the master plan for human beings whose interdependence is a requirement for life on the earth? The authors of the
second Club of Rome report acknowledge that human history has no
equivalent to the master plan which an organism receives through
natural selection. "The organic growth of mankind is *not* inherent in the
present trend of world development. There is nothing to suggest
that the transition from undifferentiated growth to organic growth will
result from the present direction of development. Nor can it be assumed that a plan will be injected by a deus ex machina."[12]

The Symptoms and Prognosis of Undifferentiated Growth

The United States as a nation is by far the most conspicuous consumer of the resources of the earth. Its rate of consumption is growing
exponentially and placing burdens upon the earth which are literally
intolerable and yet they are not fully comprehended by American
citizens. The amount of energy which the average citizen requires for
daily living is actually 115 times that amount of energy required in the
form of food for subsistence.[13] A comparable figure for a Russian
citizen is forty times that of subsistence food requirements, seventeen
times subsistence food energy requirements for a Brazilian; two times
for an inhabitant of India. The energy consumed for air conditioning
in the United States is more than that consumed as a whole by China.
When Americans consider the massive populations of Asia they are
more inclined to think of the problem of over-population in that area
of the world and not of over-consumption by American citizens. One
American consumes as many resources as fifty Asians. The per capita
lifetime consumption of a baby born today in America is staggering,
and all of it is dependent on the use of energy resources which are
being rapidly depleted.[14] In light of the exponential growths in consumption, coupled with increased population and urbanization, the

projections are that we have fewer than fifty years before we reach the limits of undifferential, nonorganic growth.

In any case, the increasing dependency of the United States on resources not available within its own borders is becoming more and more clear. The exponential growth in population and in gross national product would mean that the U.S. will need three to four times more energy by the year 2000 than in the mid-seventies, and at the same time the demand for energy elsewhere in the world will be increasing. The rising demand for energy is on a collision course with the limited supply. The greater the appetite for energy in the United States, the more severe and complicated are the stresses between nations as massive wealth is transferred to the oil-producing nations and the United States is forced to sell such items as food to achieve a balance of trade.

The growth of population and consumption patterns is also putting great pressure on availability of resources other than oil. It is now estimated that "the United States lacks self-sufficiency in 25 of the 32 materials needed to make a great industrial power. Of the top 72 materials, we lack self-sufficiency in 60. Some 40 of these are imported from 'politically unstable' or 'unfriendly' countries."[15] The United States currently consumes about thirty-five percent of the nonfuel mineral resources produced in the world, indeed the U.S. stopped being an exporter of such resources and became an importer in 1915 so that by 1974 the trade deficit of the nation in nonfuel metals and minerals was about $3.5 billion. Many of these materials are found in the so-called underdeveloped nations. Curtailment of imports in these commodities, through a trade war for example, would spell severe difficulty for whole industries in the United States. "If the U.S. steel and auto industries had to be curtailed because of mineral shortages, the chain reaction through other industries would certainly mean flatout depression."[16] Again, the economic power and stability of the United States is dependent on maintaining access to materials found elsewhere. A self-sufficient United States is impossible.

Attempts at prognosis are demonstrably difficult when dealing with the exponential growth in energy consumption. For example, the churches have entered in the debate concerning the feasibility and desirability of developing energy sources through nuclear technology, specifically fission reactors. Interestingly, two reports from church bodies—involving panels of prestigious persons from science, engineering, public policy groups—came to differing conclusions. The National Council of Churches of Christ in the U.S.A. issued a statement entitled "The Plutonium Economy: A Statement of Concern," and the World Council of Churches published two reports entitled "Facing Up to Nuclear Power" and "Report on Nuclear Energy."[17] The National Council writers tended to take a negative view toward the option of fission energy whereas the World Council urged keeping that option open. Both the NCC and the WCC acknowledge a need for options to fossil fuel sources of energy, but the NCC is much more skeptical that sufficient long-range safeguards can be developed to make the risks involved in nuclear energy morally acceptable. By implication at least the WCC report seems to argue that it would not be morally responsible to ignore *any* option for future energy sources. And indeed, it does appear that there is a moral obligation to preserve fossil fuels for an indefinite future to make them available on a restricted basis for food production (fertilizer, pesticides, etc.) and chemical production (especially for medicine-related uses).[18] If future generations have a moral claim on long-term available fossil fuels, then arguments against alternative sources of energy must show that the risks of nuclear energy really are greater than a future without fossil fuel for agriculture and medicine.

The exponential increase in energy consumption is interrelated with increases in population and the increased demand for food production. Again, the disparities and inequities between nations and peoples are impressive.

It is estimated that every person in the world would be undernourished if all the food produced today were uniformly distributed. The necessary increase to provide an adequate diet for all persons is between thirty and sixty percent.[19] Whereas up to seventy percent of the people living in underdeveloped nations are mentally or physically stunted because of low protein intake, people elsewhere in the world overeat or waste food in scandalous proportions. For example, if all the available food in the world were consumed at the level of intake in the United States, only one-third of the world's population would have anything to eat. As it is, the United States consumes twenty percent of the world food supply even though the U.S. is only six percent of the world population. At the same time, the amount of fertilizer used to maintain lawns, golf courses and ornamental plants in the United States equals all the fertilizer used by farmers in India. The grain used annually to make liquor in the United States would equal the annual grain consumption of 500,000 people in South Asia. In 1973 Americans spent $1.6 billion to feed forty million pet dogs and thirty million pet cats.

Furthermore, the inequities may increase to frightening proportions when we project the increase in world population. At current rates of increase, the population will double by the year 2000, which means that in less than twenty-five years the need for food could be three to four times what it is today if we were to accept the goal of an adequate diet for all. Great investments of money will be required to open new land for agriculture and to make it productive. Enormous amounts of energy will be required if modern farming techniques are used. In 1910 the production of one calorie of food in the United States required the output of one calorie of energy. Today to produce the same one calorie of food absorbs ten calories of energy using modern methods of tilling, fertilizing and harvesting. In addition, in the United States, millions of dollars are spent each year on advertising food products many of which have been produced in such a way as to make them "convenient" if not altogether nutritious. Some observers report that these same foodstuffs, if that is what they are, are exported to overseas nations where again, under the influence of advertising, people are urged to purchase them and consume them.

Increased population, increased use of energy in food production, processing and transportation have conspired to make it unfeasible for the United States to continue its Food for Peace program. The policy is now "food for crude." The multiplied cost of Arab oil has meant simply that a barrel of oil that used to trade for a bushel of wheat now trades for three bushels of wheat.

The deadly equation of energy, population and food might seem utterly defeating if we did not have a remarkable instance of one nation which has managed to avert disaster even as its population was increasing and its productive capacities were steadily modernized. The prognosis for resolving the deadly equation is perhaps not so bleak in light of the experience of China since 1961. In that year the leadership of China realized bad management and unfavorable weather had brought disastrously low crop yield in the 1959–61 harvests.[20] A slogan was adopted: "Agriculture is the base of the economy, and industry is the leading factor." They quickly moved to modernize agriculture by directing industry to meet agricultural requirements, promoting agricultural sciences, producing huge amounts of fertilizer, developing new strains of rice, installing irrigation systems. The agricultural revolution in China was not totally dominated by investments of capital, however; rather, the modernization was accompanied by massive amounts of human labor which has enlarged the capacity of modern techniques. Millions of people have shared in the labor, leveling farmland to simplify irrigation, terracing hills to arrest erosion, physically removing salts from the soil and replacing them with organic material, constructing dams, dikes, irrigation canals and wells. Today "China is self-sufficient in grain and all other foods. While population gained 60 percent, from 500 million to 800 million (1949–73) grain production has more than doubled, from 100 million tons to 250 million tons."[21]

The average Chinese diet would not please most Americans but it meets basic health needs. To the Chinese people, who remember recurring famines when they had to survive on grass, leaves and bark, it is a major improvement. But adequate production of food is not the only factor in China. Distribution is another factor. The benefits of modern agriculture are not all drained away from the area of production but are allowed to improve conditions in rural China, bringing better health services, housing and education to the countryside. Of course only through revolution were the Chinese able to break the former power of urban and rural elites so that new policies of distribution and equalization could be implemented.

It is sobering to reflect on the possible implications of the Chinese experience. "China's self-sufficiency in food is a product both of transformed attitudes of the peasant population—which still includes 80 percent of China's people—and of modernized and collective methods of agriculture."[22] Before we shrink from the thought of how those attitudes were transformed and how those methods were established, we have to remember that a large proportion of the world's people live on the brink of disaster. Indeed, they may

> conclude that the risks and sufferings of revolution and dictatorship are less than the tragedy of the present. They may see no other way to convince the rural elite and the urban classes to relinquish control over the benefits of agricultural modernization. To solve the food question

in many impoverished regions *without* force and violence requires the willingness of privileged groups to sacrifice short-term interests and to create new solutions for the whole society. Such far-sighted enlightened policies are tragically rare.[23]

The Chinese experience throws a different light upon the question of overpopulation too. The conventional wisdom is that overpopulation is one of the principle sources or causes of poverty, and that the only way to reduce consumption is to reduce the number of consumers. China does not see its **huge** population as a problem but rather takes the position that overpopulation is the *result* of poverty, not the cause of poverty. China's approach to poverty was not to restrict the growth of the population but to destroy the old order and replace it with an order in which the earth's resources are most equitably distributed. Population planning in the new order, then, is not a means preserving the privileges of the few but a means of greater sharing. Thus population planning is comprehensive and not restricted to isolated measures such as birth control. At the World Population Conference China's Huang Shu-tse said, "The Chinese people do not approve of anarchy, either in material production or in the growth of population. People ought to be the masters of nature and of their own race."[24] Comprehensive population planning includes:

the distribution of food, the provision of child care facilities and comprehensive medical care, and the allocation of jobs, housing and educational opportunities. It also means measures that are at times unpopular, such as curbing mass migrations to the cities and the assignment of youth to the countryside to participate in agricultural production. . . . It means curbing the infant mortality rate as well as the birthrate. It means promoting birth control in the densely populated areas and encouraging population growth in national minority areas.[25]

In this section we have been noting the symptoms and gauging the probable prognosis if exponential growth were to continue in the consumption of resources, in the demand for energy and food, and in the swelling of the human population. Conceptually there is an alternative model for thinking about growth, the organic model. Historically we have, in China, an instance of a nation which has transformed not only its social system but also its attitudes. The rest of the world may not choose to take the way of China, but the Chinese people have shown us that it is not necessary or destined by fate that the patterns of growth which have been in effect for the past 150 years continue unchecked until some natural or international holocaust devastates large portions of the world's people and land. There are those, however, who would say that if the *only* way to survive is to sacrifice most if not all individual liberties to a new social order, such as China's, it would be an intolerable capitulation to tyranny.

Survival, Liberation, and Development

The identity crisis of the church in the United States is related to the conflicting, indeed clashing, interests and values implied in the terms *survival, liberation,* and *development.* The relation of these values to the human use of the earth's resources is obvious. Each of these terms when considered as a discrete value has such an obvious claim on human interests that any one of them can, and sometimes does, lead to a form of tyranny. In the name of "survival" all other interests are sometimes disregarded or suppressed. Likewise "liberation" movements can be mounted in nearly total disregard for some human rights, or the cause of social "development" can be pressed in ways which overrule the decisions of those for whom the development is intended.

It is axiomatic that everything which humans live for depends on whether there is human existence as a basis. Survival is necessary, but we would hasten to say that mere survival is not sufficient. The perplexities arise when one asks, What is necessary in addition to survival if existence is to be worthwhile?

The limits or outer boundaries of the question are more easily discerned than the inner contours. For example, too much can be claimed for survival as a value, and there have been occasions when these excessive claims have been politically successful precisely because the value of survival is self-evident. The need for survival escalates into abuses of the survival need to the point where tyranny is permitted for the sake of survival. Daniel Callahan illustrates this point:

> The purported threat of Communist domination has for over two decades fueled the drive of militarists for even larger defense budgets, no matter what the cost to other social needs. During World War II, native Japanese-Americans were herded, without due process of law, into detention camps. This policy was upheld by the Supreme Court in *Korematsu vs. U.S.* (1944) in the general context that a threat to national security can justify acts otherwise blatantly unjustifiable. The survival of the Aryan race was one of the official legitimations of

Nazism. Under the banner of survival, the government of South Africa imposes a ruthless *apartheid*, heedless of the most elementary human rights. The Vietnamese war has seen one of the greatest of the many absurdities tolerated in the name of survival: the destruction of villages in order to save them.[26]

These and other abuses of the appeal to the necessary value of survival ought not to be forgotten in the discussion of the church's identity in an age of ecological crisis. One check against such abuse is to put the question of survival in a broader context. The issue is broader than whether the earth will survive or whether the human race will survive. Total extinction of the human race is, of course, imaginable if there were worldwide nuclear warfare together with a long-term, life-destroying level of atmospheric radiation, but overpopulation itself, for example, would not spell extinction. People would die in sufficient numbers until a population remained which could be supported by the earth's productivity. If the aim is to build a base of concern, or to motivate widespread discussion about the necessity to control growth, then "the spectre of total human extinction" is a poor and too narrow base for such an effort. "The central question is not so much whether the human species will survive, but how it will survive."[27] To be sure, there is no guarantee for the survival of the human race because massive catastrophes are always imaginable; but the fear of extinction is not an adequate or useful basis for the quest for acceptable means to control growth.

Among humans the drive for survival draws its power from biological, psychological and social sources. These sources would have to be examined if we were to define those other values, besides survival, which are necessary to make life worthwhile. People fear death, but not death only. As Callahan points out more people commit suicide because of a blow to their sense of self-worth, or their identity, than because they are seriously ill. Indeed, people have risked death in war not simply to survive but in defense of values such as freedom, religious liberty, justice, or the dignity of their humanness. Survival as a value has curious properties. When it is excessively or exclusively emphasized to the degree that all other considerations of value are suppressed, survival is itself jeopardized, as one might observe when considering the effects of modern medicine on population growth rates. Contrariwise, when survival is not considered at all or is minimized, then it is again in jeopardy. Again, Callahan provides the telling example: "Both Jews and militant blacks . . . have perceived that their survival will always be in jeopardy as long as it is dependent upon the goodwill or toleration of others."[28]   Either excessive stress on, or neglect of, survival will place survival in jeopardy. There is probably general agreement on these curious properties of survival as a value.

The disagreement centers on what else is necessary besides mere survival. It is a disagreement which ranges over many complex themes, subtle issues and interrelated factors but a disagreement which can perhaps be described for our purposes as clustering around two poles: liberation and development. Perhaps few people would argue for liberation alone or for development alone as the sole necessary condition in addition to survival, but these two poles represent emphases which can assist in understanding the current debate on how to secure a human future in light of the crisis in resources. They are complementary themes; each is necessary if we are both to analyze the current plight of humankind and to find guidance for the future, but neither is adequate for analysis and decision making. Yet, to the degree that the churches take sides and favor one over the other, the identity of the church is fragmented.

The theme of liberation is the theme of discontinuity. The theme of development is the theme of continuity. Liberationists would argue that only as one is alienated from the bondage of the social system is it possible to throw off the enslaving practises and policies which give rise to inordinate consumption on the one hand and economic inequities on the other. The religious theme here is exodus from bondage, which also implies wandering in the wilderness; there is risk and adventure and a resolute refusal to stay within the securities of the old system. There is something "irrational" about the liberationist theme because, from the view of the old order, there are no antecedents for the new life, no rules, no regular patterns of nature and government. Today this theme is announced most compellingly in the churches of the Third World, among the blacks and within the women's movement. Liberation theology, when it is heeded in affluent American churches, is a call to declare solidarity between the Christians and the poor of the world; and also to declare a moratorium on offering help *from* America on behalf of the poor. Liberationists reject that "answer" because it often alienates the poor all the more.

Traditionally, developmentalists would rationally trace out the distinct steps from problem to resolution, arguing that all persons, rich and poor, have some interests in common by which the differences can be resolved. If liberationists emphasize political action, developmentalists would favor economic models for dealing with the problems, and would insist on coming to terms with the hard issues of employment, production, resources, management, food, and planned change.[29] If liberationists tend to ignore these hard realities, developmentalists tend to forget how decisions which they themselves regard as realistic, rational and sound actually favor the rich and powerful. Liberationists stress the right of the people to participate in decisions while developmentalists tend to make decisions for the people, arguing that only after certain stages of development are achieved can the people be in a position to make wise decisions.

The American churches need the complementary emphases of liberation *and* development if they are to participate in the search for a viable human future. They need the emphasis on liberation as a challenge to easy assumptions about the American way of life to which American Christians have become very accustomed. Liberation forces upon Americans a reexamination of American answers to every human question. Liberation reminds Americans that one of the best things they can do "for" the rest of the world is to "stop stealing."[30] Liberation is a call to free oneself from a style of life which can easily become normative and "rational" but which in fact is lethal for the future. Liberation is a summons to reconsider what it is to be poor and to ask if our national wealth has not impoverished us too much in terms of dissatisfaction with jobs, family life, and alienation from one another.

Likewise the American churches need the emphasis on development. Liberation will require a reordering of priorities so that what is now needed is to put unceasing pressure on the American political, economic, military, agribusiness and media communities so that development can be turned from undifferential growth for its own sake (or the sake of privileged interests) to organic growth to serve the needs of the world's people. The need is for the development of interdependence among nations and for that we need more, not less, ingenuity in terms of management skills, planning capabilities, educational opportunities, skills in communication, sensitivity and mutual appreciation. If there is to be a new order, or more accurately a reordering of our social life, there need not be a loss of liberty or dignity even though old privileges will have to be traded in for new sense of responsibility. For such a task or reordering the very best developmental talent will be necessary. Perhaps the church can embody proleptically *both* of these emphases: liberation from the old and developmental experimentation in the new.

A DILEMMA:
ITS DIMENSIONS AND THEOLOGICAL IMPLICATIONS

Humanity and Nature: A Widening Gap?

The current interest in the ecology seems to imply that Americans are coming to terms with the apparent threat to human life brought on by dangerous misuse of human and natural resources. Recent American presidents, for instance, have spoken of the need to make peace with nature, to save the redwood forests and to "make reparations" for the harm inflicted upon the land, air and water. Some theologians, on the other hand, point out that the recent concern for the environment and for a wise use of resources is an easy distraction from the urgent business of seeking equity and justice for the people of the land.[31] H. Paul Santmire has argued that, in reality, there is a deep schizophrenia affecting the American people, a conflict of ideas and attitudes which has distinctive roots in the American historical consciousness.[32]

Drawing upon the analyses of Perry Miller, Leo Marx, Lewis Mumford and others, Santmire offers his own interpretation of the dilemma. Americans simultaneously hold two conflicting notions about the relationship between humanity and nature. The first is represented by Thoreau who described his life at Walden in this way, "I am convinced that if all men were to live as simply as I did, thieving and robbery would be unknown."[33] Thoreau's sentiment bespeaks the tradition of nature against civilization. Nature is the true home of humanity rather than the city. Nature when uncorrupted will heal humanity, will give people access to God. God is not in the city of human institutions and corrupt structures of society, but with nature. Although this theme is not so clearly expressed today as with Thoreau, John Muir, or the popular poets of the nineteenth century, Santmire finds evidence of the same attitudes among contemporary Americans who, encouraged by mass media and a popular ideology, share in what Santmire calls "the cult of the simple rustic life." There are aspects of this cult, which, while largely unarticulated, are found especially among the affluent. The popular art of Norman Rockwell and Andrew Wyeth, the advertising appeals made for trips to Hawaii, the many journals given to conservation and wildlife, the mass media image of the rugged and clean life of the skier, the surfer, the mountain climber, and of the blissful life of lovers in the open air—these and other features of the American culture suggest the attraction which the simple rustic life has for Americans. Among young people, there are such phenomena as life in communes, or the lifestyle of alienation. Kenneth Kenniston called them "wanderers, walkers, and hitchhikers; when confronted with a major or even a minor problem they are likely to 'take off,' sometimes for a long midnight walk, sometimes for a few years."[34] Indeed, Santmire says "the cult of the simple rustic life" is much like the nineteenth-century "religion of nature." It brings with it an implicit social irresponsibility. Although it is for some an expression of social protest against consumerism and against the ineffectiveness of modern social and political institutions, it reenforces for many "a prior commitment to the status quo, especially in the ranks of the small town, suburban and affluent urban citizenry."[35] The devotees of this cult believe that the problems of the city must wait until nature is healed, restored, and available again as a refuge from the ills of society.

If many Americans are still devotees of a religion of nature, however unarticulated it may be, they are also simultaneously loyal to a religion of civilization. The new faith in civilization's superiority over nature was expressed in a nineteenth century magazine article praising the railroad.

> And the Iron Horse, the earthshaker, the fire-breather, which tramples down the hills, which outruns the laggard winds, which leaps over the rivers, which grinds the rocks to powder and breaks down the gates of the mountains, he too shall build an empire and an epic. Shall not solitudes and waste places cry for gladness at his coming?[36]

The contemporary expression of this religion of civilization is, in Santmire's analysis, "the cult of compulsive manipulation." Again there are hints of this cult in popular literature, media entertainment, and widespread social habits. Americans admire the cool, efficient, technical, and competent approach to problems. As we shall note later, there are assumptions about nature and humanity which are conducive to the cult of compulsive manipulation, and which have cooperated in the assault on nature in the name of civilization. There is a certain unquestioning compliance to compulsively manipulating the environment. Santmire states it well:

> If we need a fast avenue from here to there, let it be. If that super-highway throws thousands of poor people out of their homes and destroys landscapes and forest preserves, so be it. If we need, or think we need, chemical weapons to fight the next war, we will have them and let the overflow fall where it may. Once Americans have the expertise to get a certain job done, all it usually takes is an impulsive decision to begin and the project is well underway.[37]

Americans seem to be taken in by both these attitudes, both these cults, even though they seem to be contradictory. We see here a conflict of attitudes which touches on the schizophronic identity of American churches. These conflicting attitudes in turn reflect those deep intuitions and motives which guide the way people act, perceive, think, and make decisions. We are hard put to demonstrate conclusively what guides human behavior but the assumption we are making here is that no account of human behavior is adequate which does not identify those intuitions, motives, and beliefs that constitute the dominant world view. For our purposes, this amounts to speaking of the images of nature and the images of humanity which dominate or are at least prominent in contemporary society.

The Image of Nature

We have just noted that there are contrasting attitudes toward nature expressed as the cult of the simple rustic life and the cult of compulsive manipulation. These two attitudes seem utterly opposed to each other. In fact, however, they share a common assumption, namely that nature is simply there to be used for human purposes, that nature's "value" is in its value *for* humankind. Whether one uses nature as a refuge and escape from the problems of urban and technological society, or as a resource by which to fuel the exponentially growing demands of that society, one is using nature for *human* purposes. The image of nature, which prevails in either attitude, is that nature has no value in and of itself, that nature has no intrinsic value.

It is customary to trace the origin of this notion of nature back to the influence of Descartes and the philosophical tradition which followed. This tradition distinguished two types of reality in the finite world: human minds and that which was not mind, a broad second category which included matter, life, and all things physical. Accompanying this distinction between mind and matter there was also developed a way of distinguishing among the qualities associated with things. Primary qualities are those which exist in physical things independent of any human perception of the things, for instance size, shape, mass, motion. These tended to be the quantitative aspect of things. Other qualities, the secondary ones, were those which seem to depend on some mental activity or human perception, such qualities as sound, or color. Secondary qualities, it was supposed, are projected *onto* things by the mind. How they arose in the mind—that is color, scent—was never satisfactorily explained. The mind did, marvelously, generate these qualities and in such a manner that there could be agreement about secondary qualities among various perceivers or scientific observers. What was assumed was that a nonmental thing could not itself communicate those qualities to the mind. The mind projected the qualities *onto* the thing because of sense-data associated with the thing being observed. To this distinction between primary qualities (those which are independent of perception) and secondary qualities (those which are dependent on perception) one had also to speak of tertiary qualities which seem to reside neither in things in themselves nor to be dependent on sense-data in any obvious way, namely such qualities as emotion, pain, pleasure, moral, aesthetic, and religious feelings. This third category might be termed the realm of value.

When the scope of reality is thus described, the effect is to assign to "nature" that which has only primary qualities. Nature (and natural objects) does not perceive, does not think, does not feel, does not make value judgments. Only human beings have the secondary and tertiary qualities because only human beings have minds, only humans therefore can perceive secondary qualities or experience subjective emotions or hold opinions or make value judgments. We may be amused at cartoons or fables in which animals and trees communicate with each other and with persons but we "know" that such images of nature are in violation of "reality." The point is, the prevailing notion of nature as utterly depersonalized or totally quantifiable is simply not an option for most people in the Western world. It is not even thought of as a notion or an image of nature. It is *assumed* to be the way things are, to be an accurate representation of reality itself.[38]

We have, then, become accustomed to an image of nature which is widely assumed to be an accurate "scientific" description. It is not that we have "reduced" nature to a machine. A mechanistic view of nature has indeed been held by some, and there are some occasions when the image of nature as a machine is a serviceable one. Rather, the contemporary Western view of nature implies a radical difference between nature and humankind. It is a difference that primitives could not hold as their image of reality. As Ernst Cassirer remarks about primitive consciousness in *An Essay on Man:*

> In his conception of nature and life all these differences are obliterated by a stronger feeling: the deep conviction of a *fundamental and indelible solidarity* of life that bridges over the multiplicity and variety of its single forms. He does not ascribe to himself a unique and privileged place in the scale of nature. The consanguinity of all forms of life seems to be a general presupposition of mythical thought.[39]

The effect of the view of nature to which most people are accustomed is that nature is utterly objectified, placed "out there," removed from what is peculiarly "human." Whereas the primitive sought to participate in nature, to seek some harmony or balance with nature, we have tended to distance ourselves from it. This is not to romanticize or idealize the primitive for whom nature was also full of terror, but to recognize how far we have gone to the opposite extreme. The arrogance toward nature which drew the criticism of Lynn White is not totally attributable to Christian beliefs but can also be traced to a very influential, philosophical, and scientific tradition. This tradition has had two baneful results. It has encouraged an exclusivistic humanism and a practical materialism.[40]

On the one hand, exclusivistic humanism has assumed that only humans have any intrinsic worth because only humans can experience that which is valuable. One consequence is that humans have given little attention to the impact of their lives upon that which is not human. Ironically, though, this view of nature, while it does not ascribe any "value" to nature except as it serves human beings, also implies that the only entities which are really "real" are not what we have usually called our values (values are merely tertiary as we have seen). Material entities—not values—are real. Thus, the only real "value" is not the tertiary values (which are merely subjective and therefore ephemeral or unreal) but material goods. The view of nature we are considering here, then, really promotes an exclusivistic humanism which, rather than seeking the good in terms of justice, or peace, seeks the good in terms of accumulating material things (since they alone are thought to be "real"). In short, this view of nature really undergirds the very habits of exponential growth which we have seen to be dangerous because it brings together both an exclusivistic humanism and a practical materialism which yield the deadly credo of modern America: "the greatest good is the greatest possible amount of *material* goods for the greatest number of human beings, preferably Americans."[41]

What is needed is not a new revelation or even some renewed effort at showing how the Christian revelation can resolve all these problems. Rather, what is needed is a new view of reality which will help Christians relate the gospel to the dilemma we have been discussing. To that need we will return.

The Image of Humanity

In the view of nature which we have been discussing, anything which exists in the natural realm derives its value from humankind. Human beings are the valu*ers*. That which is not human can be valu*ed*, but its value is derived from the valu*er*, humankind. Everything seems to rest, then, on being able to demonstrate the sharp distinction between nature and humanity. Without that distinction, value and meaning have no foundation. But how is that distinction itself established? How can a view of humanity be drawn such that the distinctiveness of humankind as the valuer is intact when we also recognize the obvious fact that humankind-the-valuer is part of nature? Nature, since it has no value apart from humanity, cannot be the basis of establishing the distinctiveness of humanity. The consciousness of humankind has been profoundly troubled by such implications. Western literature is full of the awareness of humankind's sense of isolation, alienation, and loneliness. Indeed for Sartre and others one would even speak of nausea while Heidegger speaks of being thrown into the world.

Twentieth-century theology has been profoundly shaped by the implications of the quest for human meaning in a universe conceived as having no inherent meaning or intrinsic value. The quest has been the foundation of some theologies which have sought to show that this quest for meaning is savingly met by the gospel message. Not only is the quest answered but also the *knowledge* of God is somehow given with faith in the gospel message as the answer to the quest for meaning. These theologies are testimony to the pervasiveness and power of the view of nature which we have described, that is to say, these theologies have accepted the assumptions which underlie such a view of nature, particularly the assumption that nature does not of itself give any clues as to lasting meaning or eternal value. Thus, the reliance upon revelation alone for a theology of nature is the way some theologies have both paid their respects to the triumph of nontheistic science and have gone on to establish theologies which are invulnerable to science and philosophy. The knowledge of the distinctiveness of humankind, in such theologies, derives from revelation. What is often unacknowledged, however, is that these theologies of revelation have uncritically accepted those assumptions which have pushed theology to such an exclusive reliance on revelation. It is unlikely that Christian theology can respond adequately to the worldwide dangers stemming from what we have here called exclusivistic humanism and practical materialism if the only alternative is exclusivistic revelation. That is, if humanity is in danger because of the extravagant claims for the absolute value of humanity in relation to nature, is there no other way to relativize or to check those claims except by the exclusive knowledge of God which comes through Christian revelation?

We must try to make clear how ecology and ecclesiology are related at this point. It is not only the ecological base of human history which is endangered by the consequences of the dominant view of reality, but the special ministry of the church is endangered as well. That is, the special ministry of the gospel presupposes that God is universally present, universally at work in the universe. The gospel does not establish the universal work of God but discloses what the intention of God's universal work is, namely to redeem. When this presupposition about the whole universe is denied, as it is by the view of reality which has come to dominate, then the presence of God and the work of God are collapsed into the ministry of the church alone. The ministry of the church *is* a specialized ministry, that is, it is based on the gospel of Jesus Christ, but the gospel is not a disclosure of God in nature or in the universe: it is a disclosure of God in Christ and in the word and the sacrament. As such, the Christian revelation is not a revelation of God in himself but it is a disclosure of the purpose of

God, the deepest intention of God. The church's special ministry assumes that God is at work and present everywhere, that "everything, everywhere is full of his glory." When the church can no longer assume that universal work of God or make it clear what it means, then the gospel message itself becomes unclear and certainly is reduced in scope. The view of nature which we have been describing cannot go unchecked or the special ministry of the church—that is, the gospel message of God's purpose revealed in Christ—is threatened. Gustaf Wingren sounded the same warning some years ago:

> This brings us to the critical point—when a man hears the word or receives the sacraments he does not then encounter God for the first time. All men have experienced the operations of God through the very lives which they live. Every day they receive life from Him and are disciplined by Him in the demands which their neighbors make upon them. But of the new relationship which is established through the death and resurrection of Christ they have had no experience before. The Church has a specific function to fulfill in the world which, apart altogether from the Church, is governed by God, the *deus absconditus* who has dealings with men and constrains them to do His will without disclosing to them His inner reality. If the Church is unable to discern this universal rule exercised by God through the law or to make it clear to men how God is already at work in all the world apart from the Church, it will inevitably lose sight of the Gospel which is its special responsibility.[42]

And so there are ecclesiological as well as ecological reasons for undertaking a criticism of the view of nature and humankind which has come to be prominent in Western cultures. The Christian revelation provides the *motive* for the criticism. Revelation does not provide the *content* of an alternative world view even though revelation does imply that no world view is adequate which precludes the reality of God as an agent in everything which happens in the universe. That is, revelation presupposes God as Creator. Revelation presupposes that the fundamental relationship in the universe is not humankind and nature but it is God and the creatures, comprising the whole created order.

Scripture and the Crisis of Meaning

In the previous section it was asserted that the special ministry of the church is in danger if the church cannot discern the universal work of God and show what such assertions mean. This has become particularly obvious in the church's work of interpreting Scripture. Scripture was written against a background of assumptions about humanity, about nature and the world which is simply alien to most modern people. In fact, Langdon Gilkey, James Barr, and others have argued that modern interpreters of Scripture seem to have assumed that anything *like* a biblical view of nature and humankind is simply impossible. They ascribe the cosmology and ontology of the Scripture to "the Hebrew mind" but in no way do they count it as a usable view of reality. The Bible has to be interpreted mythologically, especially when Scripture refers to activities of God, such as creating, speaking, acting, saving, or rescuing his people. Biblical theologians have become equivocal about what they mean, or what the Bible means, when referring to the work and activity of God. Gilkey states the situation this way:

> In sum, therefore, we may say that for modern biblical theology the Bible is no longer so much a book containing a description of God's actual acts and words as it is a book containing Hebrew interpretations, "creative interpretations" as we call them. . . . Thus the Bible is a book descriptive not of the acts of God but of Hebrew religion. And though God is the subject of all the verbs of the Bible, Hebrew religious faith and the Hebrew minds provide the subjects of all the verbs in modern books on the meaning of the Bible. . . . For us, then, the Bible is a book of the acts Hebrews believed God might have done and the words he might have said had he done and said them—but of course we recognize he did not. . . . It makes us wonder, despite ourselves, what, in fact, do we moderns think God *did* in the centuries preceding the incarnation; what *were* his mighty acts?[43]

Surely Gilkey is correct in tracing this double-mindedness among biblical theologians to the radical discontinuity between the cosmology of Scripture and the view of reality which shapes the thought of the interpreters. Gilkey's own prescription is to call for an ontology "that will put intelligible and credible meanings into our theological categories of divine deeds and of divine self-manifestation through events."[44] Clearly such an ontology would have to embrace both the biblical vision of God as Creator and the prevailing view of reality informed by modern natural and human sciences.

Christian theology ceases to be Christian theology if it is not as serious about the reality of God and God's relation to the world as the Bible is serious. The Scripture writers may not have been "scientific" in any modern sense when they told the stories of God's actions, deeds, words and ways of dealing with the world, but they were not any less serious about the reality of what they referred to than a modern, scientifically inclined person is serious when presuming to speak of reality. The reality in which the Hebrews or the New Testament Christians lived *included* God. Reality, one might say, was unthinkable without God. God was not revealed, nor did God have to "break into" reality from somewhere else in order to be known. James Barr recently summarized the relation between God, reality and revelation in the Bible like this:

> In one very central sense I would say that the *basic revelation* of God in the sense of communication between God and man, is not in the Bible, not narrated in the Bible, but is presupposed by the Bible. From the beginning it *assumes that you know who God is* and that he is in communication with man. *Unlike the situation in modern theology,* there is thus no problem of revelation which has to be solved or overcome. The whole society, and not only the Yahwistic theology, assumes that you can talk with God and hear him and receive the knowledge of his will. What you learn about God in the Bible is not the first contact with deity, it is new information about a person whom you already know. But in another way it can be said that the Bible is the locus of revelation which the Israelite tradition has in fact formed. . . . This would imply that the reading of the story is the way to meet the God whom they met.[45]

Biblical scholars will probably continue to debate Barr's assertions here about revelation, especially the implication that the biblical vision of the world as God's creation is not totally a revealed vision but is also a presupposition of revelation.[46] It is surely not debatable whether Christian theology is possible without a vision of the world as the creation of God. But the vision of God as Creator is seriously challenged by the dominant view of humankind and nature. In the next section we shall contend that a particular view of humanity and of nature, associated with American process theology, can go a long way in overcoming some of the schizophrenic conflicts which have arisen in Christian thought and practise. This view of reality is not exclusively derived from the Christian revelation nor is it a new form of natural theology if by that one means a naturalistic argument for Christian faith. Rather, this view of reality is offered as a challenge and a replacement of that which for too long has given intellectual support to the American credo of the greatest possible amount of material goods for the greatest number of people.[47]

AN ALTERNATIVE VIEW OF REALITY

As inhabitants of the earth we cannot afford to tell lies to ourselves about the nature of reality. The American credo about the greatest good is an intolerable lie. It goes against reality. Truthfulness and morality must be joined in the great issues facing humankind today. We need to change our way of thinking because the way we have been thinking about reality is practically killing us. Of course, global suicide is a conceivable but improbable option. It would be exceedingly difficult to persuade the whole human race at a given time to live only for the moment and thus to sacrifice the future if for no other reason than the fact that only the privileged minority in the world are enjoying the riches of the earth all that much at any given period. The Third World is not likely to join in that form of despair found among some privileged ones whose major fear is that they might not enjoy their privileges forever so that they are willing to contemplate ending it all. The dispossessed of the earth will probably not join the privileged in a suicide pact although they are justifiably willing to risk widespread conflict in the world rather than tolerate forever the unbearable inequalities of distribution of the blessings of the earth.

The view of reality which has come to dominate our thinking about nature and humanity is not only inadequate but it also has fostered worldwide injustice. We have referred briefly to its inadequacy in dealing with the issues of value. It is likewise more and more clear that by giving intellectual support to humanism and materialism it has exacerbated the social, economic and political injustice in the world. Finally, it is inadequate for *religious* reasons. The Bible's vision of God as Creator and of the creation of God's hand, voice, breath, and wisdom[48] are simply unintelligible according to the Galilean-Cartesian-Newtonian conception of reality so that one can only interpret the Bible (if one insists on retaining this nontheistic view of reality) by eliminating God as an actual agent in the world *today* even though the ancient people of the Bible *used to think* that way. What we are proposing here in this section is an alternative way of *thinking* about reality which is closer to Scripture's description of God's relation to the world but which does not simply reject the achievements of science and technology. There is no claim here that this way of thinking is necessary in order to believe the gospel, but that it is a way of understanding that which is implied *by* the gospel, namely that the God of Jesus

Christ is *also* the God who actually lives, acts, speaks, and imparts himself in and to the world.

Humanity and Nature

Christian faith includes within its beliefs the notion that humankind is the "crown of creation." A friend recently gave the writer the fossilized remains of a trilobite and with a knowing smile said, "This *was* the crown of creation 500 million years before Christ."[49] There was a time before which humankind was not the crown of creation and there will be a time when the human species may be surpassed. Even placing the origin of the human species back to one and a half million years B.C., as recent discoveries seem to require, does not significantly alter the judgment that within the history of *nature*, the history of humanity is very brief.

The brief history of humanity is marked by an almost universal turning away from the natural environment in order to cultivate the life of the mind, the life of the soul, the reality of the human spirit.[50] Most of the great philosophies and religions of history were represented in this movement. What was often lost was the sense of kinship with the natural environment. On the other hand, the distancing of humanity from nature opened the way for the widespread control over nature which has become so problematic for the human future. But without such control it would not have been possible to sustain the cultural achievements of history, including religion, and of course, scientific and technological capabilities. The urgent need is to recover a genuine sense of relatedness between humanity and nature but *without* the overreactions of romanticism, existentialism, and various countercultures including the cult of the simple rustic life. There is a sense of relatedness already implied in Christian notions of creation, incarnation, sacrament, and spirit.[51] Recovery of that relatedness is blocked by the view of reality which objectifies nature. If nature is a complex of objects only, it is difficult to understand how *persons* can relate to *objects* except to use them. Communion *with* nature gives way to control *over* nature. The strategy, then, is not to intensify the stress on humanity's existential difference, but to remove that which is blocking the way to the needed sense of relatedness and replace it with an alternative vision of reality.

Process theologians, especially in America, have been hard at work at the task of showing how the conceptuality of Whiteheadian meta-physics "can integrate (humankind's) cultivation of the soul, modern man's appreciation of the quantifiable aspect of nature, and primitive-romantic man's sense of kinship with nature."[52]

Probably the most daring and controversial feature of process meta-physics, or of the alternative view of reality being proposed here, is its assertion that everything in the universe, without exception, enjoys some degree of subjectivity. Nothing is a mere object, however much it may appear to be a mere object. That is, rather than regarding "sub-jective" or "human" experience as qualitatively different from "objec-tive" or "natural" phenomena, this alternative view assumes some de-gree of subjectivity in everything. Charles Birch, a biologist who is one of the interpreters of process metaphysics from the side of science, has suggested that science—for example, physics—has been successful in describing reality primarily as to its explicate order but the impli-cate order is largely hidden.

> Physics does not tell us what it is like to be an atom or an electron. Many people will say that this is a silly statement, anyway. How could you know what it is to be an electron without being one? [But] what electrons and atoms may be to themselves is not necessarily completely closed off from us. As one distinguished physicist said, "You have to sympathize with atoms to know what they really are." . . . Since Descartes, scientists have lost sight of the implicate order and just think that explicate order is self-sufficient.[53]

Instead of organizing reality according to the categories of matter and mind (or objects and subjects), the process view organizes reality in the order of past and present. Each *actual occasion* (which is Whitehead's term for the momentary happenings or events which make up reality) is, at the moment of its becoming, a subject. But each actual occasion or actual entity perishes and is succeeded by a new set of present occasions, each of them also enjoying a moment of subjec-tivity. When an actual occasion perishes it becomes available as object for succeeding occasions. That is, it then has instrumental value, it is an object, for the new subjects. No subject can perceive contempo-raries. Whatever can be taken in or prehended has already passed. It *is* object but *was* subject just as the subject which each occasion now is (for that occasion's private enjoyment or satisfaction) will pass and be available as an object for successor occasions to prehend or take in. When Charles Birch says that "what electrons and atoms may be to themselves is not necessarily completely closed off from us," he means that, by imagining all of reality in terms of events ordered temporally and each event having at least a degree of self-activity and self-value, we are really saying that all of reality is something like our own experience. What it is to *be* an atom or an electron cannot, in principle, be totally cut off from us because *we* have some access to what it is to be what we are.

Unlike the dualistic view of reality which has undergirded so many of our modern conceptual and ethical difficulties, this view conceives of reality as composed of *one* type of entity. There is no problem of the *relationship* between humanity and nature because both participate in one structure of reality. Theology would say that they are both creatures in one creation. Before we consider the implications of this view for speaking about God and the creatures, we need to explain why the dualistic view of reality has such a hold on the modern imagination. That is, if reality *is* in truth composed of *one* type of reality (events or actual occasions) and not *two* (subjects and objects), then this view of reality can help explain why we human beings have been so misguided about the truth—even though our Christian faith would have resisted such a dualism. Furthermore we might also pause to list some of the advantages that this view of the relationship of humanity and nature can bring into the current discussion about resources.

And so, can this view of reality explain the powerful attraction of the dominant dualism which distinguishes nature from humanity, objects from subjects? We must keep in mind that in process thought *all* entities are organisms which have been influenced by the past and which anticipate the future successors. All entities, without exception are both subjects and objects; as subjects they prehend or experience other entities as objects and are themselves experienced as objects by other subjects. That is why entities in nature *appear* to be "mere" objects without any inner reality: by the time they are perceived their "subjectivity" has already passed. Also, those realities which we find in our world are such that we rely greatly on our sense experience to tell us what they are and thus we miss the fact that everything around us is in reality made up of countless individuals with pulsating, throbbing energy. The inertness and static character of most things we experience is really only an appearance.

Also the dualistic view has mistaken the different ways in which actual occasions are *structured* to be different types of *reality*. That is, there is a kind of hierarchy of structures but throughout the hierarchy there is only one basic "unit," the actual occasion which is both subject and object. One type of structure would be, for example, an electron which is organized or ordered as a sequence of temporal series of occasions each rather simply repeating the predecessor. Another type, more complex, would be atoms and molecules and cells, which also are structured in a temporal series but are also "societies" of occasions. Still further, these societies can be structured to form gross enough entities in the world that they may be visible to a human eye. These are even more complexly organized structures which Whitehead distinguished as two types. There are, first of all, democratic organizations which is to say that type in which none of the member entities is in charge of the others. A plant is such a democratic society; so is a stick. The aggregate called the plant does not have any intrinsic value as a plant; the individual entities that make it up *do* have intrinsic value. The plant, as plant, has instrumental value. As David Griffin has observed, "one is not wrong to think of [such entities] as mere objects. . . . One is only wrong if one fails to realize that the aggregate is composed of true individuals that are sentient and as such have intrinsic value."[54] Second, there are organizations of individual entities which Whitehead called *monarchies*, a term which suggests that one of the enduring individuals in a given organization is of a higher level and can exert influence over the lower members. This higher-level member is the soul or psyche found in higher creatures.

Even in this overly simple description of reality composed of but *one* type of entity however variously organized, it is possible to see how a dualistic view of reality could mistake different types of *organization* as distinct types of *reality*. Thus, rather than seeing the soul, for example, as a dominant member of a society of individual entities, dualism rushes to the conclusion that souls or minds are an entirely different type of reality.

"Process thought" has its critics as one might expect. But it also has some advantages for the theological task of countering the baneful effects of the dominant view of reality. David Griffin has summarized these advantages very succinctly.[55]

First, because in this alternative view of reality the world is composed of only one type of entity, variously structured, human beings are placed completely within the natural order. Humankind does not act on nature from some supernatural or even external realm. This view fosters the sense of relatedness with all creatures which is a necessary prerequisite if there is to be any actual concern shown to nature. Second, this view allows for a real difference between humanity and nature, but it is a difference of degree, so that this view would encourage a certain reverence for the real but relative rights of other entities in the created order.

Third, reverence for being does not imply, in this view, that everything has uniform value. We have seen it as a hierarchy of structures which implies a hierarchy of value; the more complex an entity is, the more potential intrinsic value there is. And the greater the instrumental value might be for others. And fourth, the discriminating range of complexity among individuals within the world suggests that freedom is a feature of every entity but especially in the higher creatures. Human beings are part of nature, are indeed conditioned by that environment and the past, but are not determined by it. The future is likewise conditional upon the use which the creatures make of their freedom.[56]

Fifth, there is here no rejection of the quantitative or the explicate. Whitehead's philosophy of organism is, indeed, an effort to "reinstate value in nature" but not at the expense of what we usually call the quantifiable aspect of things. This is no romantic call to trust nature and let her take her course. And finally, a process view of reality enables one (and this should be particularly appealing to Christian believers) to conceptualize the reality of value . . . that is, since *everything* in existence is conceived in such a way that "subject" and "value" are real aspects of every puff of existence, then the Christian apologist need not retreat from the accusation that ideals or values or spiritual categories are somehow removed from nitty-gritty realities. Or as Griffin puts it, "Realizing certain values internally can be seen as more important than possessing certain goods externally." In this view of things, the scriptural word cautioning against gaining the whole world only to lose one's soul is given ontological framework.

God and the Creatures

Humanity and nature are related to God as creatures to Creator. One might say that process theology, by challenging the dominant conception of reality which tends always to make humankind an exception to the natural order, has returned humanity to nature. Or in Christian language, we are reminded that we are of the order of creatures and not the Creator, that we have come from the dust and will return to the dust. Since process theology is a *theology*, we might ask whether the doctrine of God found in process thought is at all helpful in dealing with the issues that are central to this essay, or does this theology return humanity to nature at the cost of eliminating God? Existentialist and *Heilsgeschichte* theologies often heighten the alienation of humanity from nature but at least these theologies, by identifying the I-Thou character of the relationship between God and humanity, have been able to address the religious question. What happens to the God-humanity relationship, in process theology which, undoubtedly, goes far in restoring the humanity-nature relationship?

Process theology offers a way of doing that which Gustaf Wingren has insisted is necessary if the church is not to lose sight of its distinctive task. That is, process theology does "make it clear to men how God is already at work in all the world apart from the Church . . ."[57] In this theology all the creatures are conceived as living, interrelated actual occasions. Reality is an organic, societal whole composed of myriads of interpenetrating individuals. God, in this view, is related directly to each of the individuals in the universe and related in such a way that God is the chief or most important cause of all the events although God is not the only cause. How God acts upon the world and the creatures is one of the fundamental and crucial aspects of the Whiteheadian view of reality and, as Daniel Day Williams has argued, "it is a topic of crucial importance for contemporary Christian theology with its emphasis in the biblical perspective upon the action of God in history."[58]

In this view God never takes a holiday from history and nature. God is necessary to every whiff of existence, every actual occasion, so that in this theology one does not speak of God intervening in history or breaking into the natural order. To speak in that way is to conceive of God as a mechanic tinkering with a mechanical world. There *are* significant events. Some occasions are "revelatory" because they are especially open to new possibilities which had been closed previously. Indeed, any novelty or newness is only possible because of the presence of God who alone presents to each creature possibilities for actualization. One has to imagine, then, that every actual occasion—that is each drop of experience which interacts with all other occasions to form the universe—is open also to the presence and power of God. None of the creatures is exempt from that influence although all the creatures, all the entities, have some degree of real freedom as they select from the real possibilities offered. God acts, in part, by offering to each occasion the initial aim, the ideal possibility, graded as to its appropriateness for that occasion in view of the ideal possibility of every other occasion. God provides something like the "seed" for each member of each new generation of occasions and yet each individual makes a contribution to what that occasion will achieve or become. The initial aim may or may not be actualized because, while no occasion is entirely a self-created entity, every member is to some degree self-created. Both God and each entity or each pulse of reality have something to do in this view. God is the Creator in this view, but God is not prior to or before that which becomes in each moment of creation. "God is not *before* all creation but *with* all creation."[59]

These few sentences can only hint at the rich—and difficult—complexity of the doctrine of God in process theology. It has been widely and variously interpreted and also vigorously disputed. Christian theologians who have adopted this perspective have usually done so because they accept the criticism which process theology directs against the traditional Christian view of God. The traditional view is not necessarily compatible with Scripture and is vulnerable to several very serious charges articulated by process thinkers. Whitehead believed that the traditional conception of God owed more to an image of an arbitrary, despotic ruler with no restraints on his power than to the New Testament picture of Jesus. In the New Testament there is, he wrote, "a suggestion which does not emphasize the ruling Caesar, or the ruthless moralists, or the unmoved mover. It dwells upon the tender elements in the world, which slowly and in quietness operate in love; and find purpose in the present immediacy of a kingdom not of this world."[60] The process critique of traditional theism, then, is largely a *moral* critique, even though its *appeal* to Scripture-minded Christians might be its possibilities for rendering the notion of God's actions in history *intelligible*. It is this moral critique against the traditional doctrine of God which is most revelant for this essay.

When God is conceived as an amalgam of the absolute and arbitrary monarch, as a ruthless moralist and as the unmoved mover—a conception often preferred in Christian theology—there are some intolerable consequences which offend the moral intuition and are incompatible to the gospel as well. First, God is the direct and final cause of everything that happens, both good and evil, the many tortuous theological rebuttals notwithstanding. Second, if God is the cause of all that happens, in a direct and final way, then human freedom is sacrificed to the tyrannical deity. Third, when God's power is absolute, then religious and ethical systems mounted in the name of God tend to be self-absolutizing. Religion, suggests Whitehead, seems always to be a synonym for hatred.[61]

Not only does the process view of God meet the condition which Wingren lays down for an adequate understanding of the special ministry of the church, but it also provides a foundation in reality itself for moral seriousness. Human responsibility for the care of the earth is, in this view, more than a sentimental urge or a romantic ideal. It is one way by which human beings serve the ultimate good. It matters supremely what human beings do: it matters to the earth, to humanity, and to God. In a television interview Rabbi Abraham Heschel was once asked why he bothered to involve himself so passionately in the many human causes that consumed his energy. He replied that he did so in order to reduce the suffering of God. It matters to God what human beings do. By restoring the intimate relationship between God and the world, process theology gives a certain conceptual clarity to human moral and religious responsibility for the care of the earth. Indeed, some process thinkers suggest that the relationship between God and the world is as intimate as the relationship we have to our bodies. The world is the body of God.[62]

Heschel's reference to the suffering of God, and the imaginative notion of the world as the body of God, point to a second feature of the doctrine of God. Not only is God here conceived as *a* necessary but not *the* sole condition or cause for everything which happens—that is, God affects or acts upon every event as we have already noted, but also everything that happens has an intimate even though slight influence on God—that is, every event affects or acts upon God. In broad and overly simple terms this is Whitehead's view of the two natures of God, the primordial and the consequent. It corresponds roughly to the biblical sense that God has determined to love the world unconditionally—

God is unmoved as to his purpose to love—and that God is also willing to adapt himself, even to repent in order to be Immanuel, to be the God who is always with the creatures even though one descends into hell (Psalm 139), God is both unmoved as to his purpose and effective will, but also deeply moved because of his intimate relationship to and involvement with the world.

The second report of the Club of Rome, we may recall, called for a new understanding of the concept of growth. An organic concept of growth is necessary if we are to plan adequately for the humane uses of the earth's resources. Organic growth in living organisms proceeds according to the master plan inherent in every cell. Cancerous growth results when that master plan is somehow overthrown and cells grow exponentially in undifferentiated fashion destroying the interrelatedness which is essential to the whole. But, say the authors of the report, the master plan for organic growth is not, apparently, inherent in the present trend of historical growth, nor will it be injected by a deus ex machina, that is by a mechanic God tinkering with a mechanical universe.

The theology which is presented here as a contribution to the discussion of ecology and ecclesiology is precisely *not* a theology of deus ex machina, nor is it a theology of an absent God who occasionally reveals himself in isolated events, either. Rather it is a theology which claims that God *is* the inherent reality in all existence, in all events, but that the way God is present is much more complex than previous conceptualities had allowed. God's power is everywhere effective but there are many forms of causal efficacy[63] just as I influence my body in various ways and the influence of my body on what I can do is various. This theology allows for God's activity to be specific to the concrete activity of every creature. God acts universally and with a fixed purpose—namely to relate to the world in love—but God cannot *act* in a uniform way and still be the God who loves. Love adapts and is specific to the circumstance. Love is what God wills and what God wills is fixed; what God *can do* is conditioned by whether the creature is a sparrow, the hair on one's head, a cancer, or a deeply spiritual person. That God will also be acted upon, that God will react to every event, is also certain. The effect on God is uniform but the quality of God's experience is specific to what happens: from the suffering of God because of evil, to the "joy in heaven over one sinner who repents." And so, while it is not apparent that there is an inherent master plan for the organic growth of the world, in this view the inherent plan is the implicit reality of God's organic interrelatedness with the creation. The question is whether human beings will continue to act cancerously or will learn to live organically according to the "seed" or initial aim which God gives to every entity.

Of course Christian piety has usually known that "master plan" as the *Logos*, inherent in God's creative activity from the beginning. The name of the one who was the enfleshment or incarnation of the Logos or master plan, is Jesus Christ. Christ is the hope of the world, for Christians, because Christ is the incarnated instance of what life-in-relationship is created to be. Christ is love incarnate. Jesus is the historical disclosure of who God is. God is love-in-action and that love is unsurpassably enfleshed in Jesus Christ.[64]

Because of Jesus Christ the world need not be in the dark about that which is necessary for hope to be real: that people be reconciled to God, to one another, and to the created order if they are to live. The reconciliation has already been accomplished. It waits only to be realized fully. And it will not be realized fully until there is that harmony with the earth which the prophets foretold, when "the leopard shall lie down with the kid," or which the hymn promises, "earth shall be fair and all her people one." Process theology is one way in which Christian piety can be helped to conceptualize the Christian faith and thus be able to participate intelligently, sensitively, and concretely in the task which belongs to all humankind, namely to live out on earth the Creator's intention captured in the vision of piety and prophecy.

Conclusion

Ulrich Duchrow has shown that Luther's understanding of faith liberates the Christian from any notion of fixed and eternal laws in nature or in history.[65] The Christian is freed to serve the neighbor so that the only fixed law is the law of love. We are more and more aware that we cannot really serve the neighbor in love unless we also develop a policy for an equitable and responsible worldwide stewardship of the earth, which is the common basis of life for all people. The view of God, of humanity and of nature which is proposed in this essay is one which knows of no fixed laws which deterministically prescribe the course of every particle of matter or every historical event. Instead, the law operative in this view is the law of relatedness. That is, the well-being of each member of God's creation, as well as the whole of reality, is really dependent on each member having regard and concern for each other. This metaphysic is one which does not see "love" as a tertiary or minor quality—somehow remote from what is really real— but sees love as the law of the universe, the greatest of all realities. As a reality love is active and effective in everything that happens. Love does not always "get its way" but is not thereby defeated. Indeed, love is shown to be invincible at the point where evil does its worst, on the cross. God is the source and reality of that love. God, as the fellow-sufferer who understands—to use Whitehead's familiar phrase— joins himself with the creatures and is joined by the world in an ever-lasting relationship. As D. D. Williams wrote, the relationship of God with the world is "the adventure of a real history where both God and the creatures have freedom to act and to respond, God supremely and the creatures within the limitations of their own creaturely status."[66]

People are not usually converted to religious faith by a conception of reality. Indeed, Christian faith comes from hearing the gospel message. But Christian faith can be immobilized when it is not clear how faith is based in reality. Faith can be misguided because of erroneous notions of reality, or faith can be intimidated by "scientific" descriptions or predictions which seem to eliminate God or the work of God from what is happening. This essay, drawing upon a subtle, complex but beautiful description of God and the world has proposed that this conception of reality can more clearly show that hope rests not merely in "faith" or even in "God," but in that which faith implies: a reliable, trustworthy *relationship* between God and the creatures. God is in the world as a real power, a power which is working slowly, quietly and by persuasiveness without calling attention to itself.[67] That power is not found *outside* the organic, interrelated wholeness of things nor is that power simply identical *with* the wholeness either. It is the power of the Spirit of God.

The church's task is to be faithful to the ministry of the gospel. But that ministry assumes a certain vision of reality which this essay has tried to make more explicit. It is a vision which can be best nurtured by the life of worship and so the worship of the church ought to be so conducted that faith is not turned away from the world of human beings and their needs. Instead, in worship the church is given that sense or experience of the reality of God-in-community which equips people for a life of service. In this day of dwindling resources on the earth, the life of service will be, especially for Americans, a life of material simplicity, a life of personal and national sacrifice, of world-consciousness and world-cooperation, of preparation for the time which must come when the demand for more goods cannot be a simple human right. The liturgy of the church—its "reasonable service"—is the church's distinctive role by which the church enacts in the present, proleptically, what is the eschatological vision of the church for the world, namely that there be a new heaven and a new earth in which harmony and peace are forever and ever.

NOTES

1. A particularly imaginative and richly researched study of the appropriation of religious symbols to support nationalistic ambition in Robert Jewett, *The Captain America Complex* (Philadelphia: Westminster, 1973).

2. Lynn White, Jr., "The Historical Roots of our Ecological Crisis," *Science,* 155 (1967):1203–07.

3. Compare Ulrich Duchrow, "Between Power and Suffering," *Lutheran Quarterly,* 27 (1975): 125–38. Whereas Luther's doctrine of faith implied liberation from damnation of the law in a religious sense, it also meant freedom to criticize the dominant view of *lex aeterna.* God does not force us or provoke us to good deeds by supposedly eternal laws but by the concrete need of our neighbor. Melanchthon, however, renewed the Stoic doctrine of *lex aeterna.* This misinterpretation often prevailed in Lutheranism and then "received a new and dangerous impetus with the triumph of modern natural science. Natural science . . . conveyed the impression of nature being guided by deterministic laws" (p. 129).

4. Joseph Sittler, "The Presence and Acts of the Triune God in Creation and History," in *The Gospel and Human Destiny,* ed. Vilmos Vajta. (Minneapolis: Augsburg, 1971), pp. 107–8, citing *Record and Revelation* (Oxford, 1938), pp. 333–34.

5. Ibid.

6. Mihajlo Mesarovic and Eduard Pestel, *Mankind at the Turning Point: The Second Report to the Club of Rome* (New York: North American Library, 1976), pp. 19–20.

7. Donella H. Meadows, et al., *The Limits to Growth* (Washington: Potomac Associates Press, 1972).

8. Ibid., p. 29.

9. Mesarovic and Pestel, *Mankind at the Turning Point,* p. 4.

19. Ibid., p. 1, cited from A. Greg, "A Medical Aspect of the Population Problem," *Science* 121 (1955):681.

11. Ibid., p. 7, emphasis added.

12. Ibid., pp. 8–9.

13. These data and figures have been provided the writer by Professor Allen

Utke of the University of Wisconsin, one of the advisory group who helped develop the theme of this essay.

14. Allen Utke, unpublished mimeographed materials, University of Wisconsin, "The Birthing of a User."

Each American baby born today will require in its lifetime:
        26,000 gallons of water
        21,000 gallons of gasoline
     104,000 pounds of iron and steel
        13,000 pounds of paper
        10,000 pounds of meat and 28,000 pounds of milk
     100,000 pounds of total food
         9,000 pounds of fertilizer
       $7,000 to $10,000 of school supplies
       $9,000 of furniture
     $10,000 of clothing

In the lifetime of this child, he/she will discard:
        10,000 no-retrun bottles
        17,500 cans
        27,000 bottle caps
           2.3 automobiles
          35 rubber tires
     252,000 pounds of garbage
      19,600 pounds of particulate air pollution

It's not a baby only; it's a super consumer.

15. Utke, unpublished resource paper.

16. *Plain Truth Magazine*, October 1973, cited by Utke.

17. The World Council reports appear in the occasional paper of the WCC, *Anticipation*, 20 (May 1975) and 21 (October 1975). The National Council report (September 1975) is entitled, "The Plutonium Economy: A Statement of Concern."

18. David J. Rose, Massachusetts Institute of Technology, unpublished paper, "Comparison of Two Important Societal Views," November 2, 1975.

19. Utke, unpublished paper, "Energy, Technology and Food."

20. *China Notes* 13, no. 2, National Council of Churches, New York (Spring 1975). Ben Stavis, "Why China Is Not a Basket Case"; Donald MacInnis, "How China Feeds 800 Million"; and Thomas Fenton, "China's Approach to Population Planning."

21. Ibid., MacInnis, p. 16.

22. Ibid., MacInnis, p. 17.

23. Ibid., Stavis, p. 15.

24. Ibid., quoted by Fenton, p. 20.

25. Ibid., p. 20.

26. Daniel Callahan, *The Tyranny of Survival and Other Pathologies of Civilized Life* (New York: Macmillan, 1975), pp. 91–92.

27. Ibid., p. 96.

28. Ibid., p. 100.

29. For a provocative discussion of this issue see Richard R. N. Dickinson, "Shifting Elements in the Development/Liberation Debate," *Occasional Bulletin* 26 Missionary Research Library, 3041 Broadway, New York, N.Y. (Jan.–Feb. 1976).

30. Ibid., p. 7.

31. Richard John Neuhaus, for example, raises this question very forcefully in *In Defense of People: Ecology and the Seduction of Radicalism* (New York: Macmillan, 1971).

32. H. Paul Santmire, "Ecology and Schizophrenia: Historical Dimensions of the American Crisis," *Dialog* 9 (Summer, 1970):175–91. This article is an excerpt from Santmire's very useful book, *Brother Earth: Nature, God and Ecology in a Time of Crisis* (New York: Nelson, 1970).

33. Ibid., p. 176.

34. Ibid., p. 183.

35. Ibid., p. 184.

36. From Leo Marx, *The Machine in the Garden: Technology and the Pastoral Ideal in America* (New York: Oxford University Press, 1964), cited by Santmire, p. 179.

37. Ibid., p. 185.

38. The philosophical situation described here is variously and widely treated. A brief account is given in David Griffin, "A New Vision of Nature," *Encounter* 25 (Spring 1974): 95–107.

39. Cited by John B. Cobb, Jr., *Is It Too Late? A Theology of Ecology* (Los Angeles: Bruce, 1975), p. 40.

40. Griffin makes this point with particular clarity in "A New Vision of Nature," pp. 100–101.

41. Ibid., p. 101. This is a variation of Griffin's phrase.

42. Gustaf Wingren, *Gospel and Church*, trans. Ross Mackenzie (Philadelphia: Fortress, 1964), p. 98.

43. Langdon Gilkey, "Cosmology, Ontology, and the Travail of Biblical Language," *Journal of Religion* 41 (1961):197.

44. Ibid., p. 203.

45. James Barr, "Story and History in Biblical Theology," *Journal of Religion*, 56 (1976):16 [italics added].

46. For a recent discussion of this question, see Claus Westermann, *Creation*, tran. J. J. Scullion (Philadelphia: Fortress, 1974).

47. The argument being made here is not that process theology is alone (or even the first) in pressing the conceptual difficulties of bringing together the exegetical, biblical, and historical material and contemporary views of reality. Rather, process theologians have been more self-consciously committed than many others in urging an alternative view of reality instead of trying to accommodate the biblical message to a presumed scientific world view on the one hand, or of disengaging "biblical thought" from "modern thought" altogether. It is for the sake of the biblical message of God as Creator, of God as redemptively active in history and supremely active in Christ, of God as present in the world, that this philosophical theology is pursued. The goal is neither to dismiss nor to replace the biblical motifs, but to interpret them by showing how a cosmic theism is necessary if the full meaning of Scripture is to be appropriated. The criticism of other theologies in this essay is not so much a neglect of the immense gains made by these other perspectives, but is an allegation that, without an adequate metaphysic (or a suitable ontology of the acts of God) they cannot meet the crisis addressed by this essay.

48. Compare quotation from Wheeler Robinson, n. 4. Of course, Scripture gives powerful support for opposition to injustice, including the injustice of unequal distribution of the earth's blessings. See Bruce C. Birch, "Hunger, Poverty and Biblical Religion," *Christian Century* 92 (June 11–18, 1975):593–99.

49. The Reverend Ken Olson of Chinook, Montana, has been a helpful and encouraging consultant for this essay. His considerable geological knowledge has stimulated his own reflection on its implications for a doctrine of creation and for the ministry of the church.

50. See, for example, John B. Cobb, Jr., *The Structure of Christian Existence* (Philadelphia: Westminster, 1970).

51. See W. Pannenberg, "The Doctrine of the Spirit and the Task of a Theology of Nature," in *New Theology*, ed. Martin E. Marty and Dean G. Peerman (New York: Macmillan), 10 (1973):17ff.

52. Griffin, p. 107. See also I. Barbour, *Issues in Science and Religion* (Englewood Cliffs: Prentice-Hall, Inc., 1966); John B. Cobb, Jr., *God and the World* (Philadelphia: Westminster, 1969); and *A Christian Natural Theology* (Philadelphia: Westminster, 1965).

53. Charles Birch, "What Does God Do In the World?," *Union Seminary Quarterly Review* 30 (1975):80–81.

54. Griffin, p. 105.

55. Ibid., pp. 105–6.

56. Robert Theobald, ed., *Futures Conditional* (New York: Bobbs Merrill, 1972). The advent of such a book, replete with the visions of the future by dozens of artists, writers, "futurists" is testimony to the fact that many thoughtful people act as though freedom as an ontological reality is a necessary precondition for a responsible life.

57. Wingren, *Gospel and Church*, p. 98.

58. Daniel Day Williams, "Deity, Monarchy and Metaphysics: Whitehead's Critique of the Theological Tradition," in *The Relevance of Whitehead*, ed. I. Leclerc (New York: Macmillan, 1961), p. 353.

59. A. N. Whitehead, *Process and Reality* (New York: Macmillan, 1929), p. 521.

60. Ibid., p. 520.

61. Williams, "Deity, Monarchy, and Metaphysics," p. 357.

62. John Rustan Clark "The Great Living System: The World as the Body of God," *Zygon* 9 (1974):57–93.

63. Williams, p. 371.

64. See Norman Pittenger, "The Doctrine of God and Its Implications in Process Theology," *Religion in Life* 40 (1971):361–75.

65. Compare n. 3 above.

66. Daniel D. Williams, *The Spirit and the Forms of Love* (New York: Harper & Row, 1968), p. 9.

67. Cobb, *Is It Too Late?*, p. 143.

As a way of thinking about reality which is an alternative to biblical and classical Christian forms, Dr. Snook proposes "American process theology." This view of reality he regards as "a challenge and a replacement being developed by such theologians mentioned in his notes as John B. Cobb, Jr. (notes 39, 50, and 52), David Griffin (n. 38), Daniel D. Williams (n. 58), Norman Pittenger (n. 64), and others. He presents a brief picture of this approach which is based on "Whiteheadian metaphysics," lists half a dozen of its advantages, and gives a "process" doctrine of God.

Inasmuch as this type of philosophical thinking is not always known as widely as it might be in its own right, and is the subject of much dispute when brought into theology—the Epilogue will touch on debate which has flared among American Lutherans over Professor Snook's own application of this way of thinking to the problem of the resurrection and life after death— it seems worthwhile to append a note concerning "process theology" and listing some pertinent titles on it.

Alfred North Whitehead (1861–1947), the son of a Church of England clergyman and brother of a Bishop of Madras, achieved fame as a mathematician at Cambridge University, and for his collaboration with Bertrand Russell on the *Principia Mathematica* (1910–13); as an educator in London; and, after appointment at age sixty-three as Professor of Philosophy at Harvard, for his metaphysical system. Reared an Anglican, he read widely on his own concerning theology, particularly in Roman Catholicism, went through an agnosticism phase in World War I, and thereafter kept no church affiliation. His 1928 Gifford Lectures, the strange terminology of which caused his audience to melt away, reached a larger and growing audience when published as *Process and Reality*. It was Charles Hartshorne (1897–), professor at the Universities of Chicago (1928–55) and Texas (1968), who made that part of his system known as "process theology" flourish, with an emphasis on God as a participant in cosmic development.

Whitehead had sought, in the face of modern scientific and mathematical knowledge, to work out a full view of reality with perhaps the most comprehensive metaphysical system developed in our century. It stood most frequently therefore in contrast to the thought of Aristotle. (Hence the parallel: just as medieval theology developed in certain schools on the basis of Aristotelian thought, so some contemporary scholars are seeking to work in theology on the basis of Whiteheadian.) A key concept was that of "becoming." While Aristotle worked with logical propositions like "S is S, S is *not* P," therefore "either S or P," in terms of "identity," the "excluded middle," and "contradiction," process thought reckoned with the possibility that "S is *not yet* P." The stress is on the process of becoming. Indeed, the process is more fundamental than the products, and the whole is future-oriented and looks continually for "creative advance."

In such a system the world is a vast collection of actual occurrences, a continual process of becoming. Events, or "occasions of experience," relate to each other in the ordered web of the space-time experience. What is "subjective" to one person becomes "objective" to another. What one experiences becomes a building block for others, as the whole moves on. *All* being thus experiences subjectivity—there is no "inert matter." It is precisely this concept which attracts Dr. Snook for speaking about "nature": everything in the universe participates in subjectivity, there are no "mere things" or "substances," and human beings are placed irrevocably in the natural order.

What of "God"? Whitehead himself devoted some space to this topic philosophically, and Hartshorne and others have developed process *theology*: God is not exempt as a kind of "Unmoved Mover" but is himself in the process of change. He is that essential structure in which all must participate and at the same time himself participates in the community of becoming and perfection of growth. Such a view enables process to take God seriously as "person" (in analogy with human growth and experience) and to see him involved in the universe. Indeed, what process theology and Christology do extraordinarily well is allow for incarnational thought and the "theology of the cross." For deity is vulnerable and can suffer. This seems to challenge some traditional views of God as "totally unchangeable" and any notions of "eternal kingship" or dominion, if that is taken to imply coerciveness, for God is said to work instead persuasively, within the process.

Pantheism is the wrong word to characterize all this. *Panentheism* is closer the idea that God includes the world as a part, though not the whole, of his being, so that there is interpenetration but not identification. In this connection Professor Snook quotes with apparent approval a phrase about the world as "the body of God" (J. R. Clark, n. 62). Such language obviously relates ecology (the care of the body of God) to ecclesiology (about the "body of Christ"). Process theology is thus proposed as a vehicle for setting forth the doctrine of God in a comprehensive way which a modern scientific world can understand and yet which resonates with themes dear to Lutheran theology like *theologia crucis*. It differs from classical salvation-history thinking in the way it involves God in the process. Thus (1) instead of Oscar Cullmann's famed and neat chart of Heilsgeschichte stretching from creation, through Israel's history, narrowing to the pivotal figure of Jesus Christ, and then expanding through apostolic and church history to "the end," we have rather a continuum, ongoing, affecting everything in the cosmos, where some "events" loom larger than others, but all are within God's plan, or, more accurately, God working; or (2) as Schubert Ogden put it, commenting on that phrase which causes Dr. Snook to see a crisis of meaning for Scripture so profound as to demand a different view of reality, namely "the acts of God": "the primary meaning of God's action" is "the act whereby, in each new present, he constitutes himself as God by participating fully and completely in the world of his creatures, thereby laying the ground for the next stage of the creative process" ("What Sense Does it Make to say, 'God Acts in History'?" in *The Reality of God and Other Essays* [New York: Harper & Row, 1966], p. 177).

INTRODUCTORY DISCUSSIONS OF PROCESS THEOLOGY
(CITED IN ORDER OF LENGTH OR DEGREE OF DIFFICULTY)

HARVEY, VAN A. *A Handbook of Theological Terms.* New York: Macmillan, 1964. Pp. 190–92.

GUNTON, COLIN. "Process Theology's Concept of God," *Expository Times* 84 (1972–73): 292–96, with comments by Norman Pittenger in 85 (1973–74): 56–57, and Gunton, p. 215.

MILLER, RANDOLPH CRUMP. *This We Can Believe.* New York: Hawthorn Books, 1976. Intended for lay people.

MELLERT, ROBERT. *What Is Process Theology?* New York: Paulist, 1975.

COBB, JOHN B., JR., and GRIFFIN, DAVID R. *Process Theology: An Introductory Exposition.* Philadelphia: Westminster, 1976. College level.

PITTENGER, NORMAN. *Unbounded Love.* New York: Seabury, 1976. With a study guide by James Fenhagen.

COLLECTIONS OF ESSAYS

BROWN, DELWIN; JAMES, RALPH E., JR., and REEVES, GENE. *Process Philosophy and Christian Faith.* Indianapolis: Bobbs-Merrill, 1971. Twenty-five articles and excerpts reprinted, plus bibliography of "significant works" which means to be complete through 1969.

CARGAS, HARRY JAMES, and LEE, BERNARD, eds., *Religious Experience and Process Theology.* New York: Paulist, 1976. Topical concerns, including "church" and "ethics."

COUSINS, EWERT H. *Process Theology: Basic Writings.* New York: Newman, 1971. Reprints twenty essays by Whitehead, Hartshorne, and fifteen others, identified with Whiteheadian "process" or Teilhard de Chardin and "evolution." Bibliography, pp. 351–69.

Encounter (Christian Theological Seminary, Indianapolis, Indiana) 36, 4 (Fall, 1975), is devoted to papers from a working conference in 1974 on "Process Philosophy and Biblical Theology," including:

LUNDEEN, LYMAN T. "The Authority of the Word is a Process Perspective," pp. 281–300;

BEARDSLEE, WILLIAM A. "Narrative Form in the New Testament and Process Theology," pp. 301–15, with a response by Bernard E. Meland;

WEEDEN, THEODORE J. "The Potential and Promise of a Process Hermeneutic," pp. 316–30;

GRIFFIN, DAVID R. "Relativism, Divine Causation, and Biblical Theology," pp. 342–60, with responses by Bernard M. Loomer and George W. Coats;

JANZEN, J. GERALD. "Modes of Power and the Divine Reality," pp. 379–406;

REITZ, HELGA. "Biblical and Cosmological Theology. A Process View of Their Relatedness," pp. 407–32.

Encounter has run separate articles on process at other times. *The Philosophical Journal, The Review of Metaphysics,* and *The Southern Journal of Philosophy* 7, 4 (Winter, 1969–70) have devoted issues to the theme. There is now a journal solely devoted to the subject, *Process Studies.* The American Academy of Religion/Society of Biblical Literature currently includes a group working on "Process Hermeneutic and Biblical Exegesis." Cf. also the issue of *The Union Seminary Quarterly Review* published in honor of Daniel Day Williams, 30:2–4 (Winter–Summer, 1975).

PROCESS PHILOSOPHY AND THEOLOGIANS

COBB, JOHN B., JR. *A Christian Natural Theology: Based on the Thought of Alfred North Whitehead.* Philadelphia: Westminster, 1965.

———. *God and the World.* Philadelphia: Westminster, 1969.

———. *Christ in a Pluralistic Age.* Philadelphia: Westminster, 1975.

———. *Theology and Pastoral Care.* Philadelphia: Fortress, 1977.

COOPER, BURTON Z. *The Idea of God: A Whiteheadian Critique of St. Thomas Aquinas' Concept of God.* The Hague: Nijhoff, 1974. It has become increasingly common to relate theologians of the past to contemporary process thought, as Dr. Snook did with Luther in his dissertation.

FORD, LEWIS S. "Biblical Recital and Process Philosophy: Some Whiteheadian Suggestions for Old Testament Hermeneutics." *Interpretation* 26 (1972), pp. 198–209. Deals with creation, providence, and biblical authority.

GRIFFIN, DAVID R. *A Process Christology.* Philadelphia: Westminster, 1973.

———. *God, Power, and Evil: A Process Theodicy.* Philadelphia: Westminster, 1976.

HARTSHORNE, CHARLES. *The Divine Relativity: A Social Conception of God.* New Haven: Yale University Press, 1948. Seminal.

LEE, BERNARD. *The Becoming of the Church.* New York: Paulist, 1974. Worship and community stressed.

LUNDEEN, LYMAN T. *Risk and Rhetoric in Religion: Whitehead's Theory of Language and the Discourse of Faith.* Philadelphia: Fortress, 1972.

MELAND, BERNARD M. "New Perspectives on Nature and Grace." In *The Scope of Grace: Essays on Nature and Grace in Honor of Joseph Sittler,* ed. Philip Hefner. Philadelphia: Fortress, 1964, pp. 143–61.

PITTENGER, NORMAN. *God in Process.* London: SCM, 1967.

———. *Process-Thought and Christian Faith.* New York: Macmillan, 1968.

———. *Christology Reconsidered.* London: SCM, 1970.

———. *'The Last Things' in a Process Perspective.* London: Epworth, 1970.

SNOOK, LEE E. "What Does Worship Say?" *Theology Today* 24 (1967–68), pp. 474–84.

WHITEHEAD, ALFRED NORTH. *Religion in the Making.* New York: Macmillan, 1926.

———. *Process and Reality: An Essay in Cosmology.* New York: Macmillan, 1929.

———. *Adventures in Ideas.* New York: Macmillan, 1933.

WILLIAMS, DANIEL DAY. *The Spirit and the Forms of Love.* New York: Harper & Row, 1968. Called by reviewers "the first process systematic theology."

TWO

THE IDENTITY OF THE CHURCH
IN LIGHT OF
THE STRUGGLE FOR HUMAN IDENTITY

Concern for the *humanum*, "true humanity," was prominent in World Council and LWF studies in the sixties. Struggles for identity broke into the open even more fully in the seventies on the part of women, youth, blacks and Hispanics in the United States, and the aging. Black Panthers, Gray Panthers, women's lib, all became a part of the scene in which most Americans live. What do these protest and self-development movements say, if anything, to the church and its anthropology (doctrine of man/woman, mankind/personkind—even the old terms are no longer without challenge)? The LWF survey of member churches in 1973–74 listed "conflicts between male and female, and between generations" as one of four major areas of concern. The relations of women, men, and youth received special attention at the Addis Ababa and Bossey consultations in 1974 and 1975, especially in self-studies from Tanzania, Ethiopia, and the Federal Republic of Germany. "Women in the Church" was the concern of a segment of Project Area I in the LWF/Studies program; the Rev. Eva Zabolai-Csekme led seminars on "Leadership Development for Women" in Ethiopia (1973) and Indonesia (1975), and 1975 was International Women's Year.

When in 1974 the response of the American Lutheran churches was sent to Geneva about current issues, it made the following judgment:

Insofar as American Lutherans still ask "vertical-oriented" questions about salvation, redemption, justification, and revelation, confessional Lutherans will remain faithful in proclaiming the Reformation witness to Christ alone, grace alone, faith alone, and Scripture alone. However, many of our people today are more troubled and divided over such "horizontal-oriented" questions as war, government, human rights for minorities, youth cultures, and natural resources. Moreover, this is not a replacement of ethics for religion as our top priority; it appears to be a different way of viewing reality in general, and the relation of the eternal to the temporal in particular. In short, questions of ultimate concern in a secularized culture are often posed in terms of the "here" rather than the "hereafter."

A note of hope is sounded in the statement, "In both the ALC and LCA individuals and groups which began with an emphasis on advancing women's interests and rights grew to the point where they talked genuinely about personhood and wholeness in the Christian community." What does this changed and changing situation say to ecclesiology?

The outline for essays developed by the U.S. Advisory Committee (see p. 25) simply spoke of "The Struggle for Human Identity," and strung out beneath it a number of specimen examples of how current quests for identity were going on currently. It was left to the essayist to choose which and how many of these would be touched upon. We wish each one might have been developed in detail, and to the list the quest for gay liberation and for new recognition of the middle class and its rights and values might now be added. It was readily apparent, however, that the question of men-women relations and the fact of sexism in society and also in the churches clamored most for attention. It is true that in the United States the search for identity, rights, and justice has especially concerned racial minorities, and has led to vigorous and sometimes beneficial manifestations of concern in churches, but worldwide the focus in the LWF study has been far more on "whether wholeness includes women" (Gerta Scharffenorth at the 1975 consultation). Obviously the roles of women become a primary topic when one considers the percent of persons in this minority group within the churches: regularly over fifty per cent, but never so in places of leadership, church councils, or committees. Hence to focus on the male-female relationship became the goal of the essay on human identity in relation to church identity. It is the area which is most likely to reshape thinking in the future about the church emerging, its ministry (need one any longer say "*her* ministry"?), and even its theology, right up to the doctrine of God. (The neuralgic point with the Missouri Synod over the ordination of women, which the ALC and LCA have accomplished with little or no upset, was not a factor in settling on the male-female relationship as crucial.) Moreover, male-female relationships, however different in different ethnic situations and however much the same, also are a problem in minority groups seeking rights today too.

The Rev. Donald G. Luck, who treats ecclesiology in light of emerging quests for human identity—particularly on the part of women—is a clergyman of the LCA, teaching at a college of the ALC (Concordia, Moorhead, Minnesota) where he has been Assistant Professor since 1969. Born at Portchester, New York, in 1933 he was graduated from Gettysburg College in 1954 and the LCA Seminary at Philadelphia in 1957. He spent a year in graduate study in Edinburgh, and, after serving in New York State as an assistant pastor for a year in Richmond Hill and then pastor in Brewster (1959–65), returned to graduate studies in systematic theology at Union Theological Seminary, New York City, specializing in the thought of Paul Tillich. He earned the S.T.M. magna cum laude in 1966 and is a candidate for the Ph.D. He has been a tutor at Union and a visiting lecturer at Manhattan College, at his alma mater in Philadelphia, and at Luther Seminary, St. Paul.

The colleagues on whom he especially relied in developing his paper included:

Dr. Larry J. Alderink, Associate Professor of Religion, Concordia College, Moorhead, Minnesota;

Dr. Eleanor Haney, Associate Professor of Religion, Concordia College;

Ms. Stephanie Johnson, broadcast journalist for Minnesota Public Radio, radio station KCCM-FM, Moorhead;

Ms. Suzanne Siemering, Instructor in Psychology, Concordia College;

Dr. David Myers, Assistant Professor of Philosophy, Moorhead State University, Moorhead.

HUMAN IDENTITY AND
CHURCH IDENTITY

Donald G. Luck

One need not look long nor hard at contemporary American[1] society to find evidence for fundamental reassessments and reappropriations of identity. What the concrete expression of one's humanity means—existentially and essentially, what one can become within the limitations of destiny and the possibilities of freedom, how one evaluates one's dignity and is valued by others, the ways in which one can perceive and constitute social roles and status, are issues that have moved into the forefront of concern for increasing numbers of individuals and groups of people. This paper represents a response to current reconsiderations of personal and social identities based on the distinctions of race, ethos, age, and sex and the implications they have for theological reconsiderations of the identity of the church.[2] More specifically, it will tend to focus on some of the implications of the woman's movement in the United States for the life and thought and mission of the church.

In examining the woman's movement in the United States as a representative expression of current reevaluations of personal and communal identity, this paper will attempt to develop the central thesis that, while the woman's movement deserves not only theological interpretation but also the concrete involvement and support of the churches, there are important qualifications. Certain developments within the feminist theology that has emerged in connection with such interpretation and involvement and support present a serious challenge to the theological enterprise itself and to the very life and mission of the church. In elaborating this central thesis, this paper aims at showing how the reconsiderations of traditional personal and social identities

1. Notes appear at the end of the essay.

represented by the woman's movement can be understood as contemporary expressions of that wider historical-cultural movement initiated in the Renaissance and flourishing in the Enlightenment which has aimed at increasing personal responsibility, self-direction and self-definition. Although the churches' unqualified endorsement for this general movement is not warranted, there are grounds for correlating it with certain biblical perceptions of the redeeming and humanizing purposes of God. On the other hand, this paper will also hold that the appeal made by certain expressions of feminist theology tends to supplant the christological foundation of the churches' thought, life, and mission.

Consequently, it will be argued, the fundamental issue which emerges out of a theological analysis of the woman's movement as a representative expression of the interrelation between the identity of the church and current reexaminations of human identity is the ultimate criterion which theology and church life invoke in determining the meaning of human identity. In this regard, the churches must avoid two tendencies: (1) to fall captive to the vagaries of changing historical movements which in the final analysis claim to authenticate and evaluate themselves, and (2) to believe the churches have access to a timeless and unchanging perception of human identity and, hence, church identity. The alternative proposed by this paper is the *ongoing struggle* of the churches (and the fact that this is a struggle and a struggle which is ongoing should be noted) to discern the "dynamic catholicity" of the christological criterion of both human identity and church identity. Such a criterion is christological since it holds itself accountable to that point within history where the Christian witness believes the *telos* of history has manifested itself. Such a criterion is dynamic because its meaning is neither exhaustively nor definitively perceived by any one generation or any one culture but rather needs to be reappropriated "kairotically," that is, in the specificity of history and culture. Such a criterion is catholic because its implicitly redemptive power and evaluative meaning address not merely the universal constants of human experience but also more particularly the uniqueness of culture and the contextual novelty of history.

This leads to the conclusion that the church must rediscover and reappropriate its identity within the dynamic concreteness of history. Such rediscovery and reappropriation emerges out of the tensions and risks involved in bringing into creative interaction its christological foundation and the immediate historical-cultural context of the churches. In the present situation the latter includes contemporary re-assessments of personal and communal identity. The church is that community which judges between the spirits and discerns the signs of the times in the light of its christological criterion; at the same time, it comes to understand the power and meaning of that criterion only by immersion in the historical-cultural struggles within which it is placed.

THE ISSUE OF IDENTITY

A helpful point at which to begin an examination of the identity of the church in the light of current reassessments of personal and communal identity can be found in the concept of identity itself.

The terms *identity* and *identity crisis* were introduced into general usage some three to four decades ago by psychoanalyst Erik Erikson and have usually been associated with the struggles and achievements of individual psyches. According to Erikson, the question of one's identity is the central psychological issue that everyone must confront and resolve at various stages of personal development, but especially in adolescence.[3] Identity entails both personal centering and communal integration; it implies the need to be "at one with oneself" and, at the same time, to find an affinity with the larger human community. Central to Erikson's analysis is his insistence that reassessing and reappropriating one's identity is a dynamic process which occurs in the context of internal development and external change. Unlike classical treatments of the more abstract philosophical question of "identity," Erikson is not interested in how the self is able to maintain a central unity amid diverse operations or what it is in human personality that remains constant within the flux of change but rather he wants to trace how individuals are able to create a continuity of self which embodies far-reaching developmental changes.[4] He believes his studies have demonstrated that the psyche is not static but rather centrally engaged in a process of growth, a process which is punctuated by a series of crises or distinguishable periods of stress and disruption which force the individual to reassess her/his internal psychological coherence and reestablish her/his relationship to the wider human community.

One implication of Erikson's analysis is that identity is more than individual and internal. It has a centrally societal dimension which is linked to the communal character of existence; it is psychosocial. This means that individuals must struggle with communal models of identity which purport to appropriate and interpret a coherent world and establish the individual's place within that world. At stake in communal identity is what Talcott Parsons has called "the internalization of the social structures" of one's world. Social identity means the individual's capacity to appropriate, evaluate and (if necessary) modify communally shared affirmations of value. It also touches on one's expanding capacity to relate both to other persons and to social institutions and deal with their readiness to include oneself. This implies that, necessarily, individual identity is bound up with the way one sees oneself in relation to the human community as a whole and the ways in which that community (or segments of it) sees the individual. In fact, it is precisely this social and cultural context that is central to the normative identity crisis characterizing adolescents and youth and which remains a continuing referent in subsequent crises.

Identity crises challenge the individual at both conscious and unconscious levels to establish a sense of personal continuity and integration in the light of contradictory mental states and patterns of value, to be open to the dissolutions of previously achieved modes of integration, and to realize undeveloped potentialities and new psychological integration. Yet it is possible not only to fail to resolve the various identity crises associated with psychological development but also to ignore the need for working through one's identity by hiding in the social and cultural identity that usually is associated with the resolution of the paradigmatic identity crisis of adolescence. By social identity we mean the identity provided by social relationships such as marriage and family, occupation, civic involvement, and religious communities. Cultural identity denotes the identity established by one's participation in distinguishable segments of society which are based on distinctions of age, race, ethos, sex, religious tradition and the like.[5] But it is possible to call social and communal identities themselves into question, thereby initiating a new identity crisis or, to put it more accurately, thereby entering into a new phase of the ongoing process of establishing one's identity.

Other developmental psychologists have modified and supplemented the schema that Erikson has proposed or have offered alternative ones, but where all agree is in their common contention that human identity is neither uniform nor immutable. On the contrary, in all of its dimensions (including those that are social and cultural) identity is subject to the possibility of ongoing alteration. What is crucial in the views of some developmental psychologists is not just that identity undergoes processing; it *is* a process. They agree with a popular slogan of the day that "Life is a journey and not a destination." The interest in seeing the self as a process has become the particular concern of the increasingly influential Human Potential Movement which, as its name indicates, focuses on the possibilities of developing untapped potentialities for personal development and what are believed to be fuller realizations of humanity.[6]

The individual is thought to be able to progress in "self-actualization" by coming to discover and embody more comprehensive and more coherent modes of human existence. Accordingly, the meaning and power ("potency") of one's being is centrally tied to the realization of one's possibilities of being ("potentiality"). The implications of this understanding of identity are summarized by Richard E. Farson when he notes: "Our personal adjustments to life have been anchored in familiarity, stability, the reliable sameness of things, the permanence of values, places, relationships. In the future our adjustment to life will be based on our ability to cope with the process of change."[7]

It is this growing association of identity and the processes of change that merits careful theological attention and which can be associated either directly or indirectly with the social turbulence that has been tied to the so-called protest movements that have emerged throughout the wider human community during the last decade and a half. It is not surprising to see an axis emerging between schools of psychology which are interested in the developmental aspects of human personality on the one hand and sociological analysis of recent social conflict and unrest on the other. Struggles with personal identity that entail reappropriation of the meaning of the self, reorganization of experience, and restructuring of values have not only theoretical but also material connections with social movements that question existing social structures and stratification, traditional social patterns, and the values and concepts of human meaning which underlie them.

The protest movements that have emerged in the contemporary American situation—the movements associated with blacks, Chicanos, native Americans, ethnic consciousness, youth, the elderly, and women —are highly diverse and have different, even conflicting aims. What they have in common is that they represent varying struggles with the issue of identity on the part of segments of the general population that see themselves as marginal and oppressed by the dominant elements (the Establishment) of a heterogeneous society. These elements can be characterized as white, male, middle-aged, bourgeoise, and northern European. Under attack are what are purported to be the discontinuities, hypocrisy, inadequacies and dangers inherent in the society which is shaped by these dominant elements and specifically the frustration by the Establishment of these subordinate social communities' attempt to realize a fully human existence. This frustration entails the denial of full human dignity in evaluating the marginal group's identity, the reduction of the marginal group to a narrow range of possible social roles, and the withholding of power from the marginal group in the assignation of social status.

To be sure, these protest movements need not have any direct connection with developmental analyses of identity. They have not necessarily subscribed to the notion that identity is more a matter of ongoing process than static realization any more than to the conviction that change is constitutive of being itself. But it is the case that each movement has been caught up in a crisis of social identity which has triggered reassessments of fundamental values and interpretations of the meaning of being human. Such reassessment has been advanced not only for the marginal subcultures or subcommunities each movement has claimed to represent but also for society as a whole. Moreover, such reevaluation and reappropriation of identity have occurred with specific reference to the material conditions of society and, thus, to what Erikson has called one's capacity to relate both to other people and to social institutions, and the readiness of these to include oneself. At stake are both "theoretical" and "practical" issues—the nature of one's being and the values it embodies on the one hand and the nature of one's concrete social roles and participation in power on the other.

In addition, protest movements and schools of developmental psychology meet in their common conviction that confrontation with unquestioned or static identity and the corresponding attempt to reconstitute identity is synonymous with the liberation of repressed potentialities for richer realizations of being and the actualization of greater personal fulfillment and self-direction. What is important to underscore is that there has usually been as much concern with "*internal*" transformations of self-perception and self-evaluation, or what has been called "consciousness raising," as there has been with the *"external"* transformation of the material bases for existence.[8]

With historical movements as complex as these it is difficult to determine with any sense of confidence why they have emerged at this stage of world history in general and American history in particular. Several factors, however, seem to suggest themselves as significant correlates. One theme that seems to be singled out again and again is the one captured in Dietrich Bonhoeffer's oft-quoted reference to "a world come of age." Since the emergence of the modern era of Western history in the Renaissance there has been a gathering sense of humanity's capacity to investigate, evaluate, and modify not only its world but also itself. There is a growing sense among people today not only of the extent to which their individual lives in society are conditioned by external factors but also of the extent to which each person is an active participant in history. This includes her/his own personal history and the common history of all.[9] Increasingly, in terms of the broad ranges of history, individuals and groups of individuals are daring to consider not how things are but how they might be. They are gaining a particularly *historical* sense of the nature of being and, consequently, have made the issue of identity (in "internal" and "external" terms) an increasingly central one.

Daniel Boorstein believes that this development was precipitated by the discovery of the "New" World and the effect it had on European consciousness. In this connection he points out that the United States was the first "prosaic nation" in world history, the first independent political and social community which was brought into being by the will and rational deliberations of men. There are no "mythological" origins for the American nation. Accordingly, the United States represents a community of human beings whose corporate identity is something that has been established self-consciously and which is, therefore, continually open to the ongoing modifications and reconstitutions that will and reason can dictate in each new generation.[10]

Interestingly, Erikson agrees with this contention and notes that it is precisely this phenomenon of a society conscious of creating itself and open to the possibilities of redefining and reconstituting itself in succeeding generations that has resulted in a typically American self-consciousness about and a preoccupation with personal and social identity.[11] Moreover, he believes the issue of identity has a central place in "the mental baggage of generations of new Americans" who were forced to integrate their former identities (which were grounded in their homelands) with the new identities which emerged in a new land.[12] Thus, if the crisis of self-definition is that associated with adolescents and youth, there is enough of the adolescent in every American so that expansive openness to the new tends to be a national characteristic and the impact of spreading Americanization causes segments of affected societies, especially the young, to begin to take seriously the stance of "self-made" persons.

Therefore, current protest movements in the United States and other societies may be seen as extensions of those "protean" expressions of identity that emerged in the American and French Revolutions and which found philosophical expression in the tradition of "the rights of man." In this connection it has been observed that this movement marks a transition to that phase of Western civilization which is characterized by the historicizing of life and consciousness. Until this point protest movements called for a restitution of what was held to have been lost or betrayed. Moreover, this was done on the basis of formal religious justification. The two hallmarks of the protests emerging out of the Enlightenment and ranging through the nineteenth and twentieth centuries are that they appealed in progressive fashion to the unrealized possibilities which were held in lie in the *future,* to new rights and social orders, and did so on overwhelmingly *secular* grounds.

As a result it has often been true that these protest movements have met opposition from the churches which not only resented their a-religious or even antireligious character but also resisted their disregard for either established tradition or already-existing visions of human fulfillment. At the same time, ironically enough, the semi-Christian and quasi-Christian character of the inherent values and visions of human identity which these movements have espoused express substantive connections with the churches, their traditions, and their biblical foundations that both sides have usually ignored or denied.[13] The result has been a chequered history marked by ambivalent relations between protest movements and the churches.

An additional result of the dissolution of direct connection between social protest movements on the one hand and the churches and their traditions on the other has been the necessity these movements felt to create and articulate specific philosophies of protest. This has been the particular function of the intellectual advocates of protest who with their formal rationales have tended to fill the gap left by the loss of religion and religious leadership (whether such leadership came from the ranks of the established clergy or from charismatic figures) as the link between formal ideas and popular political, social, and economic protest.[14] This implies that tensions and ambivalence characterize not only the relation between the churches and various protest movements but also the responses within the churches themselves. The lines of connection between formal religious leadership represented by the clergy, lay leaders, and the governing hierarchy on the one hand and the leadership of these movements on the other, as well as between the interpretation and articulation of church tradition and formal rationales of protest, are the subject of internal ecclesiastical conflict and debate.

What the rational and secular character of this turn in the history of protest movements in the West especially signals is the recognition of the mutable character of social identity. Whether one considers rationalism's appeal to an inherent rational order in nature, romanticism's belief in the divinely-inspired creativity of the human spirit, Marxism's concern to change the world and not merely understand it, or existentialism's insistence on the necessity of self-definition, what are presupposed are the assumptions that reality can be transformed and that knowledge is tied to the possibilities of transformation. In light of this relation between knowledge and modification of what is known, some insist that truth is "verified" in the etymological sense of the word. It is made (*facere*) true (*verum*). Knowledge of reality that does not transform it is an unverified interpretation.

Another correlate to the emergence of protest movements is the dialectic of ideological self-criticism. Just as Marx believed that the very ideological principles of middle-class liberalism contained within them the seeds of the economic criticism of the very society which espoused them, so too the protest movements which have emerged recently on the American scene have grounded themselves in the ideology espoused by the Establishment while calling attention to the disparity between the implicitly or even explicitly *universal* nature of those principles and their particularist or delimited realization. Consequently, one can understand such protest as protest by the marginal elements of the general population which have been systematically excluded from the rights, benefits, and dignity which American ideology holds are meant for all. At the same time, however, such movements can be seen as extensions of the protean character of earlier movements in their willingness to go beyond the existing implications of the dominant ideology and express new principles and visions of genuine human identity. Therefore, their relation to the dominant American ideology is both clarifying and creative. To be sure, they are by no means agreed as to the neglected implications of the existing ideology or as to what modifications or transformations are necessary.[15] They are agreed, however, on the marginal character of their position in society and their being denied recognition of full human dignity.

Because of the diverse goals and the diffuse analyses associated with these different protest movements, it might prove more helpful for our purposes to focus on one of them as a "test case" of how the current struggles which attempt to reevaluate, reinterpret, and reconstitute social identity have a bearing on the life and thought of the church. Such delimitation has the disadvantage of ignoring the careful analysis of the existing social situation and the alternative visions and values which each movement represents. Yet the examination of only a single movement can provide us with a *pattern* of theological interpretation which can be subsequently applied to other movements and to the phenomenon of social protest as a whole.

This paper has chosen to focus specific attention on the impact of the American woman's movement on the churches. It has done so for particular reasons. It is not simply the fact that, potentially, the woman's movement addresses the identity, roles, and status of half the world's population. It is more centrally the fact that the most fundamental distinction which establishes human identity and, therefore, the most pervasive basis for cleavage and alienation between human beings, is that of sex. Rosemary Radford Ruether goes further and argues that social alienation begins as a self-alienation experienced as an estrangement between the self and the body. This fundamental alienation is then associated with the genital distinctions of human physiology and projected, socially, as sexism. In this way, biological differentiation is connected with existing power relationships and given "natural" justification.[16] While it may or may not be true that the origins of self-alienation are physical and, specifically, sexual it is hardly debatable that the appeal to "natural" distinctions gets to the very crux of human identity and the protest movements concerned with it. Distinctions which are "natural" should be self-evident and should be exempt from the mutable character of existence which concerns historicized consciousness. In addition, appeals to "nature" in respect to male and female identities have obvious religious implications. What is "natural" is theologically understood to imply what is "God-given" and, therefore, inviolable. This puts into the sharpest focus possible the revolutionary and historicist character of recent protest movements and their significance for the church's interpretation of its life, thought, and mission.

DISCLOSING THE REALITY OF SEXISM

In 1922 Ernst Troeltsch published an essay in which he contends that the centrally characteristic expressions of the modern era which differentiate it from others are the differing though related modes of thinking and of perceiving the world which he calls "naturalism" and "historicism."[17] Both are more than general intellectual methodologies, he asserts; they are *Weltanschauungen.* Historicism deals with both the dimensions of human experience centrally characterized by flux and development and also the role of the unique and the particular. But even more so, it is a mode of perceiving reality which recognizes that all social and cultural phenomena are dominated by relativity, uniqueness, and transformation.

By recognizing that reality is "historical" as well as "natural" one must face in a very central way the admission that, to use the words of Peter Berger and Thomas Luckmann, "humanness is a sociocultural variable."[18] This only reinforces the "protean" readings of social and cultural identity to which we have already referred. Historicism reveals the historically and culturally relative character of the fundamental values upon which social institutions, cultural communities, and, hence, communal identities rest. Not only are these values historically and culturally contextual, they are open to radical question and transformation.

The effects of historicism on traditional identities, role assignations, and social standing are obvious. It will no longer do to appeal to longstanding precedent, to seemingly "universal" patterns, and to what is assumed to be an unchanging human "nature." This helps to explain why, for example, highly effective critiques of traditional concepts of the nature of being female, the proper role of women, and the social status of women have been mounted in the modern era. It also helps explain why even appeals to the religious sanction of such traditional views have been ignored. These religious legitimizations are seen to be themselves historically and culturally relative. Religious legitimizations of existing social values and social patterns are examples of the historically and culturally relative symbol systems underlying particular epochs and communities, systems that Berger and Luckmann call "symbolic universes." They are symbolic because they go beyond immediate experience to provide theoretical interpretations of human existence; they are universes because all sectors of institutional and communal existence are integrated in an all-embracing frame of reference which claims to be capable of containing the whole of human experience.[19] But they are neither universal nor immutable. The function of providing symbolic universes is filled both by acknowledged religious traditions whether they be broadly or narrowly conceived (for example "the biblical view," Christianity, Lutheranism) and by the influential quasi-religions of the modern world (for example Marxism, American civil religion).[20] By unearthing the relative and mutable character of symbolic universes, historicism has provided protest movements such as the woman's movement with leverage for overhauling existing social patterns and creating new ones despite the "universality" or "sanctity" claimed for existing traditions.

Historicist grounds for criticism and reconstruction of existing social and cultural identities have been strengthened by Karl Marx's contention that the underlying interpretative grid of a society is invariably inadequate since it is grounded in the concretely biased patterns of the social order. Symbolic universes are "ideologies," distorted or at best partial readings of the human condition which are used to justify and extend the interests of the dominant social class. As Marx and Engels put it, "The ideas of the ruling class are in every epoch the ruling ideas: i.e. the class, which is the ruling material force of society, is at the same time its ruling intellectual force."[21] This means that the symbolic universe of the dominant segment of a society comes in a subtle fashion to have as wide a "subjective" dominance and influence as its beneficiaries gain in "objective" power relations. In this way a particular ideology comes to be the fundamental intellectual shaping force for the whole of society and gains subscription and support even from those it helps to oppress. What is particularly relevant to the analysis of sexism is Marx's observation that, despite the fact that ideologies are historically and culturally relative, they present themselves as "natural" and therefore inevitable, unquestionable, and immutable. Ideologies legitimate the concrete social relations within a society; they engage in "mystification."

It is important to keep in mind that, according to Marx, the absolutizing of existing social relationships embodied in the dominant ideology is done unconsciously. Ideology is, in Engels' words, "false consciousness," an inadequate or biased reading of meaning, value, and reality in general; it is not necessarily what Sartre would call "bad faith."[22] This means that exposing the ideological character of the assumptions of the dominant class does not mean having that class confront its duplicity and hypocrisy but rather enabling it to discover its own self-deception. One might say that recognition of ideology as ideology amounts to disclosure (*apokalypsis, revelatio*). The transcending of ideology entails liberation of the oppressors as well as of the oppressed.

Representatives of the woman's movement claim that traditional notions of the nature, role, and status of women are expressions of the ideology of male dominance. Sexism refers not only to the material and structural social patterns which oppress women but also to the male-originated, male-perpetuated, and male-justifying ideology which supports and legitimizes this oppression. As in the case of other ideologies, traditional portrayals of the nature, role, and status of women are viewed as "objective" readings of "natural" (or even "God-given") conditions which are self-evident.[23] Also, like all ideologies, the popular and professional rationalizations and the religious endorsements of sexism have gained the general support of all segments of society, including the very women that they oppress. Therefore, the recognition of sexism amounts to a discovery that demands a shifting and even a radical transformation of one's perception of reality. Consequently, it is not surprising that the impact of the woman's movement often begins as a process of consciousness raising which is the prelude to wide-ranging disruptions of marital, familial, and wider social relationships. As Rosemary Radford Ruether notes, "From their earliest years, women are culturally conditioned to be willing cooperators in their enslavement and unconscious of their objective situation. Thus their liberation begins as a terrifying explosion of consciousness, a self- and world-transforming experience."[24]   Moreover, the process of liberation implies that men as well as women will come to discover the oppressive character of a male-dominated society and the ideological nature of its justification as "disclosures" that startle and broaden awareness.

It is instructive to note in this regard that Erik Erikson believes the emergence of identity is inevitably linked to a positing of a "negative identity." We come to define ourselves, he says, not only in terms of what we are but also in terms of what we are not.   That is why individuals and social groups tend to assume new perceptions of their identity with reference to an "otherness" which is consigned to the bottom of the social scale "as the sum of all that must not be."[25]   Such negative projections not only provide the dominant class with a sense of superiority and a kind of brittle wholeness but also attach a social stigma and a justification of subordination to the irreversible differences which distinguish dominant and suppressed classes.   It is blacks, youth, and women in our culture who embody the negative identity of the dominant class, according to Erikson, and must endure "an intrinsic, an inbuilt psychological unfreedom...not resolved by the mere promise of political and economic equality—although, of course, impossible without it."[26]   As a result, subordination means not only enduring existing power relationships but also living with the frustration of being unable to change into the dominant type while at the same time being unable to decide freely to remain as and where one is.   Such frustration can express itself in subtle forms of self-hatred or in a blind hatred of one's oppressors which does not really overcome the negative character of one's imposed identity.[27]   This means that liberation must rest on the capacity of persons to be what they understand themselves to be and not merely what others say they are.   It must begin with a reappropriation of what Vann Woodward has called the "surrendered identity" of the oppressed.   Therefore the unconscious or dimly perceived collusion of the oppressed with their oppressors in accepting such negative identities must be exposed.[28]

It is not surprising, therefore, that the leading edge of the woman's movement consists of a frontal assault on well-established and largely unquestioned notions concerning the nature, role, and status of women and their ideological justifications.   The powerful and even traumatic nature of this "demystification" accounts for the considerable agreement one can find in the woman's movement with Engels's assertion that "the first class oppression coincides with that of the female sex by the male."[29] Understandably, for some the woman's movement has assumed an almost messianic character since the liberation of women is viewed as the overcoming of the *fundamental* or *paradigmatic* form of social oppression.[30] Other analysts are more moderate in their claims but hold, nevertheless, that the liberation of women is *representative* of other expressions of human liberation.[31] In either case there is the assertion that an understanding of the oppression and liberation of women has wider, and perhaps universal, significance.

One fundamental aspect of sexism against which the woman's movement protests is stereotypical readings of the nature of women.[32] Such traditional characterizations have a central role in the establishment of the identities of women and men. Genital differentiation has usually been associated with differences in personality traits, interest profiles, and modes of temperament. The nature of being a woman (or a man) has been given normative and therefore unquestionable form on biological, psychological, or anthropological grounds. Biological justification usually centers on alleged effects of hormones or the effects on women of their capacity for childbearing and nursing. Psychological arguments assume there are psychological implications inherent in the physiological distinctions which exist between the sexes. Anthropological support is given to what are held to be "universal" personality characteristics to be found among women in otherwise varying human communities.

These characterizations and their justifications are increasingly being challenged as expressions of ideology, the projections and rationalizations of male self-alienation and social dominance. Where it is admitted that such characterizations are typical it is also contended that they have a cultural and social base rather than a natural one and, consequently, are open to modification and even radical transformation. Significantly, according to feminists, there is no absolute agreement as to what constitutes the normative nature of women; and even where there is a general consensus specific characteristics are singled out not as absolute distinctions but as general tendencies. Moreover, true to their character as ideological rationalizations, outright contradictions can be found in popular characterizations of female nature. As Cynthia Ozick has pointed out, because women are understood to be over-emotional and sentimental one has a ready explanation why there are so few women serving in roles requiring mechanical skills or aggressive leadership. At the same time the disproportionate absence of women from the arts is explained as being due to the fact that it is in the nature of women to be prosaic, unadventuresome, and unimaginative.[33]

There have been only a few attempts to establish personality differences in a central way on genetic or hormonal grounds.[34] The growing consensus of scientific investigation, however, is that there is only at best limited evidence for such a possibility.[35] Far greater support, though, has been given to traditional personality differentiation on the basis of psychoanalytic theories which echo, on varying grounds, Freud's famous dictim that "anatomy is destiny." Even Erikson who holds that "Freud's general judgment of the identity of women was probably the weakest part of his theory"[36] believes that genital morphology corresponds to particular male and female personality types that reflect distinguishable modes of relating to space.[37] To be sure he qualifies this distinction by holding it points to general tendencies of personality only and by insisting upon the capacity and even necessity of one sex to assume personality characteristics typical of the other.[38] Yet there is growing clinical evidence which suggests that personality differentiation is overwhelmingly the result of processes of socialization that begin even with infants. This implies, as psychologist John Money puts it, that personality differentiation based on sex is established in much the same way as a native language. It represents learned patterns of response.[39] Increasing numbers of psychologists are suggesting that even if there are natural personality differences between the sexes it is social conditioning more than any other factor that maximizes these tendencies to the point where it is this culturally variable element that is the determinative shaper of personality.[40] Increasingly, studies in behavioral psychology seem to show that a high degree of influence is exerted on personality characteristics by social expectation.[41]

This evaluation has gained general support from anthropological investigations which also tend to claim that stereotypical readings of male and female personality types are culturally variable.[42] Margaret Mead sums up these findings in her often-cited study of three New Guinea tribes whose sexuated personality characteristics differ not only from each other but also from those which are stereotypical of European societies: "Many, if not all, of the personality traits which we call masculine or feminine are as lightly linked to sex as are the clothing, the manner, and the form of headdress that a society at a given period assigns to either sex."[43] Obviously this growing body of observation and analysis is strengthening the hand of feminists in their criticism of the ideological character of stereotypical readings of the nature of women.

The feminist movement is also presenting a related challenge to traditional sexuated assignation of social roles and their closely related correlate, social status. Criticism of such stereotyping of roles and status is complex, however, because the roles that are understood to be subordinate and demeaning in one society may carry a larger measure of significance, prestige and even power in another.[44] Marxian analysis holds that the evaluation and the status associated with particular roles within particular societies are directly proportionate to the economic significance that each role has for that society. At root, both sexuated division of labor and sexuated social subservience are economic in nature.[45] The more economically significant a particular woman's role is, the more social status and actual power she has. Yet, anthropological study once again shows that the assignation of particular roles on grounds of gender—even that of caring for infants and raising children—and the corresponding social status of these roles are cultural variables. The traditional patterns of Western societies are by no means universal. Therefore, argue feminists, justifications for such assignation of roles and for the granting of related status are ideological.

The central implication of this growing body of criticism is that an assertion of male dominance, even when sanctioned by long-standing tradition or religious legitimization, is an expression of political ideology. Its function is to maintain the concrete power of the socially dominant group. Rosemary Radford Ruether argues that in the final analysis sexism does not so much rest on the weakness of women as on the suppression of the power of women. Sexism is "an elaborate system of handicaps that males erect around women to make female potency appear to be the point of their weakness and dependency, thereby suppressing from cultural consciousness the truth of male dependency." What is needed is the rediscovery of the power inherent in female identity.[46]

Not all analysts agree with economic explanations for the basis of male social dominance and for the general sexual delimitation of roles that typifies most societies.[47]   But a growing number do agree that the heretofore unquestioned assumption that a natural division of roles and status can be empirically discovered and theoretically justified cannot hold.   Even if such roles and status are "natural," critics ask, Why, for example, are social barriers erected to restrict the flow of women into particular jobs?   If "natural" implies "universal," why is there no unvarying uniformity of roles or status reported by anthropologists—even in regard to child rearing?   If "natural" implies the absence of human intervention, how then can one condemn feminism on those grounds and yet justify birth control or health care or even the male custom of shaving?   As a consequence, the sexuated assignation of particular roles, the typifying of normative male and female personalities, and, above all, the endorsement of the socially subordinate status of women are coming under increasing attack.   Also under fire are their religious legitimizations which appeal to natural theology, biblical precedent, and readings of what are assumed to be the fixed "orders of creation" (*Schöpfungsordnungen*), legitimizations which have tended to typify most responses from the churches in the past.

THE WOMAN'S MOVEMENT CONFRONTS THE CHURCHES

These broad considerations are linked to the ways in which the woman's movement has specifically confronted the churches.   Initially, it must be recognized that the woman's movement is anything but a coordinated enterprise.   It even spills beyond the borders of a working coalition to reflect differing and, sometimes, conflicting views of what "liberation" entails.   The National Organization of Women (NOW) which came into existence in 1966, for example, originally reflected the interests of middle-class professional women who demanded that women be given equal opportunity to participate and prosper in existing economic and educational systems.   Other women's groups such as the Redstockings were formed by women involved in the New Left. But even leftist expressions are not uniform.   Groups which identify with Marxian critiques of the competitive and hierarchical character of capitalist society assert that traditional Marxian theories overemphasize economic determinants and fail to provide an adequate analysis of the subjugation of women.[48]   Assertions that New Left organizations are themselves sexist have led to the splintering of participation within these movements and the creation of alternative programs. Socialist-oriented feminists, for example, stress the economic oppression of women and assert that male dominance is rooted in certain historic economic factors. Radical feminists on the other hand stress the personal and familial oppression of women and locate its source in the sexuated distinctions in physical strength, reproductive roles, or the like.[49]

The pluralistic and even fragmented character of the woman's movement is heightened when one moves from giving exclusive attention to the American scene to an examination of the international situation. Here, one encounters not only parallels to the divergent character of the American movement but an even wider spectrum of views which emerges out of cultural diversity. Merle S. Goldberg has pointed out, for example, "Western women do not seem to understand that one woman's sexual stereotype may be another's sense of security, a traditional role that provides identity, continuity—even survival."[50] This only suggests further that there is no universally acceptable or generally applicable theoretical interpretation of the nature, causes, or remedies for the oppression of women.

This divergence of views should sensitize the churches to recognize, therefore, both the opportunities and the limitations of potential lines of connection between the theoretical and active expressions of the woman's movement on the one hand and theological interpretation and church mission on the other. Historians of the woman's movement point out that the concrete struggles for women's liberation have often been tied to other movements and that feminists have tended over the years to use whatever ideology and terminology were familiar and available to them. The resulting diversity of interpretations concerning the nature and causes of women's oppression should be approached dialectically by the churches. Christian interpretations of the nature and origin of sin can provide a point of contact *and* a source of qualification in evaluating these differing interpretations.

The effects of the woman's movement on the life and the thought of the churches are also diverse. Closer examination seems to show that the concrete goals and theoretical interpretations of the woman's movement that have emerged within the churches have tended to shift in the same general directions as the wider movement itself. The earlier concerns of granting suffrage to women and enabling their full economic participation in American society can be paralleled in movements within the churches aimed at allowing women to participate in church governance and admitting them to the ranks of the clergy.[51]   These earlier goals, however, are being superceded.

Increasingly voices are being heard within the woman's movement that the movement is itself too representative of the values and presuppositions of a sexist society.   The ultimate goals of feminism are not to be reached, it is contended, by admitting women to the ranks of patriarchally dominated social structures or by equal participation in a society which continues to express the supremacy of traditionally "masculine" values.   Women are now called upon to preserve and mediate many of the particular values and social patterns which they have traditionally embodied and to abandon only their subservient status. In a pattern remarkably similar to that of other movements championing the cause of marginal and oppressed segments of society such as blacks, the attention of feminists is turning from integration into the existing American society to a transformation of that society by admitting to equality and even preeminence alternative values and social patterns preserved by women.   In addition, the woman's movement is being subjected to close scrutiny to see how it can itself express the alienation and oppression of a society not only dominated *by* males but given to the domination which is stereotypically the concern *of* males and identified with them.[52]

In parallel fashion, representatives of feminist theology have raised far-reaching questions about the unchallenged perpetuation of essentially patriarchal churches.   At stake is not merely the admission of women to equal participation in the existing patterns of church life and church thought but the very transformation of those patterns by the particular insight, experience, and perception of human identity that has been associated with women and suppressed along with them.   At points, this challenge goes to the very heart of these existing patterns by insisting that expressions of church life, of theology in general, and of central Christian understandings of God and salvation which have any hierarchical character at all are expressions of a sexist perception of reality and must be set aside.

As a result, the emerging critique which is being advanced by the woman's movement within the churches is double-edged.   On the one hand, it calls into question the institutional realizations of sexism which can be found in churches as in other social structures. In this regard, its chief criticism is that the churches are male-dominated and inhibit the full participation and contribution of women. On the other hand, it levels an even more fundamental and far-reaching criticism at the general ideological support that the churches offer to all social expression of sexism, including their own. Because the churches both mediate symbolic universes and provide ideological justification of existing social patterns it has been charged that they have helped create the internal and external expressions of sexism, perpetuate them, and give them the strongest possible justification by sacralizing them.

For these reasons the woman's movement, both inside and outside the churches, has been especially critical of the sexist character of religious language and imagery and mythos. This may seem to be a petty preoccupation to some,[53] but it must be recalled that language always reflects a fundamental mode of perceiving human experience and interpreting and evaluating what is seen. This becomes immediately apparent when the need for translation reveals the different sets of mind, the nuances of emphasis, and the alternative ways of understanding and evaluating which are embodied in differing languages. Language has power. It has a formative role in shaping people's perceptions of themselves and their world and in this way can become a hidden but highly effective instrument of social oppression.

Examinations of the churches' language have noted that its highly patriarchal character reflects the overwhelmingly patriarchal character of the societies with which Christianity has been historically identified. As Krister Stendahl has pointed out, the identification of God as masculine is as equally "a cultural and linguistic accident" as the masculinity of the Christ.[54] Yet it is instructive to ask what possible connection there can be between the overwhelmingly patriarchal nature of the language of the Bible and of church tradition and the generally patriarchal societies out of which they emerge. What is even more telling is the evidence of a definitely patriarchal bias in English translations of original biblical texts which reflect no sexual differentiation themselves[55] and a detectable shift within original texts toward masculine-oriented terminology.[56]

Critics point to several implications. The patriarchal character of original biblical texts, of biblical translations, of the language of worship and spirituality, and of theological language represents a subtle and yet highy effective endorsement of sexism by associating the divine with male symbols and images. To be sure, Christian theology has usually been sophisticated enough to assert that God transcends the inherent limitations and particularities of the human language which faith must employ, even if popular notions have not. Accordingly, God lies beyond the masculinity of language about "him."

Yet the point remains that such male-oriented language *is* used, and it is used precisely because of its suggestive character. Aspects of being which are culturally identified as masculine are seen to have symbolic power and in a way that dominates or excludes the symbolic character of feminine aspects of being. Associating the divine with male symbols and images while denying or minimizing its connection with female symbols and images tends to legitimate the subordinate status of women. At the same time it tends to deny the potentially symbolic character of what are understood culturally as predominantly female experiences and perceptions of existence. The sexist language of the churches divinizes the masculine and masculinizes the divine. Therefore, what is needed, according to some proponents of feminist theology, is what Mary Daly has called the "castrating" of religious language and symbols, "cutting away the phallus-centered value system imposed by patriarchy" and legitimated by the patriarchal language of the churches.[57]

The woman's movement is also challenging the more direct support the churches have offered internal and external expressions of sexism by giving divine sanction to the subordination of women or by associating women in a rather particular way with the reality of evil and sin. The latter has been especially true, it is held, in the cases of male theologians who link sin with the feminine characteristics of emotion, irrationality, and sexuality, and thereby legitimate their own self-alienation as passionate, intuitive, and sexual beings.[58] To be sure, unqualified negative readings of women and sweeping endorsements of patriarchy are more difficult to find in Christian and Jewish traditions than some of the more strident critics charge. Careful analyses by theologians sympathetic to the feminist movement have shown that these traditions can be seen to provide significant support to attempts to overcome the oppression of women.[59]

Perhaps one of the most important criticism of the churches being advanced by the woman's movement is that the very notion of the hierarchical nature of being upon which all subordinationism rests is itself the expression of sexism. At stake are fundamental understandings of the nature of power and authority. Patriarchal readings of power and authority expressed in social structures and legitimated in supporting ideologies do so by assuming a fundamental pattern of superordination and subordination. This means that dominance and dependence are both considered ontologically necessary. Even more importantly, their interrelationship is given a claim of unquestionable ultimacy by Judaism and Christianity in being made the theologically essential expression of the relation between God and humanity.[60]

On the one hand, this may imply that dominance and dependence have ontological validity but have discriminatingly been associated with men and women respectively through historical and cultural accident. It would not be surprising, then, that the relationship between God and humanity is described in patriarchal terms. In this case the relationship itself is allowed to stand but is disassociated with male dominance. On the other hand, this may imply that assertions of dominance and dependence *as such* have no ontological validity but are rather expressions of human self-estrangement. Such views of power and authority themselves call for redemption. What is needed is not simply the depatriarchalizing of life and consciousness but their dehierarchalizing.[61] Accordingly, this latter view assumes an inseparable connection between the "feminine" character of the woman's movement and the goals of liberation movements generally. The heart of liberation lies in the denial of dependence, even if that dependence is sacralized by being seen as the characteristic relation of human beings to God himself. Being dependent means being less than fully human. Being dependent—or dominant—means being in sin.

This line of analysis challenges, therefore, more than the alleged sexist character of church life and church thought. It views the churches' hierarchical treatment of the nature of God and of covenantal relation with God as being itself the expression of alienation, of misrelation to the order of being and, hence, to God. Theology informed by the experience of female oppression and liberation rejects the tradition of the orders of creation in favor of an ontological egalitarianism and pluralism. This implies an attempt to transcend the tendency of Western consciousness to divide reality into opposing and hierarchically-related polarities: "masculinity" over "feminity," "man" as the ruling class male over creation, history over nature, ego over body, spirit over matter, whiteness over blackness, self over society, heaven over earth. This also implies that the fundamental understanding of God must be reconstituted.

> The God concept of Western religion is an extrapolation of the "upper" pole of each of these alienations, thereby becoming the reflection and justification of all the relations of social domination expressed in these polarities: sexism, class hierarchy, racism, ecological destruction. Each of the various liberation theologies exposes an aspect of this theology of domination. Together they constitute a total assault upon its reality principle.[62]

What is being proposed by so-called feminist theology, therefore, is an alternative vision of the nature of God, humanity, covenant, and redemption forged out of the historically concrete experiences of liberation, particularly women's liberation.

This has led some proponents of feminist theology to attack the entire symbol system and pattern of thought that has shaped traditional Christian theology as the expressions of a patriarchy which has ignored the experience of women. As an alternative, some have begun to explore current possibilities of drawing on traditional feminine symbols and myths in biblical and church tradition[63] or discerning the theological implications of the experience of being a woman whether that experience is thought to be biologically grounded and genuinely unique or historically determined and culturally relative.[64]   Not the least important expression of the latter is the experience of being oppressed and relegated to the margins of society.

A related issue which is also being raised by feminist theologians is the contention that traditional appeals to the centrality of divine revelation are themselves expressions of patriarchal alienation. In its place these theologians propose to place the experience of liberation itself, including liberation from the constraints of theological traditionalism. In contention is not merely a theology whose focus is liberation from dependency but one whose very method expresses this liberation. Such theology grows out of the restoration of the Adamic power of human beings to name themselves, their world, and even God. It reflects the discovery of the primordial capacity to establish one's own identity in relation to images nurtured from within as opposed to a "fallen" state of seeing oneself in relation to images imposed from with-

out. Such a theology has taken seriously the methodological implications of the manifestation of God not as an authoritarian source of
divine truth but what Daly calls a dynamic, verbal reality, "the form-
destroying, form-creating, transforming power that makes all things
new."[65]

What Daly, Sheila Collins, Penelope Washbourn, and others are
advocating is more centrally theological than it is feminist. It goes
beyond concern with the feminist movement to the very heart of the
church's self-understanding. They are contending that divine revelation is fundamentally found not in the historical witness of the past to
the christological foundations of the church but in the historical experience of present spiritual and social transformation. They are choosing
to turn to their own experience, in this case their particular experience
as women. Some do so because they believe there are no adequate
models from the past which can guide them since the concept of a
model or authoritative paradigm is itself the reflection of sexist religion.
Others, such as Letty Russell, are more receptive to a kerygmatic approach to theology but believe that the immediate experience of liberation is the hermeneutical key for understanding the church's witness to
its christological foundation.[66]

Moreover, in the opinion of some theological analysts, the woman's
movement is creating for itself what Daly calls "a new space on the
boundary of all patriarchal institutions," including the churches. They
see this movement bringing into being a new community that has lines
of spiritual connection with all other marginal communities struggling
out of their subordinate and dependent status while at the same time
maintaining themselves as universally significant alternatives to the
oppressive character of current society. In its most radical expression,
the confrontation of the churches by the woman's movement asserts that
the concrete experience of liberation and the recognition of alternatives
to the currently oppressive character of society are enabling women—
and men—to discover the core of a spiritual community, generally unrecognized by the institutional churches, which is struggling into being.
It is this spiritual community (the "invisible" church) which represents
the true identity of the church, not the institutional churches from
whom it is hidden. They generally represent not the liberating and
humanizing power which is God but the alienation against which that
power struggles. These are some of the more far-reaching and radi-

cally disturbing claims with which the woman's movement has confronted the churches. Yet special attention should be given to the criticism which the feminist movement and feminist theology are directing at stereotypical readings of male and female identity. In place of the traditional characterizations which typify Western culture and which express sexuated bifurcation they endorse the concept of an "androgynous" humanity and advocate its personal and social realization.

ANDROGYNOUS IDENTITY IN CHRISTIAN PERSPECTIVE

In a very carefully argued and documented essay, Wayne Meeks claims that there is considerable evidence to show that one of the implications which the early church—and Paul in particular—saw in the eschatological reality of Christ was the transcending of the differences between male and female and the creation of a new reality.[67]   In this new reality both men and women were understood to share a common identity and common roles both of which expressed themselves in the concrete life of the church. The implication of what God had done in and through Jesus Christ was seen as the inbreaking of an eschatological order so radical that it set aside the claims and values of the present age, even the differences between the sexes. And it did so even when these differences were understood to have prior divine sanction.

According to Meeks, Paul's affirmation in Galatians 3:28, "There is neither Jew nor Greek, there is neither slave nor free, there is neither male nor female; for you are all one in Christ Jesus," is probably a citation from a baptismal liturgy of the early church which marked the initiation of individuals into the new eschatological age and its claims. The purpose of this liturgical formula was to place the act of baptism into its larger symbolic context and to associate it with the concrete repatterning of life associated with entrance into the community of the church. Accordingly, what is implied in baptism is a radical transformation of one's pattern of existence, the "death" of a former way of understanding and acting and the "birth" of a new. This theme of radical transformation is symbolically linked to a renewal of the original image of creation. Meeks draws attention to the phrase "male and female" and holds that it is a specific reference to the creation account in Genesis 1:27. This reference to the order of creation indicates that "Christian initiation reverses the fateful division of Genesis 2:21–22" so that in Christ's restoration of the lost image of the original creation, human beings are no longer divided, "not even by the most fundamental division of all, male and female."[68]

In other words, Meeks holds there is strong evidence that the earliest Christian community believed redemption implies entrance into a new order of existence which transcends sexual differentiation. Meeks also contends that Pauline references which maintain basic social and personal distinctions between the sexes represent a concession to the persistence of the fallen age in which Christians continued to find themselves and as a counterfoil to the Gnostics who also left behind the distinctions between male and female but did so at the price of denying the validity of the cosmos itself. Gnostics utilized the language of the androgynous reunification of male and female but did so to produce an aura of novelty and esoteric consciousness which was seen as the hallmark of "an elite, anticosmic sect." The resulting Pauline qualifications of the supra-sexual character of life in the Spirit were eagerly seized upon by second-generation Christians who were uneasy with the concept of male and female equivalence and thereby reinforced conventional stratifications of family and congregation to such an extent that it led to the misogyny of the Pastoral Epistles.

Krister Stendahl agrees with Meeks's contention that Galatians 3:28 represents a radical reconsideration of the nature of human identity in relation to socially subscribed sexual differentiations.[69] He too believes that the specific reference to "male and female" has Genesis 1:27 in mind. He adds that this agrees with the general theme of the third chapter of Galatians that in Christ the Law of Moses is transcended. The implication is that in Christ all boundaries are overcome including "the most primary division of God's creation . . . that between male and female."[70] He also argues in a manner parallel to Meeks that even though this does not amount to a Gnostic denial of the biological-physical order of existence, it does represent an alternative to the existing order of creation and therefore had significant implications for the concrete life of the Christian community. He contends that Paul's belief that the dichotomy between male and female has been overcome was not abstract ideology, referring only to the individual's relationship with God. Rather, the new unity of men and women which has been created in and through Christ "is not only a matter discerned by the eyes of faith but one that manifests itself in the social dimension of the church."[71]

Stendahl believes that the full implications of this doctrine were not seen at the time but awaited later discovery as, for example, the implications for the transcending of slavery found in the same text. Therefore, he contends, the full meaning of Galatians 3:28 lies beyond what was concretely implemented in the first-century church. The concern of orthodox theologians to defend a continuity between the orders of creation and redemption against Gnostic and Marcionite excesses, thereby upholding sexual differentiation, was laudable in its time. However in the present situation of the church, the problem may well lie in the opposite direction. Today it is not difficult for Christians to recognize in looking at the world around them that they have not entered into the complete realization of ultimate fulfillment. But they do need a vision of that fulfillment which calls their captivity to the present age into question and sets free in their midst the impact of Christ's redemption. At present, the meaning of androgynous humanity must be discerned in its concrete implications for the life and thought of the churches. According to Meeks, the implications of God's eschatological action in Christ was too radical, too dangerously ambivalent for the early church to sustain. "After a few meteoric attempts to appropriate its power, the declaration that in Christ there is no more male or female faded into innocuous metaphor, perhaps to await the coming of its proper moment."[72] Representatives of feminist theology believe that that moment has come.

There are a number of voices today, both inside and outside the churches, which claim that the overcoming of sexism requires more than the elimination of the subordinate status of women. Both individuals and society as a whole, it is asserted, need to transcend the stereotypical separations of male and female personality traits and roles and realize the personal and communal possibilities of an androgynous humanity. However, they are not all agreed as to what this implies.

The theories of Carl Gustav Jung typify one view which supports the movements of individuals and society as a whole toward wider realizations of androgynous humanity.[73] According to Jung the male and the female personalities approach reality from differing points of view and thereby give varying expression to modes of being. However, the full realization of humanity is found in the creative union of its particularly male and female forms. In order to be whole one must acknowledge the ontological significance and validity of both sexuated expressions of humanity and the presence of both expressions within oneself. Men and women both possess the characteristics which are archetypically expressed as "masculine" and "feminine" and all must discover and realize these characteristics in order to be whole. In other words, references to "masculine" and "feminine" are archetypal, not stereotypical; they apply to distinctions within the personality, not bifurcated alternatives. Differences between men and women are meant to be *in*clusive rather than *ex*cluding.

Erikson also believes that, despite genital distinctions, all human beings are fundamentally androgynous even though the personality of most tends to follow cultural differentiations between masculine and feminine personality types. Yet he insists that persons of each sex are capable of transcending these cultural differentiations and even the sexuated psychological distinctions which he believes are inherently present, in order to feel and represent the concerns of the other. Like Jung he believes that cultural differentiations do reflect certain sexually differentiated tendencies of personality, "a range of attitudes and attributes." But these are not absolute. Rather they are "predispositions, predilections, and inclinations" which can be radically modified or adopted by the opposite sex.[74] The issue is not what is our inheritance, so to speak, but rather what is our legacy, what inclinations of masculine and feminine personalities either men or women want to preserve and cultivate. This means that the basically androgynous nature of being human struggles for reconciliation within each individual.

In this connection, there is a conviction on the part of the growing numbers of analysts that greater measures of the reconciliation of sexuated modes of existence are crucial not only for the emotional well-being of individuals but also for the continuing survival of the human species as a whole. In the analysts' view the general character of modern industrial society represents the imbalanced dominance of predominantly "masculine" traits which have resulted not only in affluence and technical progress but in an obsession with unlimited expansion and a perilous international situation.[75] The inclusion of traditionally "feminine" concerns and values within the wider social identity and in individual male personalities would represent a movement toward sanity and life. It would be a transcending of the tendency to identity with what Erikson calls "pseudospecies," those delimited understandings of human identity shaped by the tyranny of "negative identity" which are driving human society toward self-destruction. Only a transcending of alienation which incorporates all of the positive realizations of human value suppressed in the "otherness" of marginal segments of humanity will save the species as a whole from the perils of its current history.

Feminist theologians overwhelmingly agree that modern industrialized society needs a restoration of human values which, in being characterized as feminine, have been as suppressed as women have been oppressed. The dominance of the masculinely linked values of aggressiveness, competitiveness, and rationality need the balance of the values of compassion, cooperation, and nurture which are traditionally associated with female personality.[76] However some are critical of the concept of androgynous humanity proposed by Jung, Erikson, and others since it aims at an interpenetration of stereotypically masculine and feminine personality traits rather than a transcending of them.[77] As an alternative they point to an androgynous humanity which is fully egalitarian, which refuses to identify personality in any way other than "human," and which encourages each individual to realize her/his own individual shaping of that humanness. Such a view holds that *all* distinctions between masculine and feminine are culturally based and are therefore questionable, mutable and of no ultimate importance. What matters is the universally human. Some of the proponents of this understanding of androgynous humanity believe it is not equivalent to an advocacy of "unisex" since the goal is not uniformity between the sexes but the maximization of differentiation between individuals on the basis of their unique potentialities. In this way, androgyny implies the encouragement of the uniqueness of each person. It rejects conventional images of human identity because it rebels against *any* standardizations of human existence.

The advocates of this radical position represent the fullest expression of "protean" affirmations of identity. Their views are compatible with the concept of self-definition which is central to Sartrean existentialism. However, like that existentialism, they end up begging the question of the meaning of human identity if they attempt to call for more than the sheer necessity of defining the self. All attempts to transcend sexism by appeals to "realization of one's potential" or "genuine humanity" or "the universally human" presuppose the reality of an *essential* humanity as well as a particular path for discovering what this is.

This is an issue which requires careful treatment and is one particularly significant for Christian theology which does assume the reality of the essentially human ("the image of God") and a context for discovering and entering into that humanity ("life in Christ").

In this connection, certain feminist theologians have presented the churches with radical reconsideration of the christological nature of the churches' perception of androgynous humanity. They assert that an understanding of androgynous humanity is not to be found in biblical revelation or in natural law but in a collective intuition of being which emerges in the context of history. They agree that the supra-sexual humanity witnessed to in Galatians 3:28, representing the realization of a redeemed humanity into which all persons are called, is neither arbitrary nor subjective. Androgynous humanity is ontological. It is that humanity which is "original" and therefore lies prior to all cultural definitions and beyond all previous intuitions. But understanding and entering into androgynous being is itself a process of becoming, of a collective and ongoing historical discovery of new dimensions of wholeness and personhood.[78]

It is important to note the dialectics of this analysis. On the one hand it rejects traditional stereotypes of human identity. On the other hand it abjures both a libertarianism which holds that individual freedom is itself an absolute (and which is interested only in what is popularly called "self-actualization") as well as an existentialism which holds that the individual is her/his own project. Moreover it does so not in the name of an understanding of human identity which the churches already possess but in the name of one which is *being* discovered in the concrete struggles of personal and social history.

It is at this point that feminist theology sees a point of contact between itself and other "liberation" theologies (and, for some, the biblical tradition as well). The discovery of lost dimensions of a genuine humanity is synonymous with the redemption of a fallen humanity. According to Ruether, this ultimately entails the recovery and reintegration, into the lives and psyches of all people, of those aspects of being human which they had previously denied themselves or had been denied or had denied to others. In other words, the vision of genuine human identity and its concrete realization is identical with the biblical hope for the coming of the kingdom of God. The question of human identity—individually and socially—is *the* eschatological question. In her analysis, Ruether believes it is ironic that the original Christian eschatological vision which challenged the dualism of Greek rationalism and Jewish apocalypticism should be overcome by them and that "the new culture-bearers" found in secular protests should now be the witnesses to Christianity's original salvation myth.[79]

All this suggests that any theological response to calls for recognizing that human identity is fundamentally androgynous must be aware of the differing meanings and implications of such an assertion. Nevertheless, there seem to be a number of grounds on which Christian theology can and should support attempts to transcend stereotypical and sexually bifurcated expressions of human identity, not only in relation to individual personalities but also in relation to contemporary society as a whole. But this in turn raises even more urgently the question of the criterion which Christian theology and church life utilize in coming to grips with the meaning of human identity and the meaning of the identity of the church.

HUMAN IDENTITY AND CHURCH IDENTITY

Theological supporters of the woman's movement seem to hold out two different visions of the identity of the church. As we have already noted, Mary Daly speaks of living on the boundary of the institutional church, that is, living in a state of a kind of estrangement-witnessing-against-estrangement. She sees the woman's movement creating a "new space" within which women—and men—are enabled to be free to break out of stereotypical identities and roles and find new measures of personal and social identity grounded in the possibilities of becoming. It is this very freedom, this daring to live without prefabricated and prescribed identities, that is itself a clue to transcendence. What Daly implies is at stake is more than a refusal to accept the sexist dictates and patterns of a male-dominated institution; it is even more fundamentally a refusal to accept male-determined understandings of redemption. The courage of women in refusing to submit to tradition, church authority, and even christologically-related paradigms is itself the deeper witness to the identity of the church. The church is essentially an event of alienation-transcending liberation or, perhaps, it is the community of those among whom and through whom such liberation is occurring.

Penelope Washbourn extends this line of thought by calling for an immersion in the immediacies of personal experience, believing that within them lies the witness to the sacred. To her way of thinking the gospel may ultimately consist of the immediate realization within the concreteness of one's own existence that life has a healing dimension which creates unity and renewal where it is neither expected nor explicable. On these grounds she believes that the woman's movement should abandon its concern to integrate women into the existing structures and patterns of the church by seeking ordination or demanding a sharing of power. Instead, she believes, feminist theology "calls for an end to all authoritarian models of truth" including the models of an ordained clergy, a divine revelation, and a focusing solely or centrally on Jesus of Nazareth. In their place she proposes a return to the experience of the demonic and the holy in the concreteness of one's racial, sexual, personal and historical existence and, with the hesitancy that is admitted by those who know they do not possess ultimate truth, a sharing of one's perceptions of the meaning of human existence.[80]

What Daly and Washbourn are outlining theologically represents more than a reading of the woman's movement. They bring into focus the many dimensions of the quest for identity which characterize contemporary culture. That quest has emerged in the context of historicist consciousness and has dared to step forward to claim not a restoration of a lost identity which once flourished openly in the past but a discovery of a potential identity which lies dimly in the future. The issue of human identity can only be worked out in the processes of personal and communal existence since reality itself is fundamentally a process. We not only realize our humanity fragmentarily, we also know and prophesy "in part." As both imply, this need not fall into the solipsism and self-definition that characterize Sartrean existentialism since one can affirm that human identity *has* an ontological grounding. But the discovery of the human "essence" can only be worked out in history— and in fear and trembling.

Such an analysis would have us turn to the concrete attempts to discover personal and communal identity to find not simply the meaning of the church's identity but the very communal reality of the church itself. What is emerging in the struggles for identity in American society and in world society are communities of persons, not just individuals, who are breaking loose from traditional images and patterns of what is understood to be meaningful existence in an attempt to live newly structured lives. In the argot of the time, they are "subcultures," that is, alternative cultures within the dominant culture. As such, they are identifiable communities of persons who are transmitting a fundamental perception of reality and a way of organizing it into meaningful categories and patterns of action. In this sense, they are "religious" communities. They articulate particular perceptions of the identity of the world and the identity of the self with which they reinforce one another and which they communicate to others. To be sure, such groupings of persons are having to face the problem of creating new kinship relations, new rituals and symbols, and new forms of community. But a variety of forms seem to be emerging: family-like communes, new marital and familial arrangements, networks of continuing contacts with those of a like mind, "consciousness-raising" groups, political collectives, and the like. What is being suggested by theological interpreters of many of the varying "liberation" movements is that within these subcultures one finds not only the *meaning* of the church but the *communal reality* of the church. The church is the community of those who are being liberated from the confines of oppressive social structures and oppressive ideologies in order to find new realizations of a more authentic human identity and are, in turn, mediating this liberation to others.

There is an alternative view which is also represented by proponents of feminist theology. This is a view which shares the fundamentally historicist presuppositions of the view outlined above. However, even though it agrees that the full meaning of human identity is something which can only be known and appropriated fragmentarily and imperfectly in history, it believes human identity has manifested its meaning and power in Jesus the Christ. The revelation of human identity has been given even though the understanding and appropriation of that revelation is (by the necessities of human finitude) historically and culturally relative and (through the reality of sin) ambiguously realized. The general context of this theological analysis is not an ontology of becoming but a biblical eschatology.

Ruether, for example, speaks of the church's identity in terms of its "sisterhood." Like the patterning of the woman's movement itself the church's essential identity is that of a redemptive and revelatory cohumanity which enables individuals to express their repressed alienation and discover a more whole humanity. The essential identity of the church is that of a community of persons who have been raised in consciousness to discern a fuller humanity than that represented by the alienated social structures and their complementing ideologies. For this reason, however, the church is the representation of a community of whole persons which transcends even the "sisterhood" of the women's movement—and, by implication, the communal particularity of other movements—since "the community of the oppressed against the oppressors . . . cannot represent the community of reconciliation. That can be represented only by a community which brings together oppressor and oppressed in a new relationship that liberates both from their previous pathologies in relation to each other."[81] In other words, it is not enough to affirm the significance of current movements and the subcultures they are creating since they, too, are expressive of human alienation in their alternation. "Rather, women's consciousness, indeed the consciousness of all oppressed people," Ruether notes, "becomes redemptive when it reveals a co-humanity beneath the master-slave distortion as the authentic ground of our being, and fights its battle in a way that takes its stand upon this ground, and constantly reaffirms it."[82] In contrast to Washbourn, the penetration of one's own isolated experience, even the experience of "liberation," is not sufficient. What is needed is the revelation of a "co-humanity," which lies as much beyond one's own particularity as it does beyond one's own alienation. That ultimately implies an eschatological vision of human identity. What is needed is the revelation of a redeemed community. "The church represents our present vantage point on this redeemed community," she notes. "It is both a real foretaste of that community and the party of redemptive struggle against the power structures."[83]

But two crucial questions remain: (1) What is the criterion of this *vision* of a redeemed community, of co-humanity? and (2) What is the source of the *power* which effects an ultimate reconciliation that transcends the alienation embodied in both the oppressor and the oppressed? The traditional Christian term for this criterion of meaning and source of power is *the Holy Spirit* who proceeds from the Father and the Son.[84]

SOME THEOLOGICAL IMPLICATIONS

Certain theological interpretations of various struggles with the question of personal and communal identity, discerning the cultural captivity of the churches and their ideological character, have sought to find new grounds upon which to interpret the nature and mission of the church. Suspecting that the distortions of this captivity and ideology are inextricably linked to the heritage of the churches and seeing appeals to tradition or church authority as themselves expressions of alienation, they have sought to build a theological base in the experience of liberation itself or within the unfolding patterns of particular movements. We have seen examples of this in the theology which is emerging out of the impact of the American feminist movement. However, the very discernment, suspicion, and vision that mark such theological movements needs to be turned on their own emerging base. To what extent do they represent a kind of cultural captivity? To what degree do their theological interpretations represent ideologies? In what ways might they still be subject to alienation? As Marx noted, ideological subscription is unsuspecting and well-intentioned; it reflects a legitimate but narrowly held—and hence distorting—perception of human existence. The only road open is to assert that within the vicissitudes and vagaries of history, a redemptive process and its corresponding image of authentic human identity is struggling to have its way. But where and how?

Fearing the limitations of traditionalism and not willing to abandon the risks of an experientially based freedom of inquiry for the deceptive security of authoritarianism, these theological interpretations have chosen to trust the immediate experience of what they see as the processes of growing humanization. If faced with the charge that this amounts to sheer subjectivism, they have responded by appeals to an ontological grounding to this experience and have called upon the intra-subjective witness of a community of those who are being redeemed as a check against an unrelieved individualism. Yet two questions remain: (1) What is the source of the criterion or set of standards that determines the ontological validity of one's claims? (2) If one appeals to the experience of others, what is to prevent that from being another instance of the blind leading the blind?

These particular theological appeals and the wider intellectual currents they reflect are the expressions of a neoromanticism which ultimately holds that final arbitration—the final determination of the meaning of human identity—is found in the ongoing historical struggle of the human spirit. It would be unfortunate enough if this pattern of thought begged the question of the criterion and source of that struggle in an abstract way, but it is even more so in light of its concretely aberrant effects in recent history. It may be true that the Nazi movement represents the monstrous offspring of such romanticism, but it is a *legitimate* child. To be sure, it may be argued that the perverted concepts of human identity hideously advanced in history by the *theoria* and praxis of the Nazis were lies, the creations of the "father of lies" who hates the truth, who rebels against the ontological order. But such an objection assumes that we do have access to an ultimate criterion of truth whose light is already dispelling the darkness. If this is so, we are faced with the question of where, in the context of historicized existence, such a criterion can be found. A related issue is whether, in the final analysis, it is we who seek such a criterion in our personal and corporate histories or instead whether this criterion seeks to break through into those histories.

The experiences of liberation, of fuller personhood, of greater self-actualization, of wider self-realization need a broader context if they are not to degenerate into egocentric self-preoccupation or the equivalent of an appeal to *Blut und Boden*. They cry out for an *ultimate* criterion of human identity and a *universalizing* of that criterion. Some insist that an ultimate and universal criterion of human identity cannot be given in history. Yet this is precisely the issue upon which hinges the relation of the identity of the church to the current struggles for human identity which are occurring in American society and societies throughout the world.

Has the "end" of history manifested itself within history or not? Is that event the criterion of human identity, or shall we look for another —or any? Has or has not the truth of *ontos* ("being") shined in the darkness so that the darkness has not been able to put it out?

The alternative to a submergence in immediate experience need not be mere submission to an alien authority or an alienating one. Beyond the Oedipal conflict between romanticist "autonomy" and traditionalist "heteronomy" can be found the affirmation of a "theonomous" manifestation of the Word become flesh and dwelling among us. Daly speaks of patriarchal authoritarianism reducing not only women but also the autonomous self to an object, "the Other." Accordingly she fears submission to what she believes is a Christolatry and turns instead to personal and communal experiences of liberation. But in doing so her perception of Christ is itself the reflection of alienation and not the overcoming of it. For if the Word is truly the Word, then one of its effects is to restore us to ourselves.

"Lord, to whom shall we go? You have the words of eternal life" (John 6:68). As Paul Tillich has noted, the law of God is the deepest law of our *own* being. At stake is whether or not we are alienated *from* the depths of our own being only by the ideologies and social alienations of our existence so that, when these are toppled by historical forces, we are redeemed; or whether we are also alienated *in* the depths of our own being at the very heart of being itself, so that we need a redemptive Word from *without* to break in and liberate us from a strange self-captivity, thereby restoring us to our *genuine* selves. The Christian tradition has been clear at this point.

To be sure that word is always becoming enfleshed in the concreteness of personal and communal history. It is "kairotic." It is neither culturally limited to Bethlehem nor historically limited to Good Friday. It is an eschatological word for all places and all seasons. And the idolatries that absolutize past expressions of the reception of that word must give way. In the final analysis, the churches must recognize they are not the "possessors" of that word any more than they are its guarantors. The church (much less the church*es*) does not possess the truth but yet it may dare believe with Luther that the Holy Spirit will keep it *in* the truth. Therefore, without being triumphalistic, the church should acknowledge its divinely-given and irreplaceable task. It is to test the spirits of the time by the power and meaning of the Holy Spirit.

In the final analysis, the identity of the church in the light of the current quests for human identity is found in its being the bearer of the word, the faltering witness and ambiguous representative of the eschatological humanity which it believes to have broken into history and brought this odd earthen vessel into being. The church is not the sole locus of God's redemption, "the ark of salvation." The Lord of history is present and active at the margins of society and at the margins of Israel, as the emergence of the New Covenant testifies. Nor is the church the community of the specially redeemed. God is able to raise up children for himself even from the stones of the desert. Nor is the church the exclusive agency of redemption in the world. That is amply demonstrated by the wider history of human communities which shows the capability of "secular" movements to effect liberation as well as by the history of the churches which reveals their cultural captivity and ideological character. Rather the church is the community which witnesses to the manifestation of the genuinely human in the eschatological event of Jesus the Christ and allows that witness to find its own redemptive way in human history. It points to the "center" of history as the "end" of history and in that light enters into the concrete struggles of the historical moment to discover what implications the center and end of history have for particular moments within history. Yet the church does so recognizing that the living power and meaning of this eschatological event are not something that the church has readily at hand. On the contrary, as the analyses of Galatians 3:28 by Meeks and Stendahl demonstrate, the concrete historical-cultural context of the churches' life is the necessary catalyst for opening up relevant but otherwise unknown dimensions of the ultimate criterion of human identity.

In other words, it is the eschatological event of Jesus the Christ which acts for the churches as the ultimate criterion for their examination of and involvement in the reappropriations of personal and communal identity which can be found in our contemporary world. Yet it is only the concrete context of these movements which can reveal to the churches otherwise latent or dimly perceived dimensions of that criterion. This means the church should neither undialectically identify with emerging liberationist movements nor turn its back on them or on the wider social currents they express. It should neither unparadoxically identify these movements with the inbreaking of God's reign nor fail to see the possibilities of their interrelationship.

The witness to the christological criterion of human identity is never final, just as it is never absolute. The church is not "absolved" from the limitations and ambiguities of historical existence. It never can hope to speak the final word; it can only struggle to speak a faithful word, "a word in season." It points to an eschatological human identity given in Jesus the Christ that is not itself static or ahistorical but rather is what we might call "dynamically catholic," able to enter into fruitful interaction with the novelties and vicissitudes of history. Such eschatological human identity continues to manifest its hidden dimensions within the ongoing historical and cultural changes that the churches experience in the world around (and within) them.

In this dynamic historical context it is possible for the church to be a witnessing community which creates new visions of human identity; but it need not. Much less does it need to take the lead in such an enterprise, though often it should since no other agency will. Rather, accepting the creative tension and the existential risk which reappropriation of its own christological foundation within the immediate historical-cultural situation implies, the church's indispensable task is to clarify, judge, and support wherever possible those emerging visions of human identity to which the human spirit is giving birth, and to do so in the light of its unique and irreplaceable criterion.

Certainly current reassessments and reappropriations of human identity should stimulate the church to reassess and reappropriate its own identity. But its identity is authentic and a source of benediction for the world only when it remains faithful to its unique christological foundation and criterion. To be sure, this has been and will continue to be misconstrued as grounds for Christian imperialism and obscurantism; yet it is ultimately that very foundation and criterion that calls such abberations most severely into judgment. Since it is Christ who is the final foundation and criterion of the identity of the church, he identifies a church which lives under the cross out of a theology of the cross. The christological foundation of the church's identity establishes it as a community of the interpretative and renewing word of the cross; the christological criterion of the church's identity provides it with the criterion by which to proclaim that word as a word of concrete judgment and concrete promise. But the church cannot presume to know in what accents that word will speak tomorrow, for that is something that must be discerned—and risked—in history itself.

NOTES

1. Although struggles with the issue of identity by individuals and groups of persons find international and even global expression, this paper will focus on developments in the United States in the belief that the particularities of the American scene hold implications that have wider, even universal significance.

2. The term *church* is used to refer to the theologically defined and eschatologically constituted spiritual community which is the concern of ecclesiology. The term *churches* refers to those sociologically and historically concrete communities which represent, witness to, and exist in eschatological tension with this spiritual community. Theological analysis of the "church" is meant to provide the "churches" with a context for self-evaluation, renewal, and establishment of purpose.

3. For a helpful summary of Erik Erikson's views see his "Autobiographic Notes on the Identity Crisis," in *The Twentieth Century Sciences: Studies in the Biography of Ideas*, ed. Gerald Holton (New York: W. W. Norton & Co., 1972), pp. 3–32. His most comprehensive presentation can be found in *Identity: Youth and Crisis* (New York: W. W. Norton & Co., 1968).

4. A helpful summary is provided by Avrum Stroll in *The Encyclopedia of Philosophy*, ed. Paul Edwards (New York: Macmillan Co., and the Free Press, 1967), vol. 4, pp. 121–24.

5. Erikson himself has given particular attention to such cultural identity in *Dimensions of a New Idenity: The 1973 Jefferson Lectures in the Humanities* (New York: W. W. Norton & Co., 1974), pp. 114ff.; "The Concept of Identity in Race Relations," *Daedalus* 95, no. 1 (Winter 1966): 145–70; "Reflections on the Dissent of Contemporary Youth," *Daedalus* 99, no. 1 (Winter 1970):154–76; and *Identity: Youth and Crisis*, chaps. 7, 8.

6. A helpful compendium of essays which touch on some of the implications of the Human Potential Movement for the church can be found in the June 1973 issue of *Event*, a magazine which until recently was published by the official men's organization of the American Lutheran Church.

7. Richard E. Farson, "The Education of Jeremy Farson," a report to the California State Committee on Public Education, March 1967, cited in Hubert A. Otto, "New Light on Human Potential," *Psychology and Personal Growth*, ed. Abe Arkoff (Boston: Allyn & Bacon, 1975), p. 303.

8. Current schools of theology which tend to "bracket out" concern with existential questions by insisting they are luxuries which the church cannot afford in the light of the pressing need for the material transformation of society would do well to make note of this fact and its implications.

9. Claude Geffré and Gustavo Guttiérez, eds., *The Mystical and Political Dimension of the Christian Faith* (Concilium, 96; New York: Herder & Herder, 1974).

10. These observations can be found in "From Pilgrim Fathers to Founding Fathers," the second in the series of 1976 Reith Lectures commissioned and broadcast by the British Broadcasting System in honor of the American Bicentennial.

11. Erikson has provided extensive treatment of this thesis and tied it closely to the fundamental American ideology which was hammered out by Thomas Jefferson in *Dimensions of a New Identity: The 1973 Jefferson Lectures*.

12. Erikson, "Autobiographic Notes on the Identity Crisis," p. 21.

13. For an analysis of the hidden Christian elements and influences in secular humanism, see Paul Tillich, "Kirche und humanistische Gesellschaft," *Neuwerk* (Kassel) 13, 1 (April–May, 1931), pp. 4–18.

14. This also raises the question of the inherent connections between the formal ideas of protest and the material protest itself. Peter Stearns believes that intellectuals all too often exaggerate the importance of the intellectual origins and justifications of particular movements and neglect the variety of material interests that those ideas serve and the material conditions that give rise to the movement. Nevertheless, he observes, it seems that protest movements inevitably tend to justify themselves by appeals to what are assumed to be self-evident or universal principles. Philip P. Wiener, ed., "Protest Movements," *Dictionary of the History of Ideas* (New York: Charles Scribner's Sons, 1973), 3, 676–77.

15. One can, for example, find a struggle over priorities of interest and interpretations of existing conditions on the part of black women who must deal with the marginal condition of both their blackness and their femaleness. Cf. Theressa Hoover, "Black Women and the Churches: Triple Jeopardy," *Sexist Religion and*

Women in the Church: No More Silence!, ed. Alice L. Hageman (New York: Association Press, 1974), pp. 63–76; Rosemary Radford Ruether, "Sexism and the Theology of Liberation," *Christian Century* 90, no. 45 (December 1973):1224–29, and "Crisis in Sex and Race: Black Theology vs Feminist Theology," *Christianity and Crisis* 34, 6 (April 1974):67–73. This same tension can be seen in the varying goals of the feminist movement in Third World countries in comparison with North Atlantic nations. Cf. Ceciwa Khonje, "Liberation for an American Woman," and T. Omas Ihromi, "Social and Cultural Background of Concepts of Roles of Women: Reflections on the Indonesian Scene," in *Ecumenical Review* 27, 4, (October, 1975):352–56 and 357–65 respectively; E. Maxine Ankrah, "Has the African Woman Settled for Tokens?" *Lutheran World* 22 (1975):22–31, and the reports of the World Council of Churches, Berlin Consultation on Sexism, in "Words to the Churches: Voices of the Sisters," *Risk* 10:2, (1974), and articles by Marnei Mellblom, Sun-Ai Park and Yoshiko Isshiki in *Lutheran World* 22, (1975):89–94.

16. Ruether, "Sexism and the Theology of Liberation," p. 1224.

17. Ernst Troeltsch, "Die Krisis des Historismus," *Die Neue Rundschau,* 33 (1922):572–90. This is a brief and untechnical presentation of the central elements in Troeltsch's classic study of historicism, *Der Historismus und seine Probleme* (Tübingen, 1922).

18. Peter Berger and Thomas Luckmann, *The Social Construction of Reality* (Garden City, N.Y.: Doubleday, 1966), p. 14.

19. Ibid., p. 88.

20. The term is Paul Tillich's and refers to secular systems of meaning and value and the communities which they create that function as do the more traditional religious communities in expressing questions of "ultimate concern" and "answers" to those questions.

21. Karl Marx and Friedrich Engels, *The German Ideology* (New York: International Publishers, 1947), p. 79.

22. As a result, Marx is not concerned about assigning "blame." The fundamental issue is the concrete transformation of the social situation, not the assignation, admission, and expunging of guilt. Some representatives of protest movements, including the woman's movement, and their theological allies would do well to consider this aspect of Marx's thought.

23. Compare John Stuart Mill's observation, "Everything which is usual appears natural. The subjection of women to men being a universal custom, any departure from it quite naturally appears unnatural." *Subjection of Woman* (1869), cited in Barbara Deckard, *The Women's Movement: Political, Socioeconomic and Psychological Issues* (New York: Harper & Row, 1975), p. 9.

24. Ruether, "Sexism and the Theology of Liberation," p. 1226.

25. Erikson, *Dimensions of a New Identity,* p. 36. Cf. *Identity: Youth and Crisis,* pp. 295ff. Interestingly Erikson holds that the negative projection of the protean identity central to Jefferson's ideology was tied to the clearest expression of non-protean persons, persons who could not take initiative for themselves—slaves. One might go on to point out that, significantly, definitions of the legal rights and status of slaves were in the colonial period based on the precedents in English law concerning the rights and status of women.

26. Erikson, *Dimensions of a New Identity,* p. 114.

27. Compare Simone de Beauvoir's analysis of woman's existence as "the Other," the archetypal expression of oppression—including its manifestation as economic exploitation and social exclusion—in *The Second Sex* (New York: Knopf, 1953), and Kate Millet's treatment of the self-alienation of women in *Sexual Politics* (Garden City, N.Y.: Doubleday, 1970), pp. 382ff.

28. Note Erikson's specific treatment of this in reference to the oppression of women in *Identity: Youth and Crisis,* p. 273.

29. Cited by Mary Daly, "Social Attitudes Towards Women," *Dictionary of the History of Ideas,* p. 529.
p. 529.

30. This is true for de Beauvoir who contends that woman's identity as "the Other" embodied in the concept of "the Eternal Feminine" is the fundamental expression of the denial of subjecthood in its reduction of woman to an object. Rosemary Radford Ruether agrees by contending that the woman's movement "goes to the roots of the impulse to dominate"; "Women's Liberation in Historical and Theological Perspective," *Women's Liberation and the Church: The New Demand for Freedom in the Life of the Christian Church,* ed. Sarah Bentley Doely (New York: Association Press, 1970), p. 26. Compare Nelle Morton's observation that the woman's movement "carries a cosmic overtone," in "Preaching the Word," *Sexist Religion and Women in the Church,* p. 41.

31. Compare Mary Daly, "Theology After the Demise of God the Father: A Call for the Castration of Sexist Religion," *Women and Religion,* ed. Judith Plaskow and Joan Arnold (Missoula, Montana: Scholars Press for the American Academy of Religion, 1964), p. 9.

32. The terms *nature of women* or *female nature,* and their parallels *the nature of men* and *male nature* are used to refer to characterizations of personality referring especially and properly to women and men. The terms *feminine* and *feminine nature,* and their parallels *masculine* and *masculine nature* have a more asexual denotation and are meant to refer to those characteristics generally or more often associated with women, (and with men) but which can be attributed normatively as well as descriptively to men and women. In this respect, reference to *feminine* and *masculine* natures is similar to Jungian references to the *anima* and the *animus* or to Taoist concepts of Yin and Yang.

33. Cynthia Ozick, "Women and Creativity," *Woman in Sexist Society,* ed. Vivian Gornick and Barbara Moran (New York: Signet, 1971), p. 437. Compare Alan Graebner, *After Eve* (Minneapolis: Augsburg Publishing House, 1972), p. 54.

34. See examples cited in Georgine Seward and Robert Williamson, eds., *Sex Roles in Changing Society* (New York: Random House, 1970), pp. 3–4.

35. Sheila Tobias, Ella Kusnitz, and Deborah Spitz, eds., *Psychological Differences Between Men and Women,* (Pittsburgh: Know, 1969), a report of a panel discussion held during the Cornell Conference on Women January 22–25, 1969; Naomi Weisstein, "Psychology Constructs the Female, or the Fantasy Life of the Male Psychologist," *Roles Women Play,* ed. Michele Hoffnung Garskof (Belmont, Calif.: Brooks/Cole, 1970), pp. 76–77.

36. Cited by Patricia Martin Doyle, "Women and Religion: Psychological and Cultural Implications," *Religion and Sexism: Images of Woman in the Jewish and Christian Tradition,* ed. Rosemary Radford Ruether (New York: Simon and Schuster, 1974), p. 27.

37. Erikson, *Identity: Youth and Crisis,* pp. 266ff.

38. Juliet Mitchell offers a careful defense of Freud on the basis of what she holds are his similar qualifications of sexual personality differentiation, *Psychoanalysis and Feminism* (New York: Pantheon Books, 1974), pp. 310ff., 401ff.

39. Lester A. Kirkendall and Isadore Rubin, *Sexuality and the Life Cycle: SIECUS study Guide No. 8* (Sex Information and Education Council of the United States, 1959), p. 10. Cf. Elaine Donelson, *Sex Differences in Developmental Perspective* (Hopewood, Ill.: Learning Systems Co., 1975); J. L. and Joan Hampson, "The Ontogenesis of Sexual Behavior in Man," and J. W. Money,

"Sex Hormones and Other Variables in Human Eroticism," *Sex and Internal Secretions,* ed. W. C. Young (Baltimore: Williams & Wilkins, 1961), 2:1401–32 and 1383–1400 respectively; and J. Money, J. G. and J. L. Hampson, "Imprinting and the Establishment of Gender Role," *Archives of Neurology and Psychiatry* 77 (1957):333–36.

40. Judith M. Bardwick, *Psychology of Women: A Study of Biocultural Conflicts* (New York: Harper & Row, 1971), p. 216, passim. Inge K. Braverman, et al., "Sex-role Stereotypes and Clinical Judgments of Mental Health," *Readings on the Psychology of Women,* ed. Judith M. Bardwick (New York: Harper & Row, 1972), pp. 320ff.; Carlfred B. Broderick, "The Importance of Being Earnest—or Evelyn," *Psychology and Personal Growth,* ed. Abe Arkoff (Boston: Allyn & Bacon, 1975), pp. 79ff.

41. Eleanor E. Maccoby, ed., *The Development of Sex Differences* (Stanford, Calif.: Stanford University Press, 1966); Nancy Reeves, ed., *Womankind Beyond the Stereotypes* (Chicago: Aldine Atherton, 1971).

42. Claude Levi-Strauss, for example, holds that the only sexuated constant that exists universally is exogamy or the practice of exchanging women between families and class. It is on these grounds alone that "women are everywhere within civilization the second sex but everywhere differently so," Mitchell, *Psychoanalysis and Feminism,* p. 38.

43. Margaret Mead, *Sex and Temperament in Three Primitive Societies* (New York: Dell, 1961), p. 260.

44. Deckard, *The Women's Movement,* pp. 182ff.

45. Ibid., pp. 184–89. The classical Marxian position is set forth by Friedrich Engels in *The Origin of the Family, Private Property, and the State.*

46. Ruether, "Crisis in Sex and Race," p. 72.

47. Erikson, for example, believes that other motivations include the honest desire to preserve sexual polarity and the vitality of sexual difference, the male incapacity to be empathetic where necessary and see the sexuated other in oneself and vice versa, general inertia in changing the status quo, and male uneasiness about the female capacity for pregnancy and childbirth. *Identity: Youth and Crisis,* pp. 263ff.

48. See for example, Hilda Scott, *Does Socialism Liberate Women? Experiences from Eastern Europe* (Boston: Beacon Press, 1974).

49. For an extended examination of the varying groups in the woman's movement and their differing self-interpretations and goals see Deckard, *The Women's Movement,* pp. 332–64, 414–36.

50. Merle S. Goldberg, "International Women's Year: Fact and Fantasy," *Saturday Review,* June 14, 1975, p. 22.

51. Voting privileges were extended to women by the Lutheran Church-Missouri Synod only in 1969; authorization of the admission of women to ordination was not granted until 1970 by the Lutheran Church in America and the American Lutheran Church and is still withheld by the Missouri Synod.

52. Some feminists ask, for example, if a woman who rejects the identity imposed on her by a sexist society is any less oppressed if she accepts the collective identity bestowed on her by a woman's group. Freedom from male domination cannot be replaced by subservience to "sisterhood," it is argued. In similar fashion feminist criticisms of men as a class or on stereotypical grounds are themselves to be seen as expressions of sexism.

53. For example, the support given in 1973 by Harvard Divinity School students to conscious attempts to avoid sexist language in classrooms was greeted

with subtle ridicule by the popular press and professional scorn by the Department of Linguistics of the university.

54. Krister Stendahl, "Enrichment or Threat? When the Eves Come Marching In," *Sexist Religion and Women in the Church*, p. 120.

55. Ruth Hoppin, *Games Bible Translators Play*, (NOW Ecumenical Task Force on Women and Religion; privately circulated).

56. Phyllis Trible, "Departriarchalizing in Biblical Language," *Journal of the American Academy of Religion*, 41 (1973):35–42.

57. Daly, "Theology after the Demise of God, the Father," p. 9.

58. A summary of such views is given by Mary Daly, "Social Attitudes Towards Women." Cf. Ruether, "Crisis in Sex and Race."

59. Phyllis Bird, "Images of Women in the Old Testament," Ruether, "Misogynism and Virginal Feminism in the Fathers of the Church," and Jane Dempsey Douglas, "Women and the Continental Reformation," *Religion and Sexism: Images of Woman in the Jewish and Christian Traditions*, ed. Rosemary Radford Ruether (New York: Simon and Schuster, 1974); Leonard Swidler, "Jesus Was a Feminist," *The South East Asia Journal of Theology* 13 (1971):102–10; and "Is Sexism a Sign of Decadence in Religion," *Women and Religion*, pp. 167–75; Robin J. Scroggs, "Paul and the Eschatological Woman," *Journal of the American Academy of Religion* 40 (1972):283–303; and "Paul and the Eschatological Woman Revisited," *Journal of the American Academy of Religion*, 42 (1974): 532–37.

60. Joan Arnold Romero, "The Protestant Principle: A Woman's-Eye View of Barth and Tillich," *Religion and Sexism*, pp. 319–40; Morton, "Preaching the Word," *Sexist Religion and Women in the Church*, pp. 39ff.

61. Sheila D. Collins, "Toward a Feminist Theology," *Christian Century* 89, no. 28 (August 1972):796–99; Ruether, "Whatever Happened to Theology?", *Christianity and Crisis* 35, no. 8 (May 1975):109–10.

62. Ruether, "What Ever Happened to Theology?", p. 110. Cf. Morton, "Preaching the Word," *Sexist Religion and Women in the Church*, pp. 39f., Collins, "Toward a Feminist Theology," p. 789.

63. For example, Sidney Cornelia Callahan, "A Christian Perspective on Feminism," Doely, *Women's Liberation and the Church*, pp. 37–46.

64. For example, Penelope Washbourn, "Authority or Idolatry? Feminine Theology and the Church," *Christian Century* 92, no. 35 (October 1975), 961–64, and "Differentiation and Difference—Reflections on the Ethical Implications of Women's Liberation," *Women and Religion*, pp. 127–37.

65. Daly, "Theology After the Demise of God the Father," p. 13.

66. Letty Russell, *Human Liberation in Feminist Perspective* (Philadelphia: Westminster Press, 1974); Cf. Paul D. Hanson, "Masculine Metaphors for God and Sex-discrimination in the Old Testament," *Ecumenical Review*, 27 (1975): 316–24.

67. Wayne Meeks, "The Image of the Androgyne: Some Uses of a Symbol in Earliest Christianity," *History of Religions* 13 (1974):165–208.

68. Ibid., p. 185.

69. Krister Stendahl, *The Bible and the Role of Women* (Philadelphia: Fortress, 1966), pp. 32ff.

70. Ibid., p. 32.

71. Ibid., p. 33.

72. Meeks, "The Image of the Androgyne," p. 208.

73. See Ann Belford Ulanov, *The Feminine in Jungian Psychology and Christian Theology* (Evanston: Northwestern University Press, 1971).

74. Erikson, *Identity: Youth and Crisis*, p. 291.

75. Erikson, "Dimensions of a New Identity," p. 118–19; *Identity: Youth and Crisis*, pp. 291ff.

76. In parallel fashion, certain psychologists are suggesting that many of the values associated with marginal subcultures such as the blacks and the poor may be precisely those which society as a whole needs in dealing with the pressures of rapid change and the destabilization of social structures. For example, Louis Z. Zurcher, "The Mutable Self," *Psychology and Personal Growth*, pp. 16–22. Cf. Erikson, *Identity: Youth and Crisis*, pp. 304ff.

77. For example Linda L. Barufaldi and Emily E. Culpepper, "Androgyny and the Myth of Masculine/Feminine," *Christianity and Crisis* 33, no. 6, (April 16, 1975), pp. 69–71.

78. For example Janice Raymond, "Beyond Male Morality," *Women and Religion*, pp. 115–25.

79. Ruether, "Women's Liberation in Historical and Theological Perspective," *Women's Liberation and the Church*, pp. 26–36.

80. Washbourn, "Authority or Idolatry," pp. 962f.

81. Ruether, "Sexism and the Theology of Liberation," pp. 1128f.

82. Ibid., p. 1129.

83. Ibid., p. 1128.

84. Compare Frederick Herzog's important criticism of the neglect of a christological focus in certain interpretations of liberation movements in "Liberal Theology or Culture Religion?" *Union Seminary Quarterly Review*, 29, no. 3, (Spring/Summer, 1974):233–44.

THREE

THE IDENTITY OF THE CHURCH
IN LIGHT OF
ACCELERATING CHANGE AND PLURALISM

Professor Philip J. Hefner, of the faculty of the Lutheran School of Theology (LCA), Chicago, has been particularly involved in recent years—as a systematic theologian, with roots in historical study—in observing and commenting on the American scene, nationally and ecclesiologically. The essay which follows provides an analysis of his own church, the LCA, and a bold depiction of its possible future destiny, Deo volente. The pages of this essay are likely to arouse discussion and debate similar to that concerning the book he coauthored with his colleague Robert Benne, *Defining America: A Christian Critique of the American Dream* (Philadelphia: Fortress, 1974). For their reactions to that debate, compare Benne and Hefner in *Lutheran World* 23 (1976): 200–206.

Born in 1932 in Denver, Colorado, where he attended high school, Dr. Hefner was graduated from Midland Lutheran College (LCA), Fremont, Nebraska, 1954, followed by a year as Fulbright scholar at Tübingen, and then from Chicago Lutheran Theological Seminary in 1959. His M.A. (1961) and Ph.D. (with distinction, 1962) were awarded by the University of Chicago. His doctoral work led to publication in 1966 of *Faith and the Vitalities of History: A Theological Study Based on the Work of Albrecht Ritschl* (New York: Harper & Row, in the "Makers of Modern Theology" series edited by Jaroslav Pelikan). He engaged in postdoctoral research in Germany on an AATS Faculty Fellowship in 1971–72 at Hamburg. For 1977–78 he has been honored with the Franklin Clark Fry Fellowship.

An ordained clergyman of the LCA, he has spent his entire ministry in teaching in its seminaries: Associate Professor, Hamma School of Theology, Springfield, Ohio, 1962–64; Professor, Gettysburg Seminary,

1964–67; and since 1967 at Lutheran School of Theology, Chicago, as full professor from 1969 to date. He has been visiting lecturer or scholar at half a dozen colleges and theological schools, including the University of Chicago Divinity School. His memberships in learned societies are extensive. He is the author of *The Promise of Teilhard* (Philadelphia: Lippincott, 1970) and some seventy articles, and reviews. He is the editor and translator of *Three Essays by Albrecht Ritschl* (Philadelphia: Fortress, 1972), and contributed an essay to a volume which he also coedited, *The Scope of Grace: Essays on Nature and Grace in Honor of Joseph Sittler* (Philadelphia: Fortress, 1964).

The choice of Dr. Hefner was an obvious one for his assignment. Already a scholar who had published a good deal, and active in the structures of his church (though not uncritically), he was able to attend—as representative of the U.S. Advisory Committee on Studies—the LWF consultation on "The Identity of the Church" at Bossey, Switzerland in 1975, where his knowledgeableness about methodology caused the Geneva staff to invite him for the 1976 consultation in Tanzania. In this way he is the essayist in this volume most fully informed firsthand about the current way of "doing theology" in the LWF Studies Department.

The U.S. Committee was committed by its outline (see p. 22) to reflecting on ecclesiology in light of the change and pluralism so characteristic of our day. One of the conflict areas flagged by the 1974 listing of problems by LWF churches was "Church and Culture" or "secular pluralism." The analysis by U.S. churchmen of the American scene in 1974 acknowledged "wide ethical/social diversity" amid "a broad confessional unity," but, for all the difficulties "in an age of rapid social change," they viewed "the pluralism in American society as a positive quality, an opportunity to regain an understanding and a practice of our Trinitarian heritage." They cited as an optimistic example how restructuring in the LCA has brought together "the main programs of the former boards of college education, home missions, and social ministry" into a single division operating in a holistic way—a remark that sets the stage for Dr. Hefner's further probing of the LCA and its structures.

The directions from the Advisory Committee were quite general for this essay area. "Cultural pluralism" appeared, as did "pluralism in the interpretation of Scripture and in church traditions," in its list of possible directions. The decision to examine pluralism within the LCA is Dr. Hefner's own decision, but follows naturally from what earlier studies, including that of the Strasbourg Institute suggest (see above, pp. 18–20). The decision to explore the middle-class setting sociologically of the LCA is his also, but it reflects considerable empirical data and is in line with the direction of the Geneva ecclesiological study, to examine a church where and as it is. One can then either be critical of a church for too much cultural captivity and social containment or positive about that church's mission to the world in which its members live. It may well be the function of the LCA to witness where it is placed in middle-class society, while seeking also to transcend that, as was observed at one LWF consultation.

It remains a regret of Dr. Hefner and of the Advisory Committee that a similar analysis of the ALC (or LC-MS) could not be provided in this volume. He offers ample reasons for limiting himself to his own church. Obviously any such report runs the twin dangers of sounding chauvinistic and seeming to bare one's soul in public. History must judge whether visions of the future are correct.

The group with whom Dr. Hefner discussed his paper during stages of its composition includes:

Dr. G. Everett Arden, Professor of Church History Emeritus, Lutheran School of Theology, Chicago;

Dr. Robert Benne, Professor of Church and Society, LSTC;

Dr. Wesley Fuerst, Professor of Old Testament, Dean, LSTC;

Dr. Franklin Sherman, Professor of Christian Ethics, LSTC;

Dr. William Lesher, President, Pacific Lutheran Theological Seminary, (LCA), Berkeley, Calif.

THE IDENTITY AND MISSION
OF THE CHURCH:
THEOLOGICAL REFLECTIONS ON
THE CONCRETE EXISTENCE OF
THE LUTHERAN CHURCH IN AMERICA

Philip Hefner

This essay is written with the Lutheran World Federation Department of Studies project, "The Identity of the Church and Its Service to the Whole Human Being," clearly in mind. This project, as I understand it, seeks to respond to the question: "How has the church actualized itself in our communities, and what significance does this actualization have for our theology and future practice?" The assumption is that constructive advance is possible if we are both critical and lucid about what concrete shape our church existence has taken.

The question demands, however, a style of reflection that is not always easy to undertake. It requires an intimate interrelating of theological sensitivity and the total life-phenomenon which the church has become. This concrete life-phenomenon has a history, a sociology, a psychology, an organizational form, a concrete environment in which it has taken shape and continues to live, a faith centering in Jesus Christ, and a theological self-understanding flowing out of that faith. All of these must be brought together, so far as possible, in a living whole and allowed to speak their authentic testimony. The final goal, however, is to perceive the various faces of the church theologically, to provide a theological interpretation of the concrete life-phenomenon which is our church. Such an enterprise is not common in our theological work, and it places great demands upon the theologian. It requires that the theologian enter into areas of knowledge in which he is not particularly competent; it presses him to pay attention to what *is* empirically, as well as to what ought to be, theologically. The theologian is also pushed mightily to recover what he has come to know through living intimately with the church, through the "feel" that has come through the nurture that the church has provided.

The focus of this essay is the Lutheran Church in America (LCA). The author acknowledges his inadequacy to the task of interpreting the concrete life of this church. He has had to forge his own methodology for the task. The interpretation is open to criticism and disagreement at many points. The experience of the LWF study of ecclesiology has been that member churches have themselves benefited from their studies, perhaps even more than the outsiders who have read and reflected upon those studies. So it is with this essay. I hope that it will be useful to the LCA itself, as it engages in continual self-examination, even as I hope also that sister Lutheran churches around the world may gain insight into the LCA and perhaps be aided in their self-examination, just as I have benefited from reading studies produced from other churches.

I have restricted myself to a case-study of only one American Lutheran denomination because the problems of this study are so complex and the materials so vast that space and time prohibited including more than one church. Furthermore, I could hardly trust myself at this time to approach an interpretation of any church except the one that I know intimately (though partially) through my own experience as a lifelong member. Much of what is suggested here could be applied to the other Lutheran churches in North America, even though, as I shall indicate, there are unique elements in the LCA which do not exist in other churches. The reader should keep in mind that the author has no intention to exaggerate the distinctiveness of the LCA, particularly not at the expense of any other Lutheran church. This is simply a case-study which applies critical theological reflection to the LCA.

The conclusions of this study may be applicable to other Lutheran churches where they share common problems and history with the LCA. Recent history suggests that as different as the churches are, they all face the common task of relating themselves to indigenous cultures in a manner that denies neither their shared destiny with the culture nor their distinctive destiny as the churches of Christ. The basic thrust of this essay points to one way in which the church/culture issue may be approached, and this approach, whether it find agreement or disagreement, should be useful in the ongoing discussion. Perhaps even more, the method by which the conclusions are arrived at may be useful in thinking about ecclesiology.

The destiny of the LCA, like that of every ecclesial community, is to be an embodiment of the gospel in its time and place (see below, pp. 170–71). It is God the Holy Spirit who empowers the church to embody the gospel, but in his providence, God has created human beings with the capacity for reflective thinking and intentional action and he has created a dynamic environment within which his church is to grow. The Spirit's empowerment includes therefore, by God's own design, the reflective, intentional participation of the churches within the distinctive contours of their environments. The embodiment of the gospel depends on God's own grace and power, but that grace and power are carried in the earthen vessels of human thought and assessment, and those vessels are useful and beautiful only as they engage very specific environments. The present reflections, consequently, attend to how the LCA has embodied the gospel in its place, and to the issues that affect that embodiment in the future.

That the church might share most fully in the embodiment of God's gospel it is helpful to gain some understanding of its destiny in its environment and of the gifts God has bestowed upon it for its ministry. These gifts are the means with which the church may be obedient to its destiny and also the basis for judging its faithfulness or disloyalty to its destiny. In our attempt to understand these factors more fully, we give attention to (1) the background of the LCA, where it has come from; (2) what the LCA says about itself and its aims, on the one hand, and its actual present impact in its world, on the other; and (3) the challenge which faces the LCA to weigh its actual impact in the light of its stated intentions and the ensuing obligation to permit the judgments that flow from such reflection to shape its future impact on its world.

THE LCA—WHO WE ARE

The Intertwining of Pluralism and Uniformity

The LCA reveals a fascinating interplay of pluralism and homogeneity in its own origins and development. If we look at the background from which the original Lutheran immigrants came, we see the

intertwining of difference and sameness. (The LCA came into existence in 1962 by a merger of, (1) the United Lutheran Church, which
was chiefly German in origin: (2) the Augustana Lutheran Church,
which was Swedish; (3) the American Evangelical Lutheran Church,
Danish; and (4) the Suomi Synod, Finnish). The immigrants came
from settings as different as orthodox Germans and pietist Scandinavians; they included the well-educated and the peasant. The immigrants
came at different times, spanning the time from the pre-Colonial eighteenth century, through the several waves of immigration in the nineteenth century, into the twentieth. And they settled over a wide area
in America. Some remained in the East, others in the South, while still
others put their roots down in the midsection of the country, and even
these latter stretched from Ohio to Nebraska to Minnesota. One has
only to note the differences between the eastern Pennsylvania Lutheranism of Muhlenberg and Krauth and that of the Grundtvigian Danish
settlements in Minnesota and Nebraska to recognize that pluralism is
indigenous to the groups that formed the LCA.

To the hypothetical visitor from another planet, however, or to an
American black, this diversity might seem overdrawn. The LCA Lutheran immigrants came, after all, from a very particular corner of the
world, almost entirely from four European countries—Germany, Denmark, Sweden, and Finland, with a smattering of Baltic and eastern
Europeans thrown in. North of the Alps, roughly from the Oder to
the Rhine, extending through most of the Nordic countries—not what
one would call a broad segment of the world, or even a broad segment
of the European world. Not only geography, but also values and culture were surprisingly similar. Close up, the beer-drinking Lutheran
and the pietist abstainer might seem different, but they both worked
mightily to improve themselves, succeed in business, farming, or the
professions, to keep themselves clean, and to build a community that
was stable in the New World. Most importantly, for all their differences, their religious heritage was grounded in a common source—the
German Reformation of Martin Luther.

We ought to exaggerate neither the diversity nor the sameness of the
immigrant Lutherans, nor should we subordinate one to the other.
Rather we must see the scope of both diversity and sameness. In
proper perspective, however, the homogeneity of European backgrounds must surely stand out as the primary characteristic of the

Lutherans who formed the LCA, whereas the diversity exists as a counterpoint.

A similar intertwining of sameness and diversity is revealed when we look at the American experience of the Lutherans who formed the LCA. Their backgrounds and values from Europe led them to the same basic niche in the American society—the niche that may be designated by Lloyd Warner's social class identifications of upper-lower class through upper-middle class.[1] These classes are well described by Joseph Kahl:[2]

> *Upper-middle.* The moderately successful business and professional men and their families. . . . Some education and polish were necessary for membership, but lineage was unimportant.
> *Lower-middle.* The petty businessmen, the schoolteachers, the foremen in industry. This group tended to have morals that were close to puritan fundamentalism; they were churchgoers, lodge-joiners, and flag-wavers.
> *Upper-lower* (later we will substitute the term *working class* for this group). The solid, respectable laboring people, who kept their houses clean and stayed out of trouble.

Owners of farms are included in the two middle-class categories, depending on the size and success of their farming enterprises. Kahl is insightful when he characterizes the value-orientations of these groups as "career" and "respectability."[3] Their values and abilities led these immigrants and their descendants into those places that prized their desire for success, their ability to organize and manage, their responsible and serious attitudes towards life, their faithfulness to family and friends, their desire and ability to participate in voluntary organizations, their drive for independence. The social class-designation is imprecise and not of central importance. We may call it "middle class" (see the more careful discussion below, p. 155), but the key is that these Lutherans migrated within American life to basically the same sector of social stratification, because their values and skills performed the same kinds of services in society, as I have just described. If this is what we mean by "WASP" (White, Anglo-Saxon, Protestant), then Lutherans fit into that category. It would be difficult to imagine that the predecessor denominations of the LCA could have been anything except predominantly white.

However, within the American Lutheran scene, the LCA denomina-

1. Notes appear at the end of the essay.

tions have represented a distinctive thrust that has had certain observable consequences.   The historian, E. Clifford Nelson, has traced some of these important characteristics as an openness to modern knowledge, a willingness to accept the American experience, and an ecumenical stance towards other Christians.[4]   We shall elaborate these characteristics in more detail below, but we can point here to two important characteristics that go hand in hand with the elements Nelson has noted: (1) a progressive theological stance which allows the LCA to face the modern world in freedom, and (2) a penetration of the city which involves the church in urban possibilities and problems.   For our theme of diversity, the theological openness means that the LCA is thrust directly into contact with modes of thought and intellectual forces that are not necessarily familiar to traditional Lutheranism whereas the penetration of the city has opened LCA membership to small but growing and significant numbers of persons (chiefly blacks, but also Hispanic-Americans) who do not share the European background of the denomination and who also bring with them in many cases a long Christian heritage that is non-Lutheran in important ways. While the LCA could not be considered a radical or avant-garde group, it is distinctive among American Lutheran groups in characteristics we have just observed.   Futhermore, each of these characteristics opens the door to greater diversity within the LCA—diversity that comes from the American environment in which we live.

The LCA's Characteristic Thrusts as Openings for Secular Pluralism and Change

Every group in the American society experiences the pluralism and change that permeates society as a whole.   How that pluralism and change are received, however, and the impact they make, are shaped by the peculiar character of the group in question.   The peculiar character of the LCA has opened the particular windows by which the breezes of change and pluralism have entered.   We are instructed by a closer look at this process.   We can describe in some detail how the LCA statements of faith, under the distinctive modes that we have borrowed from Nelson's interpretation, are correlated with the LCA's own encounter with change and pluralism.

1. *The LCA's understanding of its faith.*   The present Statement of Faith of the LCA is in continuity with at least 150 years of history and

reflection in the predecessor bodies that have contributed to the present denomination. We call attention to this long tradition, because we must acknowledge that despite diversity of ethnic groups, different style of leadership through the generations, and different types of polity in the predecessor bodies, a common conception of the faith under-girded their history and eventual merger into the LCA in 1962. As G. Everett Arden, the historian of the Augustana Lutheran Church has said, the understanding of the faith carried by the Muhlenberg tradition is the same in substance with the faith that was "grounded in Scripture, measured by the Person and mission of Jesus Christ, elaborated in the historic Lutheran confessions, and personalized in the great evangelical awakenings which swept through all the Scandinavian lands in the 19th century."[5] This common possession of faith made possible the birth of the LCA.

An almost quintessential statement of this understanding of faith appears in the landmark document of Frederick H. Knubel, first president of the United Lutheran Church in America, entitled, "The Essentials of a Catholic Spirit."[6] This document was prepared for inter-Lutheran discussions in 1919 and became the basis for the ULC's "Washington Declaration" of 1920.[7] Knubel and other leaders of the ULC, including Professor Charles M. Jacobs, believed that "the issues of Bolshevism and other anti-Christian forces in addition to the ecumenical discussion of Faith and Order demanded that the Lutherans think through the problem of catholicity."[8] As he looked over the historical process that had brought the Christian community to its understanding of God the Father, Jesus Christ, the Holy Spirit, grace and justification through faith, Knubel understood his own time as a part of that same process, but now challenged by the task of defining the church. He writes:[9]

> That [the historical working out of the faith from God the Father to Justification] in brief has been the progress thus far. Now we are in the midst of or moving toward a further struggle. It is the effort to know what these believers are in this world. It is the effort also to understand what the agency is which brings the salvation of God to men for their acceptance in faith. In other words, Christendom now must experience the doctrine of the Church.

Efforts to define its faith in the context of defining the church have characterized the twentieth-century efforts that have culminated in the present authoritative documents of the LCA. These 20th-century efforts are of a piece with nineteenth-century trends, which we shall not go into here. The characteristic faith of the LCA is embodied in the Constitution of the LCA (1964–72), especially Articles II, IV, and V, and also in the 1972 Report of the Commission on Function and Structure. The Washington Declaration of 1920 and the Baltimore Declaration of 1938 are also significant. These last two documents are of ULC origin, fashioned in explicit attempts to define itself over against other Lutherans; they are, in other words, somewhat polemical in purpose. The provenance of these two documents in the ULC does not diminish their significance for the LCA. The Augustana historian Arden, once again, speaks of them as elaboration and clarification of the tradition that the Muhlenberg Lutherans share with the Scandinavian groups that formed the LCA.[10]

We may summarize the LCA understanding of its faith in this way: The LCA takes its stand firmly in the catholic tradition of the church, insisting that the final authority for interpreting this tradition is Jesus Christ, the incarnate word of God. This tradition exists as the instrument of the Holy Spirit for actualizing God's presence in the world and therefore the forms that it takes are always to be tested through the church's engagement in mission in an ever-changing world. This statement of faith has certain very specific implications that challenge our present church life and on occasion bring the LCA into tension with other Lutherans and other Christians.

First, while insisting on its deep loyalty to the revelation of God in his incarnate word, Jesus Christ, the LCA tends to relativize the specific witnesses to that revelation, even though it cherishes those witnesses and acknowledges their authority. Even though the LCA seldom achieves proper balance between loyalty to the witnesses and their relativization under Christ, such balance is a norm to which the LCA holds itself accountable. Scripture, creeds, Lutheran confessional writings, as well as catholic liturgy and tradition are witnesses which the LCA thus acknowledges as authoritative and yet subordinate to Christ. The Baltimore Declaration of 1938 devoted considerable attention to establishing this authority of Christ. The document defines the "Word of God" in three ways: (1) "in its most real sense the Word of God is the Gospel, i.e., the message concerning Jesus Christ"; (2) in the "wider sense" the Word of God is the salvation history which is

God's "revelation of himself," reaching its fullness in Christ, but beginning with creation; and (3) "because God continues to make himself known through them, we believe that the Scriptures also are the Word of God." This is definitely a historical understanding of the Word and tradition. Yet it is emphatically Lutheran in its concern for the primacy of Christ, in the light of whom we measure the tradition, even Scripture as to its "more important and less important parts." This understanding is neither free from controversy nor is it wholly non-polemical, but it is carefully stated. More recent theologians and official statements have elaborated and reaffirmed this position.

Second, the LCA insists on its basic catholicity. In his pivotal document, Knubel explicitly rejected a narrow definition of Lutheranism which would equate Lutheranism with generic Christianity. The Washington Declaration defined catholicity as universality and insisted that the catholic church is raised "above all local and temporal forms of expression in organization, rite, and ceremony." Article IV of the present Constitution states:

> This church, therefore, derives its character and powers both from the sanction and representation of its congregations and from its inherent nature as an expression of the broader fellowship of the faithful. In length, it acknowledges itself to be in the historic continuity of the communion saints; in breadth, it expresses the fellowship of believers and congregations in this our day.

Although the norm of catholicity is honored far too often in the breach rather than in the observance, the LCA does hold itself accountable for a catholic expression of Lutheranism. This has been evident for more than a century in its stated goal of Lutheran unity in North America, its role in official ecumenical organizations and in interconfessional dialogues, and in liturgical renewal.

Third, the LCA wants to follow the leading of God's Spirit into the world, to be a part of God's actualizing of his gospel of grace. In the Washington Declaration, "works of serving love" were mentioned as one of the four marks of the one, holy, catholic, and apostolic church (the other three: professing faith in Jesus Christ, preaching the word and administering the sacraments, and attempting to secure universal acceptance of its truth). Of these works, it is said that they are themselves "a creation of God the Holy Spirit" and "a proclamation of the Gospel. In outward form they may appear to be merely humanitarian and altruistic; in motive they are Christian, born of the love of Christ and performed in His name and in obedience to His command." In its current statements of purpose, the LCA images itself as an instrument of the Holy Spirit (Constitution, Article V), and it recognizes that the Spirit moves out into the world where the gospel is to be related to "man's every situation" and extended "to all the world" (Article V, Section 1a). In its 1972 restatement of purpose in the Commission on Function and Structure study, the LCA asserted that this charge as instrument of the Spirit involves working for justice, meeting human need, and communicating to nonchurched persons. In an impressive statement of its willingness to follow the promptings of God, the church affirmed that it would judge every statement of its purpose by the test of its fruitfulness in "the church's engagement in mission in an ever-changing world."

In conclusion, what we find in the LCA understanding of faith is the product of a generations-long attempt to define a position that is unmistakably Lutheran while at the same time insistent that Lutheranism is not divisive within Christendom, but rather open, willing to reach out to other Christians in its understanding of Scripture and tradition, and in its desire for unity. Furthermore, it includes the conviction that service in the world is essential to belief in Christ and the proclamation of the gospel. We note in this position elements of catholicity, confessional Lutheranism, renewed Pietism, and the desire to relate positively to the American environment.

2. *The LCA's encounter with change and diversity.*

a) *Openness to modern knowledge.* What Nelson points to as openness to modern knowledge, coupled with a tradition for progressive theology which relativizes all authority to Christ and desires to be the instrument of the Holy Spirit, provides a natural entrée for a number of secular forces. These forces are both cause and consequence of change and diversity. Historical-critical study of Scripture and tradition, for example, have been characteristic of the LCA stance; even when there was opposition to critical study, prestigious figures in the denomination have not only allowed it to take its course, but have taken steps to funnel its insights and method into the church, including even the church school curricula that are used at the grass roots.[11] This critical study could find its way into the church, because the Christ of Scripture and its text was the supreme authority. It could be embraced, because it is through the proclamation of Christ *from* the text of Scripture (Constitution II, 3 and 7) and not the text by itself that the Spirit "creates and sustains faith" and God "realizes his redemptive purpose."

The introduction of historical study into the church's life was not restricted to a method of interpreting Scripture, however. It was also a manifestation of critical thinking as such at the very heart of the church's existence—the reflection upon sacred Scripture and its revelation. Critical thinking, in turn, is a powerful force for pluralism and change, because it encourages free inquiry, independent judgment, and trust in the process of discovering new knowledge. These engines of thought cannot be easily tamed, and only a strong conviction that Christ is authority above all and that the Holy Spirit uses the thought and proclamation of his faithful servants could sustain the encouragement of critical thinking without splintering the faith altogether. A good deal of the history of the LCA traditions has occurred precisely within the struggle to affirm the freedom of critical inquiry and yet turn that inquiry into channels of edification.

Critical thinking was also brought to bear upon the postbiblical traditions of the Lutheran church. As a consequence the LCA has been willing to relativize Luther's thought itself and also the dogmaticians of the century that followed upon Luther. This critical spirit has not only resulted in making careful distinctions between the various confessional documents of the Book of Concord and their relative authoritativeness, but also in considerable diversity on the question of what constitutes "confessional theology." Although it is public doctrine among Lutherans that only the Scriptures and the Confessions have normative status in defining what Lutherans believe, there has frequently been an assumption that a certain line of German theologians (sometimes designated as those who stand in the line of Hengstenberg and Erlangen) is closer to Luther and the Confessions than any other theologians. This strand of theology is often considered to have an exclusive claim on the term *confessional*.[12] The LCA has not accepted this assumption, partly because of its willingness to apply historical-critical method to the Lutheran tradition and partly because some of its predecessor bodies—the Lundensians of the Augustana church and the Grundtvigians of the American Evangelical Lutheran Church, for example—simply could not give primacy to a narrow stream of German thought and maintain their integrity as Lutherans in their own right. Theology which subscribes fully to the Lutheran Confessions and yet defines *confessional* in broader terms is at home in the LCA.

The opening of the door to critical thinking brings, eventually, an encounter with the whole of modern thinking about the world. This opening leads unavoidably to a confrontation with modern modes of understanding history, human being, nature, and the knowledge and method of the sciences. The LCA has grappled with these modern strands through most of its history, seeking both to articulate the faith in the context of modernity and also applying contemporary thought to analyze its own faith, its structure, its ministry, and its mission.[13] As a consequence, the LCA has acknowledged, whether explicitly or implicitly, a certain authority in modern thought per se. This authority is not conceived as power over the gospel, but rather as a factor that cannot be ignored and must be dealt with constructively.[14] In a slow, groping, sometimes torturous manner, the LCA has come to understand and to affirm that doctrinal and evangelical faithfulness are not enough as criteria for judging and shaping its life. That life must also be informed by what our best thinking knows is true and desirable, and it must make sense accordingly. Biblical study, theology, organizational structure, social action, evangelism, stewardship, and parish and seminary education have been subjected to this dual authority of doctrine and modern thinking. This is not to say that the LCA has always understood either doctrine or modern insights adequately or applied them wisely, but it cannot be gainsaid that the dual authority has been a reality in the LCA and its predecessors.

This acceptance of the two authorities has been documented by historians, it has proven to be a thorn of controversy in relations with other Lutherans, and the effort to relate the two authorities properly has absorbed much effort. The proper relation of the two is as yet an unresolved problem. This effort will occupy our attention in a later section of this essay, but here it is important to underscore the existence of the double authority and to understand that this dualiy can be tolerated because of the conviction that Christ stands above all, above both doctrine and modern thinking, and that the Holy Spirit uses the process of the church's life—however that process is shaped—as his instrument. If we are to understand how diversity and change are making and have made their impact upon the LCA, we must recognize that they gained entrée and force in the denomination through its traditional legitimatizing of modern knowledge through a progressive theological stance. The intention has never been to permit the gospel to be compromised, but the struggle with compromise has been real.

b) Openness to ecumenism. What we have just observed applies strictly to the intellectual encounter with diversity and change and their impact on church life. In another dimension, the LCA and its predecessors were opened to ecumenical diversity and its force for change. Certain of the predecessor churches had strong ecumenical thrusts in the 19th century.[15] Through its predecessors, the LCA was not only on the scene at the formation of the inter-Lutheran groupings that have led to the Lutheran World Federation and to the National Council of Churches of Christ in the U.S.A. and to the World Council of Churches, but it has at times also played a leading role in the formation and continuation of those groups.

This ecumenical involvement has made its mark in many ways upon the LCA, beyond the energy and financial support that it has consumed. The LCA has been influenced by theological input, social ministry outreach, liturgical renewal and cooperation, and educational interrelationships in its encounter with other churches. The international dimension of ecumenical relations and the specific dialogue with Roman Catholics may be the two most important elements for LCA Lutherans. The former has reminded the church of its membership in the worldwide fellowship, many of whose members live in situations that both inspire the LCA and call into question the directions that the LCA has taken with respect to the American society that seems imperialistic to Christians in other parts of the world. The Roman Catholic opening not only revises many assumptions that have grown out of the Reformation critique of Catholicism, but it has also furnished input for creative change in liturgy, theology, and cooperative ventures.

It is an understatement to say that the impact from ecumenical involvements is yet to be assimilated and understood by the LCA itself. Issues raised, e.g., by the international involvements and Roman Catholic conversations will take much reflection and could result in momentous changes. The former challenge bids us to reconsider our relation to American society and to American foreign policy; the latter has led to fundamental consideration of the larger issue of what the Reformation of Luther stands for, as well as the issues of the nature of the ordained ministry and the papal authority.

c) Penetration of American life. At still another level, diversity and change have entered LCA life through its penetration of American life. Whether due more to intention or historical accident, or to both, the LCA and its antecedent groups have been characterized as the "most" American of the Lutheran denominations in the United States. In this respect, as in others we have discussed, the developments have not been in a straight line or monolithic. Some observers would insist that it is more accurate to say the LCA *has been penetrated by* American life, rather than to ascribe such purposefulness to the church itself. When we do speak of penerating American life, we must recognize that we speak relatively. Not even the LCA is "American" in the sense that the Congregationalists and Presbyterians have been, for example. We are in many areas still only a generation or two away from our ethnic origins. Furthermore, we have never been at the levers of power and influence in America. We cannot speak as a noted Presbyterian leader speaks of his denomination: "Style and interest in everything from colonial architecture to the running of the American economy and government were directed by our traditions and our ancestors."[16]

Recognizing this relative sense in which we have penetrated American life, we can point to several important consequences which that penetration had on the LCA—each of which has provided an occasion for America, with its diversity and change, to penetrate us. First, we may speak of involvement in the cities. By "city" we refer to metropolitan areas ranging from the inner city to the outer ring of suburbs. The LCA is the least rural of the American Lutheran denominations, and this has had certain results for the LCA. The church is sufficiently involved in over twenty-five metropolitan areas that we have attracted some of the diverse groups in the cities to our membership. These new members make diversity and change *actual* in the very midst of the church. Their religious background is often vigorous, but it is significantly non-Lutheran—we refer particularly to blacks and Hispanic Americans. Their associational patterns, worship life, and culture are often different from LCA tradition. In some cities black congregations are the fastest growing, indeed the only growing congregations.

The thrust into the city means, in the second place, that the LCA is faced with ministry and mission in financially less affluent situations. This not only places severe demands upon the synods and national church to support such ministry, but also places new demands on the interrelationship between financially strapped eastern seaboard areas and the southern and midwestern areas, where affluent support is more available. The situation also compels us to probe new forms of ordained ministry—for example, tentmaking, cooperative, and the like, which place less financial burden on the church.

With respect to the impact of change and diversity, the penetration of the city means that the LCA is immediately subject to developments in the most febrile and sensitive area of American life. It is no exaggeration to say that as the metropolitan areas of America go, so goes the LCA. This statement is accurate, in spite of the fact that substantial numbers of farmers and small towns are included in the LCA.

Third, penetration of American life is correlated with the high interest that the LCA and its predecessor bodies have shown in social issues. It is not an overstatement to say that through its various denominational offices having to do with social concerns the LCA has produced a fairly extensive study of nearly every issue of significance that faces Americans—world community, ecology, abortion, penal reform, racism, to name a few. A recent study by the Lutheran Council in the USA has revealed the relatively large investment of time and energy that the LCA has put into the study of these issues and into informing its constituency of the implications of these issues for church life.

What is the conclusion to be drawn from this description of the LCA, where it has come from and where it stands today? Obviously, our brief sketch of the LCA has been highly selective and interpretive, precisely so that we could lift up definite conclusions that seem significant to the efforts of the LCA to be faithful as a church of Christ in America in the years ahead.

First, we can see that, like every group, the LCA has its own peculiar stance, growing out of the contours of its own history. Since this peculiar stance has emerged oftentimes in conflict with other Lutherans in North America, we have not avoided at times speaking of the distinctiveness of the LCA. This is important, so that our sister churches of the Lutheran World Federation will understand more of the diversity among their Lutheran cohorts in America. This expression of distinctiveness would be misleading, however, if it gives the impression that the LCA stands in stark contrast to other Lutherans in North America in every respect. Although the LCA does represent a definite tradition, which E. Clifford Nelson calls "eastern Lutheranism" and "neo-Lutheranism,"[17] it holds no monopoly on those designations and it has members who share much with more conservative Lutherans in other bodies. Furthermore, on many issues there are more similarities than differences between the LCA members and those of other Lutheran churches in America. From another perspective, misleading impressions may be conveyed by our largely positive evaluation of the LCA up to this point. Such a positive attitude is explained by our description of the LCA largely from its statements of its own intentions, which always assert the best aspirations of the church. These statements become, however, very important precisely because of their tone of high aspiration, because they are the statements to which the LCA must be held accountable and on the basis of which it is to be evaluated later on in our discussion.

Second, our sketch shows how inseparable the interior theological self-understanding of the church is from the world in which it lives. At various crucial points in the history of the LCA and its predecessor bodies, there was scarcely a self-conscious understanding that efforts to define the faith and practice of the church would prove to be levers by which the secular world would grasp the church and bend it. As we assess what it has meant for the LCA to be an ecclesial community, however, it is essential that we be aware of how interior faith-image and external pressures from the world interact with each other.

Third, the challenge faces us directly to reflect upon the future course of this ecclesial body that lives under the impact of a definite Lutheran identity which is working itself out in engagement with modern knowledge, ecumenical interaction, and American life—an engagement which it has openly pursued through the course of its history. Such reflection will require a theological interpretation of LCA history and prospect. It requires a holistic theological interpretation of what is the significance of the form the church has taken in the LCA. The remainder of this essay is an attempt to provide a contribution to such a theological understanding.

As we begin this reflection, we summarize the gifts which we believe the LCA has been given in its history, gifts which serve as foundation for its life in the immediate future. These gifts are the resources that have developed, under God, for the LCA to meet the challenges of its present time and place. We enumerate these gifts seriatim. We remind the reader that while the distinctiveness of certain gifts is obvious from the historical sketch we presented above, we do not imply here that other American Lutherans do not share some or all of these gifts:

1. A progressive theological self-understanding which allows for openness to advances in knowledge which are radically reshaping the contemporary understanding of the world and human beings

2. A tradition for openness for involvement in American culture, rather than Lutheran ghetto existence

3. An explicit ecumenical orientation, which includes both an edifying thrust for its internal life and outreach with other Christians, particularly the more "catholic" churches

4. A sophisticated organizational structure, with the undergirding conviction that such organization can be used freely for the church's mission

5. Liturgical ferment, with a general trend to recovering the worship life of the patristic churches

6. A relatively deep involvement in the urban areas of America, with the result that the future of the LCA is tied intimately to the future of the metropolitan areas

7. A significant, small but growing, black membership in the northern and western urban areas

8. A large body of analysis and interpretation of social and cultural issues that confront the church in America today

9. An increasing number of competent women in seminaries preparing for ordination and other full-time church work, together with increased participation by laywomen in the policymaking areas of the church's life

10. Ties with the international Lutheran community

THE LCA PLACEMENT IN AMERICAN SOCIETY

The characteristic LCA understanding of its faith, acted upon by the secular world, stands within a still larger social context which exerts its own pressure upon the LCA and which also lends its own coloring to the concrete manifestations of that faith, whatever the LCA's explicit intentions and motivations may be. This larger social context we refer to as the "middle-class modulation," and we consider it so all-encompassing that it becomes a chief category for this interpretation of the form "church" has taken in the LCA. Middle-class concerns and characteristics have become an inescapable medium in which the LCA lives

—hence the term *modulation,* which bestows its own inflection on what the LCA is and does.

We must be as precise as possible when speaking of the middle-class modulation, since *middle class* has become a catch-phrase for so many different reasons in recent times. Sociologists and social anthropologists in America have established a pattern of class structure that has remained fairly stable in its categories.[18] We referred to this structure earlier, with reference to Joseph Kahl. Joseph Bensman and Arthur Vidich have provided simpler class designations: Upper, upper-middle class, lower-middle class, working class and subworking class. These class designations refer to *social and economic* phenomena. The class designations have remained stable, even though the economic basis of the various classes has shifted and the social content of each class has undergone rather dramatic change. Social class refers to a style, a life-way (to use a phrase of John Bowker's) which an economic or social group develops in the context of its particular success or failure, ascent or descent in the society. As a consequence, when we refer to the middle class, we are not indulging in popular pseudo-Marxist rhetoric, nor purely economic interpretation, although social class is inseparable from economic factors. We focus rather upon the style or lifeway of the middle class, its character and significance. There is plentiful material upon which we can rely, since sociologists and social anthropologists have themselves devoted a great deal of their study to these factors.

It is the middle-class lifeway to which the LCA Lutherans have largely migrated. The LCA has not intended to be so fully middle class, but the power of its living faith has been poured, by historical accident, into a middle-class mold. Its faith and life are strong, but very definitely bearing the middle-class modulations.

What is the middle-class lifeway? Earlier, we mentioned the characteristics of a desire for success, ability to organize and manage, a responsible and serious attitude toward life, faithfulness to family and friends, the desire and ability to participate in voluntary organizations, and a drive for independence as appropriate to the middle-class life-way. Kahl has included these characteristics in his colder, less suggestive terms *career* and *respectability.* His terms may have a one-dimensional and pejorative ring, but his more extensive elaboration of these terms reveal a rich and dynamic lifeway. For example, his description of what *career* denotes as a middle-class value:[19]

A career is interesting and satisfying. It may be that the contemporary [careerist] feels somewhat less inner complusion to work than the driving entrepreneur of the Puritan past, but nevertheless he feels that his work is important and challenging. He grows as his career advances and he assumes larger responsibilities; he has a sense of accomplishment and of continuity. He keeps up to date in his field, and he feels progressive, creative, and in control of important affairs. He senses that he is doing the big work of his culture. He is not alienated from work . . . he wants to feel that the competitive rules were fair and that he won through superior ability and energy.

This middle-class value is not aimed only at production and the driving business ethos of a past generation, but it is also embodied in consumption-orientated and service domains, including social service, teaching, and the like.

Bensman and Vidich put in historical perspective the character of the middle class as it has emerged since World War II.[20] The upper-middle class is now almost exclusively comprised of higher managerial, administrative, professional, intellectual and bureaucratic persons. These are the successful groups, who flourish, because the form of wealth which is dominant today is one which demands their functions. The key, new characteristic forming their lifeway is their college and university education. Because higher education for the first time has become the prerequisite for the successful entrance into the upper-middle class, "the university now became the major center for the production of culture and for setting new styles of cultural consumption and leisure."[21] Edward Banfield fills out this lifeway even more by pointing out that the ability to imagine a distant future and discipline oneself to work for it, acquire the necessary skills, etc., is indispensable for membership in this upper-middle class.[22] Kahl's description of *career* and Bensman and Vidich's description of who comprises the middle class corroborate Banfield's emphasis upon time-orientation as a mark of this class, since future-orientation and discipline are precisely the characteristics that are required by the forms of wealth which upper-middle-class persons have so successfully served.

This middle-class lifeway has become important, not because it controls absolutely the economic and political life in our society, nor because it possesses great wealth, but rather because it has become *indispensable* in the society that America has forged and to the maintenance of the forms on which that society is based. The middle class is not first of all a group of greedy and power-hungry persons who pull the strings in society. It is the group of persons whose lifeway has infiltrated the warp and woof of our common existence, so that if it were suddenly to disappear, the society would crumble. The middle class is comprised of engineers, doctors, teachers, lawyers, social workers, managers, small and medium-sized businessmen, successful farmers, leaders and managers of voluntary organizations. These persons are those who literally keep the society operating through their planning, organizing, and managing skills. The lower-middle class is also indispensable, as is the working class, but for different reasons. Their relation to the upper-middle class must be described later.

The pivotal role of the middle class can be illumined in another way. America has not created traditional styles of living that were indigenous to itself.[23] It has borrowed—from England, from the successive immigrant heritages that furnished lifestyle options until the immigration was stopped in 1924. One of the great challenges since that time has been for Americans to develop their own lifeway. Since the twenties other significant changes have taken place in American society—the rapid contraction of rural society, the decline of traditional upper-class styles, due to the changing base of capital formation and wealth, and the drastic changes in the occupational structure, which have catapulted the college-bred new upper-middle class into prominence that many of the successful persons never expected.

The upper-middle class that has emerged since World War II has not only shared in the American challenge to fashion an authentic and indigenous style of life, but as a consequence of its indispensable role in American life, it has borne the burden of creating lifestyles for all of American society. In a sense, the upper-middle class has had to pioneer for all Americans, in that all Americans see middle-class values as a reference point for themselves. If we understand the lines of development in other parts of the world as well, we can see that by virtue of its encountering the problems of contemporary technologization and complex social organization first, the upper-middle class of America (and also of Europe) is also carrying out an experiment that is international in its significance. We are not indulging in ethnocentrism nor in a glorification of the upper-middle class. Rather, historical developments have placed it in this crucial position, and its destiny is to do what the times demand as creatively and wholesomely as possible.

If we comprehend this leading-edge position of the upper-middle class, then a number of other issues are more intelligible. We can understand, for example, why one might be inclined to say that American *is* middle class, since America does live by the values of the middle class. Simply because the upper-middle class is indispensable and because it bears the burden of forging a style that is authentically American at a time when there are few models to emulate, it would be strange if its values were not dominant in America.

We can also understand why so many Americans who are not, strictly speaking, middle class identify themselves as such and why middle-class styles are important for the lower-middle class, the working class, and the lower classes. Obviously, middle-class values and styles will be normative for society, because the upper-middle class is the crucial class for the functioning of the society. The lower-middle-class and working-class persons will aspire to upper-middle-class styles and values, particularly in educating their children, because they aspire to share in the creative life of American society. Those who do not or cannot aspire to such sharing will, whether justly or not, be marked in invidious ways. This also explains why the working classes may be greatly alienated from society and from the middle classes. They are indispensable to society, but they are outside the mainstream of where the cultural, economic, and value-formation action is.

One final characteristic of American society (and here America is not unique in its functioning—indeed, all societies share with it) needs to be noted, namely, the underlying *principle of cooptation*.[24] The very success of the American economic system keeps expectations high that increasing numbers of people will share in the wealth and rewards of the system. Thus, at the same time that more people do share in these, the grounds for hostility and discontent also grow stronger among those who do not receive the financial or status rewards they think they should have. The American system deals with this potential discontent by cooptation, beginning with the middle class and extending to all sectors of society. The principle of cooptation does not always work, but its operation is clearly in evidence. Private or public philanthropy is used to effect this cooptation. The most significant efforts at cooptation have been directed to: (1) individuals with little or no income, with the emergence of direct relief as a major item in the national budget and in local state and municipal budgets; (2) individuals of higher social status whose share of the rewards of income or status seems lower then it should be, with the result that intellectuals, professionals, academics, and administrators have risen dramatically since World War II in their share of the rewards; (3) individuals and groups whose spiritual expectations are potentially disruptive, including religious, educational, cultural, recreational, and political expectations.[25] It is chiefly the new use of the greatly expanded federal budget and the adoption of Keynesian economic policies that has enabled this cooptation, but private philanthropies have also been involved.

In this framework of cooptation, we must remember that our society always aims first at coopting, rather than disappointing or destroying persons and groups. Furthermore, not only is the middle class one of the groups most dedicated to coopting others, but it is itself very largely a coopted group.

Finally, we can understand why the criticism of the middle classes has been so bitter in recent years. That criticism rests not only on the injustices that the middle classes have perpetrated, but also it finds its roots in a sharp awareness that the experiment in style that is carried on in the middle classes is immensely significant for America and the world as a whole. The successes of the middle-class experiment are applauded, but the failures and distortions dare not go unchallenged, simply because too much is riding on that experiment.

We may now usefully summarize the middle-class modulation which comprises the larger social context in which the LCA is placed. That modulation is the lifeway that has developed among the managerial, administrative, professional, intellectual, and bureaucratic class which in turn has become the "successful" group in our society, largely because it serves an essential function in assuring that American society, which is now built upon a technological, highly productive base, survives. Precisely because this group has become the successful and indispensable group, its task is to form the style and values for the whole society, and all the classes below the upper-middle class recognize this, even if they do not always accept the leadership of the middle class willingly. Is everyone in the LCA middle class? By no means. However, this fact ought not cloud over the basic middle-class character of the LCA. We note here that in today's society, farmers, for example, who are often not considered middle class in the common mind, definitely fit into that class, since they often share the college education base of the middle class, share its values of future-orientation and self-discipline in planning ahead, and possess the managerial and administrative skills of the middle-class style. Furthermore, we must not lose sight of the fact that the leadership group in the LCA, in both national and local circles projects the ethos and style of the middle class as we have described it here. This will become clearer in what follows. *The Lutheran,* for example, the chief media force in the denomination as a whole, consistently projects middle-class images for its readers. The typical delegate to the 1972 convention of the church was male, between the ages of forty and forty-nine, owned his own home, possessed a graduate or professional degree and had an annual income of $24,000.[26] Lower middle-class and working-class members of the LCA, therefore, must come to terms with the middle-class style, in the way that every American must. This style is set as the norm for these classes and the church is largely managed by persons who live in the middle-class style. To assert that this is so is not to approve it, but it would be an error not to recognize how middle-class the LCA has become.

The Middle-Class Modulation at Work

We are not always accustomed in the church to perceive how our very best expressions of faith are possessed by the social milieu in which the church lives. In this section we propose to describe three examples of how the LCA has been so possessed. Such concrete description is necessary if we are to understand how the church has actually manifested itself among us.

1. *Ministry—doctrine and practice.* The character of the middle class prizes organization and effectiveness. At its worst, this is "efficiency" at the expense of human values. At its best, it is an effort to focus resources on the achieving of goals that free individuals within a group have decided are central to the purpose of the group. It is this focusing that engenders what we call "organization." Organization tends to be downgraded today as undesirable and inhuman, but such attacks are misplaced if they really believe that organization per se is evil or even expendable. Organization does require discipline and commitment to the rules of the game by which the organization operates and makes its contributions. In a subsequent section we will elaborate on the seriousness with which the LCA takes organization. On the other hand, the LCA has given considerable attention to its doctrine

and practice of the ministry, producing over the past three decades (including the work of the predecessor churches) a sizeable body of reflection on ministry. When we look at that theological reflection alongside the middle-class context of the LCA, we see that the theology has become a rather impressive rationale for practice which reinforces LCA organizational existence, an organizational form that is itself characteristically middle-class (as a later section will describe). The theology has come very close, in other words, to becoming *ideology*. The theology has claimed to be reflection upon the Word of God and its implications for ministry; in actuality it has the effect of grounding a complex organizational manifestation.

In 1938, 1952, 1966, and 1970, the ULC and the LCA produced official statements on the doctrine of the ministry, and the subsequent years continue to see much attention devoted to the issues raised by the doctrine. The official statements contain rich and admirable theology, not to mention the large number of unpublished background studies that undergird the official statements. What does this theology of the ordained ministry emphasize? It speaks of the ministry proceeding from the Word of God, instituted by God to make the promise clear, as the Augsburg Confession, Article IV, enunciates. The LCA documents counter Baptist and other free-thinking traditions which were threats to the ULC in earlier decades. These documents emphasize that the ministry is not a freelance operation of the individual pastor, *it belongs to the church*. This means that the pastor cannot freelance without a call from a local group and that he or she cannot function at will without the church-at-large approving the ministerial activity. Individual pastor, local parish or agency, and national church are linked indissolubly together. The pattern of clergy selection, nurture, ordination, and installation is instructive. The ministerial candidate presents himself or herself to synodical committees that approve candidacy and pronounce the candidate suitable for ordination. Ordination cannot take place until a call from a specific parish or agency is received. Calls are monitored by the bishops, and ordination is an act of the bishop, in behalf of the whole church. Installation is also an act of the bishop, but the parish or agency is involved intimately.

This theology and practice are substantial, well-grounded in the catholic tradition, rejecting errors, providing a kind of order and freedom that free-lancing, exclusively parish-oriented doctrines did not have. In the context of American Protestantism it has several advantages for combining freedom-in-order that protects both pastor and parish from transient whims. This theology and practice have also, however, reinforced LCA middle-classness, leading to the question whether they have also been shaped, in part, by the middle-class milieu. In a denominational structure moving towards centralization and organizational firmness, both in the New York-Philadelphia headquarters and in the Synodical Presidential (episcopal) offices, a structure increasingly adopting a "line-of-command" system of accountability, with financial, educational, promotional, and programmatic weight in these headquarters, this theology has served to integrate the ordained person fully into the organizational system. This person is beholden to the microcosmic element of the organizational system—parish or other agency—and to the macrocosmic element—the church-at-large. The parish, in turn, is made dependent for leadership on the larger unit—synod and national church. The theology has in a sense been coopted, although quite unwittingly. Neither the theologians who wrote the theological statements nor the bishops or denominational leaders consciously calculated this cooptation. Nevertheless, the functional consequence of the theology has been to give ideological reinforcement to a conventional bureaucracy in which all units are dependent upon those that are above them in the line of command. (Today there is considerable tension in the church, since synods and congregations are expressing their desire for more autonomy. They threaten the existence of the national bureaucracy by withholding funds from it. Their quiet protest is both a reflection of a general tendency in American life to distrust bureaucracy, and also a sign of healthy rejection of cooptation.) Earlier we spoke of how deeply rooted cooptation is in the bureaucratic structure of post-World War II American middle-class life. In its theology of the ministry, we see the LCA providing ideological reinforcement for its own process of cooptation.

It is no accident that the official documents of the LCA now do not speak of "ministry," but rather of "professional leadership." The organizational leadership elite is more aptly designated as a professional corps that can be deployed effectively. As a consequence, innovation and healthy free-lancing are difficult. For example, "special calls" (i.e., to nonparish situations) are granted by the organization at its will, and these tend to be in relatively "safe" areas—teaching, bureaucracy, chaplaincy—not in community organization, poverty work, or political activity.

The theological educational system, which also has its rich theological foundation in Lutheran concern for an educated clergy that can expound the word of God, dovetails with the clergy-organizational complex. The church system selects students, as we described above, up to the decision of their suitability for ordination. The students undergo a long, relatively rigid, closely supervised education which is in fact "acculturation" into the system. Efforts to make seminary education more uniform are in effect efforts to escalate the effectiveness of acculturation. All education is, of course, acculturation. The question is, What kind? In the last thirty years, there has been change in the theological education that students receive, but very little increase in the amount of Bible, history, or theology taught, and little improvement in the quality of the teaching. There has been an enormous increase in efforts to relate to the practical situation of the church, in making students more effective, giving them skills for functioning as the church thinks they ought to function. This practical education is also much more closely supervised. On the one hand, these efforts to relate theory and practice, to increase the practical side of ministerial education, are to be applauded. On the other hand, they are potentially dangerous, since they tie the students ever more closely to the organizational form of the church and its processes, possibly weakening their resources for remaining critical of the organizational form as such, even though they may be critical of inefficient functioning.

Organization, competence of clergy, clergy education—they all dovetail admirably into an interlocking system. The system is quintessentially middle-class, and it possesses a clearly articulated theological foundation. The question, as we shall probe later, is whether this interlocking whole is a middle-class closure that is opposed to our stated intentions of catholicity and openness to the world. We can suggest here, however, some considerations that lead us to raise the question: (a) Our system needs a professional leader who has certain skills and characteristics that tend to be homogenizing and definitely oriented toward the system-ghetto in which our organizational form and middle-class modulation might imprison us. Our polity, for example, allows for little "voluntary" activity outside officially approved programs, whether those activities be fund-raising, missionary societies, theological education, or evangelistic societies. Baptists, Methodists, and Roman Catholics are examples of groups where voluntary organizations (which have a tendency to offer a radical witness within the larger denominational body) are tolerated, often encouraged and enabled. Consequently, there is more opportunity in those churches for diversity and also for centers of critical independence. On the local level, we do not train our pastors to be comfortable with voluntary groups who would function radically within the parish. (b) Our professional leaders tend to relate best to the kind of people who fashioned our system, operate it, or feel comfortable in it: the college-education-based middle class that we described earlier. Pastors have difficulty relating to working-class persons, blacks, and minorities. Preaching style, organizational style, associational patterns, and even pastoral care is oriented toward the middle class. The principle that operates in some areas, that new parishes will be developed only in communities that have the prospect of becoming financially self-supporting, reinforces this phenomenon, since nonmiddle-class groups are the least affluent. Potential alienation between classes is also reinforced. (c) The middle class has traditionally wanted clergy to be "chaplains" of some sort or another, and our clergy tend to be chaplains to the middle class. Such chaplaining entails a view of the church as chiefly a "hospital" for the disabled or for personal growth problems (which Charles Glock indicates is the view most prevalent among us).[27] This includes not only the ordinary parish activity, but also charitable contributions to the needy. It is no accident that the most easily obtained and most common nonparish calls to ministers are either maintenance functions within the church organization or to chaplaincy positions involving social work or pastoral counseling. It is virtually impossible to obtain such a call for community organization work, for ministry to work with and organize the poor, migrant laborers, and such groups. Seminary graduates may serve as hospital chaplains, but not in the Southern Christian Leadership Council (the organization founded by Martin Luther King, Jr.), Saul Alinsky organizations, or political and social reform movements. Why? Quite possibly because we still accept as normative the old "inner mission" model for ministry in society. This model was one of bestowing charity, rather than empowering the disadvantaged to organize their own lives. The inner mission model was the closest a European church—one that was allied with the anti-revolutionary forces of the mid-nineteenth century—could come to social work. The organizations we have mentioned that are not chaplaincy organizations, which do not deal primarily with maintenance or charity activities, but rather with empowering the "outsiders" in society, often non-middle-class persons, to organize their self-interests and grievances so that they can challenge and change the American social system—these organizations seldom receive LCA clergy participation, even when they call such clergy.

2. *Organization.* The 1972 reorganization of the LCA followed the principle of "structure conforms to function." As a result, an overhauling took place, which aimed at effective embodiment of the goals of the church. As with the theology and practice of ministry, this organization and its theory are impressive and in many respects one can hardly take exception to the intention and function of the organization. There are some dimensions to the organization that deserve attention, however. The organizational theory is, as one might expect given the description of the middle class, a monument of middle-class thinking and style. It is sophisticated in its conception, so sophisticated that only a highly trained middle-class group could have put it together.

In order to implement the organizational principle—"structure follows function"—every segment of the system (the "system" in this sense is the church) must be aware of its goals and reflect on the best way to accomplish them. This intention is wholesome. From a purely descriptive point of view, however, we should recognize that this requires either the reflective experience and capacity of those who are accustomed to working such organizational structures or else the assistance of facilitators who can enable a group (parish, school, etc.) to achieve functional and structural clarity. Such experience, if not the capacity, is primarily at home in the middle class. The organization requires expertise, in other words, and that is a commodity that is by definition possessed largely in the middle class. It is not surprising that the list of congregational and pastoral functions in the LCA organizational handbook includes this facilitating function. Theologically, this facilitating aims at enabling the laity to carry out their own ministry. Functionally within the system, however, the inclusion of the facilitating function is honest and explicit recognition that someone or some group is necessary to run the organization, and that the chief facilitator should be the pastor, who is one of the accredited "professional leaders."

These comments are critical, but also descriptive. The LCA organization is middle-class in its conception and requires middle-class values and skills for its implementation. Catholic outreach to nonmiddle-class persons may be hindered by such an organizational conception.

There are additional dangers lurking in the LCA structure, stemming from its character as an ecclesiastical counterpart to the dominant secular bureaucratic style of the present middle class in America. This is not surprising, since the church holds no monopoly on the "structure-follows-function" principle; indeed, it borrowed the principle from the middle class in secular society. These dangers are outlined by Bensman and Vidich. They summarize them in these words, which should be understood in the light of the cooptation principle that we described earlier: "Bureaucracy deprives individuals of freedom and autonomy, not necessarily by coercion but rather by creating a favorable system of rewards for compliance with dehumanized, technical, and efficient patterns of performance."[28] These authors go on to designate four personal, social, and cultural problems that flow from middle-class bureaucracy: (1) The development of pleasant, comfortable, premanufactured patterns of conformity which destroy personal autonomy and individualism; (2) the overdevelopment of stylized patterns of opinion and tastes that deny not only the independence but also the capacity for independence to all individuals who are not members of the bureaucratic elites; (3) the development in the most general sense of a quality or tone of life that reflects the tone and quality of the bureaucratic milieu and becomes a dominant public style; and (4) the development of means by which the bureaucratic and administrative elites can use their key positions in their own interests.[29]

We would not go so far as to say that the LCA has fallen into these four pitfalls, but their long shadow has crossed segments of the LCA organization and its operation. Intimations of all four of these dangers could be pointed to, and indeed critics have called attention to them. At the 1974 convention of the LCA, as a matter of fact, a group of such critics ran their own candidate for the presidency of the church, and he presented a platform that could have been gleaned from the analysis of American society set forth by Bensman and Vidich.

For the purposes of this essay, it would be erroneous to observe these dangerous tendencies within middle-class organization without at the same time remembering that both in secular society and in the LCA, this bureaucratic organization has as its intention the effective focusing and mobilizing of its energies to carry out its stated purpose and goals. And for the LCA, such an organizational form can be accepted because of our tradition of freedom in matters of adiaphora, including polity.

3. *Worship.* Briefly, we point to the congruity between the middle-class lifeway and LCA worship. In this area, also, the trend is toward excellence. The Service Book and Hymnal of 1958, the current Inter-Lutheran Commission on Worship efforts at renewing worship, and other cooperative ventures reflect some of the best in the Christian tradition of ritual, music, and ceremony. However, this excellence comes in the form that the middle class can appropriate. It is for the most part wordy, cerebral, relies on printed texts, controlled innovation, little spontaneity, and it takes little or no account of local traditions. Just as the medieval liturgy was the monastery at worship and the baroque period liturgy was the concert-going public at worship, so the present and contemplated LCA liturgy (which it shares with most of American Lutheranism) represents the educated, disciplined, book-oriented middle class at worship.

Ironically, the liturgical developments are among the most authentically catholic in LCA church life, yet their middle-class modulation, their limitation to Western (meaning Western civilization, not the Western church as opposed to the Eastern church) forms, and their growth out of male-oriented traditions raise questions as to whether they facilitate or hinder the outreach of the church across class lines, as well as those of race and sex.

In summary, we may say that generally the middle-class placement of the LCA has threatened it with betrayal of its character as a one, holy, catholic, and apostolic church. We speak of catholicity as the power by which the church penetrates the temporal and spatial world, the cultural and spiritual world in which it lives and maintains continuity with its historic tradition.[30] The LCA has a very strong impulse, by its nature, towards catholic outreach and penetration, but the vehicle of its outreach is middle-class ethos and style. This middle-classness has its positive aspects. The middle-classness itself is a sign of outreach, in one respect, since it represents a step out of ethnic narrowness that has bedeviled much of American Lutheranism. Furthermore, the intellectual alertness and openness and what we might call "conventional liberalism" of the LCA's position on social issues represents an identification with the progressive elements of the middle class.

When we add to this the ecumenical thrust which overcomes much of the sectarianism of American Lutheranism, we do indeed observe an impressive thrust for catholicity within the LCA.

The danger facing the LCA in its middle-class character is that this character forms a closure, as well, which itself works against further catholic outreach and penetration. The LCA tends, as our discussion of the ministry suggested, to define itself in practice as ministering to the middle class as service or maintenance chaplaincy. This often takes the form of ministering *to ourselves*. As such, this constitutes a denial of our own purpose to be catholic and open to the world—a purpose that is part of our stated identity and historical tradition. It denies catholicity, because it cuts us off from other churches that *are* more than middle-class. It denies us openness to the world, because so much in the world today has to do with challenging the middle-class orientation, at home and abroad.

The chaplaincy image and function *is valid*, and we do not challenge this validity. But it is not enough, not large enough to define the church, specifically not the LCA, if the LCA is what it has said it is. I have spoken chiefly of the ordained clergy, but this has implications for the laity as well.

This danger is not new to the church. Since the earliest centuries, catholic presence in a specific time and place and culture has threatened to turn against itself and demonically squelch further penetration and outreach.

The same dialectical ambiguity faces the LCA when we look at its life under the rubrics of oneness, holiness, and apostolicity. It presses for oneness in the church catholic, but its efforts are blunted by its being in unity mainly with "its own kind of people." Its holiness, its belonging to God, has enabled it to transcend and criticize many of its religious and cultural shibboleths of doctrine, ethnicity, and sectarianism, but that holiness is not apparent vis-à-vis its middle classness. Its adherence to the conventional liberalism of the middle class in America is another force that mutes its expression of holiness that would offer an alternative to this American mindset. In doctrine, biblical study, liturgy, and ecumenical relations, it has pressed to maintain its apostolic character, but that apostolicity has been defective, since a genuinely apostolic preaching and ministry would not be content with middle-class closure.

LCA DESTINY, INTENTIONS,
AND IMPACT IN THE FUTURE

Destiny

The word *destiny*, as well as the idea that goes with it, has fallen on
bad times. Whether we back off from the idea of destiny more because we recoil at the chauvinistic intentions that have been rational-
ized under its aegis or because we lack the courage and vigor to enter-
tain the thought of our having a destiny is difficult to discern. It may
be that in the pluralistic setting of American society, the groups that
formed the LCA were so intent in opening themselves up to American
experience that they were reluctant to think about their destiny, lest it
seem gauche or too particularistic. One of the prices we have paid for
religious toleration in America is the tendency to believe that the various churches live side-by-side in bland sameness. Or, perhaps a preoccupation with internal affairs has kept LCA eyes lowered to the point
that we did not look up to gaze upon our destiny.

Consideration of our destiny is unavoidable, however, because destiny is but another way of speaking about "calling," and "vocation."
As a voluntary organization in American society, we in the LCA are
not simply a group of like-minded individuals whose gathering together
is an end in itself. We have a calling given us by God, within the
world that he has given us, sensitive to the changing times in which he
places each generation. Since God has given us self-awareness, the
ability to think and to reflect upon our goals and our actions with respect to those goals, we stand under the imperative to reflect upon our
destiny under God, seeking to discern its outlines, and to consider what
actions that destiny demands.

The preceding analysis of the LCA and reflection upon its character
is an important part of our reflection upon our destiny. What we have
focused upon up to this point is a description of the past whence we
came and the shape of our present life. This past and this present
shape do not determine our destiny; we do not extrapolate our destiny
from these data. However, these data do throw light on the trajectory
of our destiny, and they must be attended to if we are properly to discern what God has called us to.

We may summarize the chief configurations of the LCA trajectory,
as we have surveyed them: An original complex of groups that emi-

grated to North America mainly from Germany, Scandinavia, and Finland, settled in a period of about 250 years over the continent, with primary strength in the east coast area to the Plains states, mostly in the northern tier of states, with significant groups in the southeast. The church formed by these groups under the name of the LCA was relatively open to Americanization, came to terms with modern knowledge, was open ecumenically, and penetrated the urban areas of the country. They did, thus, participate in American diversity, inasmuch as Americanization, modern knowledge, and the city brought in persons and ideas that were different from the northern-European Lutheran heritage. Along with this development towards pluralism, the church became deeply rooted in the middle-class lifeway. This rootage in the middle class has been a force for homogeneity, countering the pluralistic tendencies in some specific ways. It has formed a closure that is diametrically opposed to the catholic character of the LCA, as well as to its claims to be part of the one, holy, and apostolic church.

If this is the trajectory, what can we say about our destiny as the LCA? We can say that our destiny is first of all that of a group of Lutherans who are, by and large, Americanized, intellectually alert, significantly urbanized, ecumenically involved, middle-class persons. Whatever our calling, it is within the framework of this setting which God has given us. The LCA's destiny under God—the one, holy, catholic, and apostolic thrust beyond middle-class closure, reinforced by intellectual, social, and ecumenical openness—will *not* be carried through by abandoning the middle-class lifeway. That lifeway *is* LCA identity in a manner that can hardly be shaken. That lifeway is part of the created time and place God has called us to. *Rather, it is as a middle-class church that the mission of the LCA, which transcends and criticizes middle-classness, will be carried out.*

Let us state clearly what the destiny of the LCA is, as we interpret it within this middle-class placement. We keep in mind that the LCA is a small group in America, numbering slightly more than three million members. To the extent that what we say applies to all of American Lutherans, we could still speak of only nine million persons. *The destiny of this LCA is to be a signal community within the American middle-class milieu.* It cannot hope to reform the entire middle class; indeed, it cannot count on being a successful group within the middle class. Its character as a signal community means that its destiny is to embody the gospel within that middle class. When we speak of "embodying the gospel," we are calling upon our Lutheran conviction that the church's whole ministry is that of proclaiming the gospel of God's promise as an indigenous reality in the place and time given to it. To embody the gospel is to participate in that *viva vox evangelii*—the living voice of the gospel that is an active, busy thing, according to Luther. But we participate in that *viva vox* with our lives. It is important today to include the word *embody*, since we are not to proclaim from afar, nor in bloodless abstraction, but we rather proclaim by the living reality that we are, and this is an embodied reality. *To be a signal community is to share in the embodiment of the gospel in our middle-class American world.* In other words, our middle-class placement provides the medium and form of our destiny, but our existence as God's church provides the content and thrust of that destiny. To deny our middle-class character, which we share with non-Christians in our time and place, is to deny God's creation which is the substratum of our lives. To deny our character as a signal community in embodying the gospel is to deny the witness to Christ's redemptive work which God has placed within us as his church.

The context of the signal community within the middle class is rendered more difficult and its witness more necessary when we remind ourselves of two factors. First, the present situation in which the middle class is under sharp attack, particularly the American middle class. It has been subjected to just criticism for exploitative, coopting tendencies, and its propensity to self-aggrandizement. It has also been made the scapegoat for nearly all of the world's ills, in a manner that is often patently absurd. In the midst of such criticism, two very dangerous tendencies are discernible: (1) a loss of morale and self-hatred on the one hand, which cuts the nerve of the middle class, and (2) a hardening of heart and mind, on the other hand, which rejects all criticism and tends towards paranoia. These pathological reactions to criticism are especially significant in the light of the second factor: that the middle class, despite the criticisms and the changes that have at times outdistanced it, is still the most dynamic segment of American (and world?) society; and precisely because it is the indispensable class—the one that bears the burden of carrying cultural norms, adapting those norms to changing situations, and creating styles and values which are the reference point for all of society—it is in the position to make a key contribution to the future of American society and of the world. The impetus for change and reshaping society may be sharpened by the have-nots, but it is the haves who possess the wherewithal to change and reshape in a powerful way.

In this context, we may say that the LCA shares in the Christian mission *to* the middle class and *through* the middle class. In other words, its faithfulness to its destiny will be a critique of the middle class in which it is ensconced. It will also be a call for that class to fulfill its own destiny as the indispensable class of society, while at the same time the LCA comforts and supports that class where it is appropriate and furthermore transcends the middle class in its own life.

What are some of the elements of the LCA destiny within and beyond its middle-class position?

1. It possesses the possibility to become an interracial church, since its blacks—although small in numbers—are strategically located in cities and are themselves chiefly middle class, with the education and resources of that class, but with the challenge to be more than middle class.

2. The LCA shares in the middle-class expansion of women's liberation, both in home occupations and in more public positions, including church leadership. There exists a large reservoir of energy, intelligence, experience, and commitment among white and black women for sharing in the LCA's mission.

3. Although significantly urban, more than any other American Lutheran denomination, the LCA has a rural constituency that is essential to its life. This mix of urban and rural-small town, provides an opportunity for catholic solidarity that permits cultural exchange and transfer, along with black-white, man-woman transfer that can open up new vistas for ministry, mission, worship.

4. The LCA's commitment to confronting modern knowledge in a constructive manner gives it the opportunity to fashion a theology and strategic rationale for articulating its mission through and beyond its present milieu.

5. The LCA's ecumenical commitment opens up relations with other churches that have experience and strength in segments of the American population that are absent in the LCA itself.

6. The LCA's expertise in understanding and interpreting current social and cultural issues, together with a progressive public stance,

give it entrée to crucial areas of American and world situations in which a liberating presence may be expressed.

7. The LCA's ties with the international Lutheran community and the World Council of Churches provide an opportunity to transcend its Americanness, as well as its middle-classness.

8. The LCA's openness to modern knowledge suggests that it can participate in efforts to shape the new intellectual synthesis that is needed in our culture, a synthesis that will relate Christian faith to the scientific world view, to new understandings of nature and human being, and to emerging new political philosophies.

9. The LCA's openness to current trends gives it the freedom and inclination to utilize effective organizational forms.

LCA Destiny: Theological Resources

The basic resource for the LCA is the faith which it affirms in its basic documents, which it has recognized as the authority for its belief and life. This faith has already been the object of our attention. In sum, it enlivens the church to receive and live out the reality of Christ in the world. To receive the reality of Christ is what Lutherans have traditionally reflected upon as justification by grace, whereas living out that reality is what we have known as sanctification. We have observed that the traditions of the LCA highlight both the centrality of Christ and his authority and also the works of serving love in the world. Equally, those traditions reiterate that the faith is catholic, which means that no matter how relevant it is to any given time and place, it rises above all particular situations in its universality.

It is appropriate to probe what specific images of the universal faith might be most appropriate to the LCA's challenge today. We lift up two images: cross and kingdom. These two images provide the grounding for the three aspects of the LCA destiny that we shall summarize briefly—inclusiveness, service, and critique:

The cross is the symbol in our faith that speaks of God's intimate involvement with his creation, the death that was the means of the decisive grace for that creation. The cross speaks, however, not only of what God has done for his world, but also of the shape of God's *continuing presence* in the world and the normative shape of the Christian's life. Thus, the cross tells us not only of God's love, but also of his very being in this world. The cross stands as a revelation that the serving style is both the vessel of God's grace for us and also the style for which he has created his handiwork. The cross of Jesus Christ reminds us that this serving is not a soft matter of convenience, but a matter of service-unto-death.

The kingdom of God is a symbol that speaks of God's power and the universality of his will. The kingdom belongs to God alone; it is not something that human beings manipulate or "bring in" by their efforts. Its final coming is in God's hands alone. This kingdom is universal, however, extending to all of creation and all of time, which means that we all participate in it. The service of the cross is part of the kingdom, which gives perspective to the service by calling our attention to the fact that God alone makes our service significant and that our service shares in a universal will larger than ours.

The Shape of the LCA Destiny: Inclusiveness

The LCA will, if it is faithful to its destiny, be a community that embodies *inclusiveness*, and this takes several forms. First, cross-cultural dimensions of inclusiveness lie before us in our middle-class American placement. We speak here, not of the cross-cultural elements on the international scale, but within the LCA itself. Within its life the LCA experiences the encounter between the largely northern-European, Lutheran, and male-oriented culture with three other cultures—blacks, Hispanic-Americans, and women. Although our use of the term *culture* may be broad, we use it to refer to the lifeways of groups that reveal patterns that are distinguishable in important ways from the dominant LCA lifeway inherited from Europe and European history. Blacks and Hispanic-Americans come into the LCA in numbers significant enough to demand attention for the mission of the church; women are obviously present in forcefully large numbers. Blacks and Hispanic-Americans bring with them secular and religious backgrounds that do not flow out of northern Europe nor out of Luther's Reformation. We have largely assumed that they will become indigenized to the background of the dominant segment of Lutherans. There is here a situation unfolding that is reminiscent of the struggle between Peter and Paul over circumcision. Is Lutheranism, specifically Lutheranism in North America, to be equated with a heritage from Luther's Reformation and northern Europe? Northern Europeanism may seem less crucial than Luther's Reformation, but we are dealing here with Lutherans who are not rejecting Luther's Reformation, but rather amplifying that heritage, which they have accepted at second hand, with traditions that Luther and his descendants did not know, which were not indigenous to their culture. These traditions are nearly as strange to contemporary Americans of northern-European ancestry.

Women stand in a different situation, culturally speaking. They share, to the extent that they are of northern-European ancestry, the culture of the dominant groups in the LCA, but they are calling for a radical alteration in that tradition at the many points where that tradition has discriminated against their feminine nature and demeaned it. Their alterations call for the introduction of something new in Lutheran experience, something new that they have not lived with for generations, as the blacks and Hispanic-Americans have. Their alterations do qualify, in our opinion, as *cultural* additions to the LCA.

The alternative to an insistence that these different cultures must be circumcised by northern-European Lutheran heritage is *cross-cultural exchange.* Such exchange affects many aspects of theology and practice: worship, preaching, pastoral care, patterns of association, style of authority, and styles of action in society. Such cross-cultural exchange is foreign to the middle class, since its highly successful strategy of cooptation is accustomed to circumcising successfully the subcultures that seek entry into its lifeway. The exchange is essential to the LCA, however, if it is to be church, and catholic church.

Cross-cultural exchange demonstrates the concreteness of embodiment, to which we referred earlier. Liturgy, for example, cannot be inclusive of women and blacks and Hispanic-Americans in the abstract. Styles of language, music, and preaching are concrete, and the effort to allow genuine exchange and reconstruction of these styles will tax our creativity, patience, and commitment to the utmost.

Second, inclusiveness means crossing the lines of social and economic class. The challenge to the middle class is whether it can forge a style, a set of values—which we have said is its burden in our present society —that does not cut off the lower-middle, working, and subworking classes. It cannot forsake its middle-classness, and it would be disastrous if it even attempted to do so. But it must evolve a style that is not exclusive of other classes. In this respect, also, the middle class has not succeeded in America. Its educational base and expertise set up blocks between it and other classes that are very real. Middle-class arrogance and pride often elicit the hatred of working-class persons.

The LCA has not avoided this class conflict, but as a signal community, it will seek to pioneer a middle-class style that does not exclude working-class persons from a more significant role in its life. The LCA, though middle-class, is not called to restrict itself to being middle-class. Evangelistic outreach is also at stake here.

Third, inclusiveness involves the wholesome interrelating of the American middle class with persons and societies around the world. The LCA bears the stigma of the American middle-class insistence that other countries are its "clients."[31] The international Lutheran community and wider Christian community can be of redemptive significance for the LCA, if it fashions its life within the Christian ecumene in a manner that embodies the gospel as a signal force for the middle class generally.

Fourth, there is an ecumenical dimension to inclusiveness. The LCA is not the only church that shares the destiny of the middle class. Its small size almost mandates that it seek out, in accord with its own tradition, other churches—Lutheran and non-Lutheran, middle-class and nonmiddle-class. The middle-class churches provide a wider and stronger context for embodying the gospel to the middle class itself, whereas the nonmiddle-class churches can teach the LCA new ways and styles that are necessary if a signal is to be sent to the American middle class.

The Shape of the LCA Destiny: Service

The gospel presses the middle class to inclusiveness, such as it has not heretofore known, and that same gospel leads into pathways of service that point to what may be the white-hot center of the destiny of the middle class. As a cutting-edge group, which bears the task of forming a style for contemporary life, and as the class that is indispensable for its resources and creativity, as well as for its managerial and intellectual gifts, the middle class exists to serve the world. The middle class is not the victim of society and history. It is not the weakling nor the disadvantaged class in the world, nor in American society. This class may be the key to the future of the world, simply because its potential contributions to the world are so significant. In many ways, the middle class recognizes this. It is the class that devotes enormous energies to keeping society afloat. In America, it is the class that keeps the essential voluntary associations alive, contributing its skills with no remuneration. In other aspects of its lifeway, however, it is self-aggrandizing and greedy. Its principle of cooptation aims at subsuming all other groups under itself, even as it has been subsumed under the societal system.

Our age is the epoch in which, to use traditional terms, the fate of the world may rest on the middle class's ability and willingness to lay down its life for the world. The middle class is faced with frightening challenges that turn it inwards, to self-preservation at all costs. In a world economy that is one of limited growth, the pie of benefits slows down its expansion, resulting in the circumstance that granting a piece of pie to the have-nots entails a smaller piece for the middle class. Only a farsighted, spiritually alert middle class will resist the temptation in such a situation to let the have-nots starve. The challenge is to find the capacity to broaden the middle-class perception of its self-interest to include service in behalf of the health of all of society through means other than cooptation with its pernicious belief that a healthy middle class benefits the rest of society simply because of its own health.

It is too much to expect the middle class to adopt in wholesale quantity the conviction that service in behalf of the whole of society is the preferred style. Nevertheless, it is urgent that there be signal communities within the middle class that do understand such a style and possess the grace and courage to practice it. The LCA, in ecumenical concert, is called to be such a community. Such a calling will demand hard thinking and creativity to devise political, economic, social instrumentalities of service that bring the resources of the middle class to bear upon the well-being of the whole society.

The Shape of the LCA Destiny: Critique

The motifs of cross and kingdom provide the basis for a creative and redemptive critique of the middle class—a critique which the signal community that embodies the gospel will bear within its file. Without this critique, service is impossible.

Critique in the light of the cross of Christ and the kingdom of God relativizes the smaller loyalties that obstruct the middle class from the destiny God has given to it and enlarges the perception of self-interest that is necessary if that destiny is to be intelligible. Parallel to the preceding line of thinking, the cross reveals that all loyalties in this world can be put to death for the sake of service and that life, not death results. At the same time, the self-interest has been enlarged beyond the self without abandoning or destroying the self. The kingdom of God proclaims that no self exists apart from the whole of time and space that is God's—a vision that also relativizes and enlarges.

Our discussion has touched at many points on the tendency of the middle class to absolutize what must be relativized and to insist upon a too narrow perception of self-interest, which in the end is really self-destruction. The critique which lives in the body of the signal communities that are the churches can show forth the fundamental freedom which the middle class can have to relativize what it once thought was too precious to relativize and to take the leap which broadens the vision of self-interest. Lutherans may have been more accustomed to refer to this theological truth as the Protestant principle. We prefer the more constructive terms of the cross and the kingdom, because they speak to the creative, shaping, active life that has been given to all creatures, particularly to the middle class.

The three directions which are opened up by our destiny under God —inclusiveness, service, and critique—point to the forms in which the middle class is both fulfilled and transcended. They point to the essential truth that the middle class must be middle-class and yet more and other than middle-class. Outside the signal community this seems absurd. That is why the signal community must *embody* the gospel, so that its concrete life may be unleashed into the stream of society.

The form which the reality of the church has taken in the LCA is full of promise and also of betrayal and closure. God has given to this community of unfit servants the traditions that point to what true church can mean in the middle-class American setting that the descendants of Luther inhabit in North America. To many of our Lutheran brothers and sisters around the world, we inhabit an inauspicious and unwholesome place. Perhaps their witness can strengthen us, not only to see how our life must be created anew in this place, but also to cherish this place as one that is not too mean for God to work in.

If we take the concrete actuality of the church in its LCA form seriously, certain new directions for faith and life present themselves to us.

We are challenged to reconceive our way of relating the church and culture, of relating creation and redemption. The tension between the church and culture dare not be lost, else cross and kingdom are betrayed. At the same time, the fundamental unity of the two dare not be lost sight of, else gospel-embodiment is rendered impossible, and with it the life and mission of the church to share in that action by which "God so loved the world that he gave his only Son." Our ecclesiology has, to this point, understood this truth inadequately, with significant consequences for both our theology and our life. The theology of disjunction has bewildered our people, leading them to build walls between Sunday and the rest of the week, unaware that in so doing they were allowing the week without God to coopt them into betraying the gospel. The LCA is afraid to move from tension between church and culture to a conception of tension-within-unity. Whether it is an inadequate emphasis upon law and gospel or upon the two kingdoms that plays a decisive role in this fear would have to be studied at some length. In any case, it is clear that in order to do justice to both the distinction between church and culture and the unity, we must recast our theological emphases. Theology and life interact upon each other: failure in one realm reflects itself in the other; new insights from the gospel of cross and kingdom in the one realm will also vivify the other.

If the reflections contained in this essay have any merit at all, they will begin to show how the ecclesiological practice and theology must be reshaped into the LCA and perhaps this experience in the LCA can be of service to our sister churches.

NOTES

1. W. Lloyd Warner, *Social Class in America* (New York: Harper Torchbooks, 1949, 1960); Kurt B. Mayer, *Class and Society*, rev. ed. (New York: Random House, 1955).

2. Joseph A. Kahl, *The American Class Structure* (New York: Rinehart and Co., 1960).

3. Ibid., chap. 7.

4. E. Clifford Nelson, *Lutheranism in North America, 1914–1970* (Minneapolis: Augsburg Publishing House, 1972), chaps. 1 and 3.

5. The quotation is from a personal letter. See G. Everett Arden, *Augustana Heritage* (Rock Island: Augustana Press, 1963).

6. Published in *The Lutheran Church Review*, 38 (1919):187–97.

7. In *Doctrinal Declarations* (St. Louis: Concordia Publishing House, 1957), p. 15.

8. Nelson, *Lutheranism in North America*, p. 23.

9. See above, note 6.

10. See above, note 5.

11. For example, in earlier years, H. C. Alleman, *The Old Testament—A Study* and also his *The New Testament—A Study* (Philadelphia: Muhlenberg Press, 1935). In more recent years, note Robert J. Marshall, *The Mighty Acts of God: A Survey of Bible Thought and History* (Philadelphia: Lutheran Church Press, 1964).

12. See Karl Hertz, ed., *Two Kingdoms and One World* (Minneapolis: Augsburg Publishing House, 1976), p. 10; Joseph Sittler, *The Doctrine of the Word in the Structure of Lutheran Theology* (Philadelphia: Muhlenberg Press, 1948); Conrad Bergendoff, *Christ as Authority* (Rock Island: Augustana Book Concern, 1947).

13. Of course, this is not to say that all such attempts were beneficial. The efforts of Samuel Schmucker in the 19th century are often severely criticized.

14. There are strands of tradition in the LCA that have opposed this thrust, but the acknowledgment of two authorities as we describe it here has also been reflected in official position.

15. See, for example, Abdel Ross Wentz, *Pioneer in Christian Unity: Samuel Simon Schmucker* (Philadelphia: Fortress Press, 1967).

16. Jack L. Stotts, "The Search for a Theological Center: Promise and Pilgrimage" (inaugural address as President of McCormick Presbyterian Seminary, October 23, 1975).

17. Nelson, chap. 3.

18. See Joseph Bensman and Arthur J. Vidich, *The New American Society: The Revolution of the Middle Class* (Chicago: Quadrange Books, 1971); and Edward C. Banfield, *The Unheavenly City* (Boston: Little, Brown, and Co., 1970).

19. Kahl, *American Class Structure*, pp. 197–98.

20. See above note 18.

21. Bensman and Vidich, *New American Society*, pp. 133–34.

22. Banfield, *Unheavenly City*, chap. 3.

23. Bensman and Vidich, *New American Society*, chap. 7.

24. Ibid., chap. 10.

25. Ibid., p. 184.

26. *The Lutheran* 12 (August 14, 1974):3. See also Edward Uthe, ed., *Significant Issues for the 1970's* (Philadelphia: Fortress Press, 1968), pp. 141–45.

27. Charles Glock, et al., *To Comfort and to Challenge* (Berkeley: University of California Press, 1967).

28. See above, note 24.

29. Bensman and Vidich, *New American Society*, pp. 276–77.

30. See Paul Tillich's discussion of catholicity in *Systematic Theology*, vol. 3 (Chicago: University of Chicago Press, 1963); Gustaf Aulén, *Reformation and Catholicity* (Philadelphia: Muhlenberg Press, 1961).

31. Bensman and Vidich, *New American Society*, pp. 272ff.

FOUR

THE IDENTITY OF THE CHURCH
IN LIGHT OF
DEVELOPING IDEAS OF MISSION

"Mission" has, and has not, been featured in the LWF ecclesiology study. It did not emerge as one of the "conflict areas" need-
ing attention in the list of "burning issues" compiled by member
churches in 1973–74. Yet dissension over church involvement in the
political realm and questions of relation to cultural environment, which
are in that list, have been very prominent in connection with recent
missiological thought. Further, many churches involved in the ecclesiological study are the product of missionary beginnings. Other
churches, long accustomed to sending missionaries out, are now becoming partners who benefit from the insights of these younger churches
and receive fervent witness from them as to what Christianity means.
Identity is especially dear, and perhaps more keenly perceived away
from home, "by the waters of Babylon," in a minority situation, in missionary tasks. It may well be in mission that the church's true identity
comes to the fore. The very origins of the whole ecclesiology study,
highlighting as it does church identity *in light of* "service to the entire
human being" reflect the soul-searching brought on by the issue of
"proclamation and development" raised in Ethiopia.

The 1974 analysis of the American scene by three U.S. churchmen in
answering questions posed in Geneva, saw the relation of witnessing to
salvation and sociopolitical witnessing as a crucial issue. They felt that
most church members would benefit "from a more holistic vision of
God's reign throughout the church and the world," so as to overcome
"the false opposition between 'this-worldly' social action and 'other-
worldly' personal evangelism." They asserted "the independence of
the church from other power structures, holding that it must be faithful

to and accountable to the Lord for the way it fulfills the mission He has entrusted."

The U.S. Advisory Committee was well aware both of the developments going on ecumenically in mission and the attitude of U.S. Lutherans towards methods for mission. The moratorium debate had raged, with some Third World leaders calling for a "holding pattern" on traditional approaches and support while indigenous churches develop their own way of doing things. "Mission on Six Continents" introduced a global team-concept whereby, for example, a group of church people from varying church situations could tour the United States, observe, and then offer a critique about better ways of witnessing. On the other hand, it was recognized that the LCA concept of "independence/interdependence" (see above, Introduction, note 2) was different in outlook from the more evangelistic approach operative in the ALC, which in this period had just completed an extremely successful appeal for funds for mission. Then, too, the long-popular slogan, "The church *is* mission," suggested a look at missiology today—in all its diversity—would be important for ecclesiology.

The guidelines for the topic offered by the Advisory Committee for the essay were rather general. They spoke of "developing ideas in mission," to recognize the ferment taking place. They suggested merely that international, national, and local levels of concern be recognized, and the only other guidance was to append some jargon terms of the day to point up possible issues.

The essayist himself (as his personal preface shows), has brought particular insights to his task, out of a varied background in many parts of the world. James A. Bergquist was born at Parkers Prairie, Minnesota, in 1932; attended Luther College, Decorah, Iowa, an institution of the ALC (B.A., 1954); and Luther Seminary, St. Paul (B.D., 1958). Thereafter he served as an assistant pastor in Los Angeles, 1958–61, and as pastor of a parish in Honolulu, Hawaii, 1961–64. He also found time to earn the Ph.D. degree in 1962 at the University of Southern California, School of Religion, in New Testament, with a dissertation entitled "The Resurrection of Jesus in the New Testament—A Hermeneutical Study."

Dr. Bergquist's teaching career began as an assistant professor of religion at Concordia College, Moorhead, Minnesota, 1964–66, followed by a period as professor of New Testament at the Gurukul Lutheran Theological College, Madras, India (1966–71). During this time, though a missionary of the ALC, he was seconded to the LCA for service in India, and he began to write on theological education in India, several volumes being published in Madras. This experience led to appointment as Associate Director of the Theological Education Fund of the World Council of Churches. Responsible for Southern Asia, the South Pacific, and parts of Africa, he worked out of TEF's London office until 1974 when he became Academic Dean at Lutheran Theological Seminary (ALC), Columbus, Ohio. He continued, by mutual arrangement, part-time with TEF through 1976.

Thus, during the time he was working on this essay, Dean Bergquist was still traveling, in contact with theological education in other parts of the world. He has had particular experience with "education by extension" work, and for TEF edited *Ministry in Context* (1972), and *Learning in Context* (1973). He has also been teaching New Testament and Missions courses at the Seminary in Columbus. Dr. Bergquist's other publications include *Jesus Interprets the Old Testament Commandments* (Minneapolis: Augsburg, 1966); *The Ten Commandments and Responsible Freedom* (Madras: Christian Literature Society —Indian SPCK, 1971); and articles in the *Lutheran Standard, The Christian Century,* and *Indian Journal of Theology.*

The two groups of persons with whom Dr. Bergquist talked and from whom he received comments and suggestions for this essay reflect his dual involvements in recent years: from the faculty of LTS, Columbus,

Dr. Arthur H. Becker, Professor, Practical Theology;

Dr. Walter R. Bouman, Visiting Professor, Systematic Theology;

Dr. Ronald M. Hals, Professor of Biblical Theology;

Dr. Merlin Hoops, Professor, New Testament;

Dr. Preman Niles, professor at the Theological College of Lanka, Sri Lanka, visiting professor at LTS, added his comments as an Asian biblical scholar; and

Dr. Hans Schwartz, Professor, Systematic Theology; and two former colleagues on the TEF staff, London: Dr. Shoki Coe, Director (from Taiwan), and the Rev. Aharon Sapsezian (from Brazil).

THE SEARCH FOR INTEGRITY IN MISSION: EXPLORATIONS OF POINTS OF DISTURBANCE AND RESPONSE AMONG LUTHERANS IN NORTH AMERICA

James A. Bergquist

Let me state as a personal preface the place where I find myself in addressing the theme of this chapter. I am an American-Lutheran Christian seized by two fundamental convictions. The first is that God's gift of dying and rising in Christ remains the single certain reality in our time. The other is that to penetrate the depth of the gospel and its power for our day we must remain open to its surprises. One of those surprises is the way in which so-called Third World realities are helping us define both the content and meaning of God's good news. From this basis, three perspectives inform the essay. (1) I am a *Lutheran* who views the evangelical heritage as a treasure offering clues to my identity and mission, while at the same time offering new possibilities in the true liberty of the gospel for fresh, ecumenically enriched understanding of the message and task. (2) I am an *American* who believes that we need help. I am grateful for the vigor and discipline which has indeed been a part of American church history. I am also aware of the ambiguities of our history—its shallow culture-faith and nativism, and above all today, of the paralyzing effect of our affluence. Whatever else happens in the future, the power to mold the future of humanity appears increasingly to be shifting to the other world—the two-thirds world in which a growing majority of the human race live in increasingly intolerable terms. Our wealth and consumption in part depends upon the poverty of others. This is no fairy tale. It is a fact which is not merely a scratch on the surface of our Western

187

society but reveals our deepest disease. (3) I am a *Christian*. The issue of mission before us at bottom is deeply theological. We can only approach integrity in mission through growing interdependence in a fully international and ecumenical sense. The gift of the gospel is a word of realism and hope. It is the way of him who "did not count equality with God a thing to be grasped, but emptied himself, taking the form of a servant" (Phil. 2:6–7). We cannot earn or discover this way. It comes by a new creation. The Christ-given identity of the church provides the sole dynamic for faithful mission, and for hope in the face of frustration. There are people in our churches who have been touched by this dynamic, many of them by what they have received "back" from the Third World in ways which unlock anew the mystery of God's grace for people in need.

It is my purpose to explore what integrity in mission today means for our American Lutheran churches, for our mission at "home" as it is disturbed and freshly defined by global realities, and for our interdependence in mission. The shape of the chapter will be to follow three lines of exploration. First, we shall probe the agitating background against which missionary thinking and action today is taking place, seeking sympathetically to understand the North American struggle to comprehend the dimensions of its own economic, social, political, and ecclesiastical domination of the Third World and to pursue integrity in mission in the light of that situation. Second, we shall try to elaborate how integrity in mission was understood and enacted in response to the social milieu of American Lutheranism in past decades—a milieu and response we shared to a great extent with all American Christians—and then examine the specific challenges arising today to confront that inherited missionary vision. Finally, in a considerably shorter section, we shall attempt to identify those movements and ideas which appear to signal the shape of integrity in mission for the future.

But what is meant by integrity? It is an appropriate word to apply to mission because there is a two-sided quality to it—identity and response. Persons or institutions of integrity are those whose outer actions and responses reflect the truth of their inner lives, at least as nearly as the ambiguous realities of either inner being or outer action can ever allow. To act with integrity is thus to act consistently, in ways that are honest and dependable because action and being are integrated, each supporting and testing the other.

Mission with integrity is the mark of a church whose outer actions and responses (its witness and service) correspond to the truth of its inner being (identity). Mission thus becomes the test of integrity for individual Christians and the church. We have been made new beings in Christ, a community formed by grace to live as the sign of God's new age. Mission is the integration of who we are and what we have been commissioned to do in the world, a connection explicitly made in 1 Peter 2:9: "But you *are* a chosen race, a royal priesthood, a holy nation, God's own people, *that you may declare* the wonderful deeds of him who called you out of darkness into his marvelous light." The church's identity and response both depend upon and test each other. There is no possibility of authentic mission without the interaction of the two in life under grace.

And yet integrity is always approximate, never complete. This is true for two reasons. (1) The Christian life itself, the new being of the individual and the community, is always a process of receiving and becoming—a process often described in Pauline terms as becoming what we are.[1] (2) Actions too—if they are to reflect the reality of the new being in Christ—need to be reshaped continually if we are to meet with faithfulness altered needs for Christian response in the world. Thus, though grounded in the once-for-all act of God in Jesus Christ and coming as a gift, mission with integrity must always be characterized as a process of growth toward a fuller realization of identity and service.

This chapter is intended to affirm that the fundamental human crisis —and of mission—is not primarily institutional, financial, and organizational, though all are involved. The issue is basically theological. The key question is how the Christian faith through its institutions may provide a dynamic and relevant focus for human renewal.

DILEMMAS IN OUR SEARCH FOR INTEGRITY

A new vocabulary of mission has emerged. It is in large measure a fighting language, designed to disturb complacency, expose inconsistencies in established North American missionary perceptions and action, and propose new directions. To some the language appears subversive; to others it contains promise. The new vocabulary holds in

---

1. Notes appear at the end of the essay.

common with established missionary conceptions the idea that mission encloses all that the church is and does, and that its dimensions embrace the near and the far. But it strikes in different directions by combining a frank sociological and even ideological analysis of the context of mission with fresh studies of the Bible and Christian tradition. It challenges the North American churches to define mission in the light of Third-World issues as measured by both uncomfortable global realities and equally disturbing pockets of the Third World to be discerned within American society. The new vocabulary declares these Third-World issues—the fundamental human questions of our day—to be the ones which today inescapably and increasingly define, test, expand, confirm, and correspond to the specific shape of mission in North America. This analysis describes the contemporary setting, both domestically and internationally, as one to a large but often hidden degree characterized by oppression, domination, and dependency. It calls for liberation as the focus of missionary words and deeds. It prescribes the task ahead as one involving risk, reparations by the strong, revolution by the powerless, moratorium, conscientizing, and dialog as the form of proclamation. Gone, or at least seemingly muted, are the more familiar (and comfortable) categories of mission—the preaching of repentance and faith to the nations for salvation, reconciliation, peace, love, joy in the spirit, unity.

Dependency as a Context for Mission

The new vocabulary of mission grows out of an emerging awareness today of how western domination of the two-thirds world has made "dependency" an inescapable issue. It will be important to define the critical impact of the fact of North Atlantic domination upon present-day thinking about mission.

An ancient tale from the Arabian Nights sums up the dependency theme:

> Somewhere off the Malabar Coast a poor Fisherman, hauling in his empty nets for the umpteenth time, caught a glimpse of a glittering object lodged in a knot of one of the ropes. He retrieved it, and after rubbing off the encrustations instantly recognized it for what it was, an otherworldly purple bottle containing a Djinn who had been condensed therein by Ormazd, Master of the Cosmos. The Fisherman shipped his oars, trimmed the little vessel, and smashed the bottle across one of the gunwales.

At once the gigantic, fiery-red Djinn leaped from the pieces and, wrapping a finger around the Fisherman's neck, began to strangle him like a boa constrictor.

"Stop! Please stop!" cried the Fisherman. "Do you know what you are doing? How can you be so ungrateful as to murder me when I have just freed you from eternal incarceration?"

"Ah," replied the Djinn, continuing to compress his liberator's throat. "There was a day when I should have agreed with you—but that day is long past. For nine hundred years I have lain imprisoned in that bottle. During the first three hundred years I vowed that the man who released me should command my powers for all time; I should make him Emperor of Creation, possessor of every lovely girl and shining jewel. No man came. During the second three centuries I had time to reflect on the superficiality and egocentricity of mankind. Why should I raise the specimen of such a race to a rank equaling my own? Granting his first three wishes should be enough for him. Still no man came. So for the last three hundred years I have burned with a consuming hatred of human frivolousness, and I have sworn to destroy the tardy scoundrel who finally sets me at liberty."

And he did.[2]

The moral of the tale, one supposes, lies in its applicability to our present historical situation. For centuries large parts of Asia, Africa, and Latin America have been captive under the domination of colonial powers. Beginning in the age of European "exploration" in the late fifteenth century with the search for gold and spices in the Indies of Asia and the New World, and accelerating in the eighteenth and nineteenth centuries with the demand for raw materials and markets to nourish the machines of industrial revolution, European domination of the rest of the world became nearly complete. The United States for its part added colonies in the Caribbean and Pacific in the late nineteenth and early twentieth centuries. The result was a threefold pattern of interlocking dependency. The first was *political*. Even where colonial governments were not established to control directly the destinies of an area, political domination was a fact in such places as China, which the Western powers carved up into spheres of influence, or as in India where the princely states were controlled by the rulers of British India (often, to be sure, with the connivance of the Rajas themselves).

The second was an *economic* captivity. As Barbara Ward has noted,

Under colonial tutelage the whole world received its first introduction to a single, unified world economy. The reason why colonialism involved this transformation is quite straightforward. The western powers had absorbed colonies precisely in order to integrate them into a wide web of commerce, and to establish a monopoly control over their resources and trade.[3]

The third interlocking dependency was *cultural,* a growing dominance of Western technology, language, education, and—it must be said—of Christian ecclesiastical forms in the "younger churches." One additional effect of the Western cultural control was the rise of ideas of white supremacy and consequent racism.[4]

Today the Third World, so long under domination, is beginning to make real its independence. Formal political independence is perceived to be only the first stage—a process begun early in Latin America and achieved only since the end of World War II in Asia and Africa. The deeper struggle today is against the economic and cultural forms of dependency (and its continuing political reality), a form of dependency more pervasive and dominating than most North Americans image but utterly real to Third-World nations and the minority peoples of the United States. And as the struggle for liberation proceeds, the long dominant powers of the West—who often today consider themselves the liberators—fear their own destruction. How one views liberation movements depends upon where one stands. To the dominated and oppressed, revolutions against domination in all of its forms appear as signs of hope. To the dominant and affluent, to us who have benefited from and even enjoyed the freedoms of affluence precisely because of our domination, liberation may well seem as a threat. Consider, for example, how most Americans have feared that Maoist China would unleash the "yellow hordes" upon the rest of the world, reviving similar fears discernable in earlier American policies toward Asian immigrants.

Thus to repeat the imagery of the tale, the Djinn is the Third World in its present struggle for liberation. The fisherman is the West, fearful for its future as the old securities of domination disintegrate. As André Malraux has described the situation: "We are at the end of a civilization, just as we were at the end of the Roman Empire. We are actually between civilizations—the colonial one and a decolonized one —which we do not really know yet but only sense."[5]

Theodore White has written of the same complex shifting of cultural assumptions. He contrasted his trip to China in 1972 to his service there during and after World War II. In 1945, he wrote, the world apart from Russia was of American design. The war had left America master of the globe, with no balance or restraint to limit "either America's power or America's generosity to deal with that world as it wished." By 1972, the thinking of one generation had been worn out and the next system of ideas was not yet ready to replace it. "The postwar world was dead and awaited burial." The world trading system North America had designed was "totally obsolete—America could no longer both sustain and drain the free economies of the world, setting the rules by its own power." Vietnam and the energy crisis exposed both the limitations of American power and its misshapen grasp of the true nature of the emerging world. Economic orthodoxies were trembling—Keynesian theories as well as the theorems of the Great Society "were demonstrably inadequate," as the government built highways, financed cheap suburbs, but strangled the cities, and ruined cheap transportation. Nor has education coped. Education was "pumped in to create an elite without responsibilities." America's systems are clogged with ideas. If intellectuals once wrote the Constitution, engineered the reforms of Teddy Roosevelt, and undergirded the ideas of Franklin D. Roosevelt's brain trust, today paper after paper, study after study, and learned paper after learned paper on urban decay, race, violence, the environment have suffocated clear thinking under a "mattress of scholarly investigation." In short, the power relationships, which not so long ago appeared so secure, are today changing under the impact of the growing self-awareness of the Third World. White comments that the change crunches "people who have no idea where the crunch and hurt come from, who cannot understand what has made them fat or now drives them from their homes."[6]

Against these signs of radical alteration of the centuries-old relationship between the first and third worlds, and the rapidly changing and shifting certainties of the postwar era, we can understand how *dependence* has come to be a key word and point of conflict and how difficult it is for those caught in its midst to comprehend. The Third World finds itself formally free but still economically and culturally captive to the rich first world, while at the same time Western institutions appear to be captive to their own myths of technological progress and growth. The post-colonial revolution has failed to bring an end to domination and create new possibilities for just societies out of new forms of interdependent relationships with the West. The post-Christian secular revolution in the West promises the skills to feed, clothe, employ, and heal the masses of the poor, but in reality appears to be producing a dehumanized and oppressive future dominated by self-interest. Traditional forms of Christian society appear helpless in the face of these deep-seated, institutional crises which appear to accentuate, not alleviate, domination.

Two Stages of Missiological Consciousness:
Toward Liberation as a Focus for Mission

Recognition of dependency as the context of mission has led to an understanding of two stages of consciousness about mission which has emerged since the 1950s and even earlier.

The *first stage* was set by the post-colonial revolution in the Third World. The coming of freedom to former colonial countries brought expectations for quick change. Beginning with India, Pakistan, Ceylon, and Burma in 1947, then Indonesia by 1950, and from 1958 onwards in Africa, it has been computed that 99.5 percent of the land area of the globe which was under colonial status prior to 1945 became free of colonial rule by 1969. Hopes ran high in the early years of the post-colonial era. Despite massive poverty and related problems in most of the newly independent countries, 1950–70 was a time of optimism. The former colonial nations of Asia and Africa expected to find their places as equal partners among the Western powers. The new nations by and large began by adopting Western models of liberal democracy, committed themselves to mixed economies which seemed to promise growth and the distribution of wealth just as they had in the West, and eagerly sought to adapt modern technology to their traditional cultures.

The 1950–70 era had as its key term *development*. Massive aid programs, both government-to-government and church-to-church, were established in attempts to enable the poorer countries to develop educational and industrial infrastructures to launch them to the economic "takeoff" point.

Policies among churches and missions reflected the new sociopolitical situation and, in fact, to some extent anticipated the era of independence and development. The leading missiological thrust may be traced in terms of slogans. One of the very earliest, which continued to hold a major position for the decades prior to 1950, was that of the "three selfs." According to this idea, when the Third-World churches became *self-governed, self-supporting,* and *self-propagating* they would then automatically become authentically self-respecting. That slogan, developed in East Africa by Henry Venn and applied most successfully in Korea, anticipated much now written about authentic interdependence. But by and large missionaires did not work themselves out of a job nor did emphasis upon self-sufficiency alter much the continuing dependency upon mission subsidies, often with distorting and corrupting effects on both sides. After 1950 other slogans emerged reflecting more clearly the end of the colonial era: "Church-to-Church Relationships" and "Partnership in Obedience," both indicating a desire on all parts to achieve equality and mutuality in mission. Yet power, largely financial but also of institutional authority, continued to reside with the more affluent and dominant partners. Other slogans along the same lines signaled particularly developments of the 1960s—"Joint Action for Mission" and "Mission in Six Continents"—both hinting at deeper dimensions of the problem of partnership. It came to be recognized that development had to be tackled worldwide. Inherent also was the realization that the Constantinian era was over in the West—Christians everywhere were in the minority struggling to serve and witness in an unbelieving world. The task was seen to be not just one of geographical expansion from established centers (often called the "salt water" theory of missions) or of church growth (for example, McGavern, Winter, Glasser, and the Fuller School) but of a task involving six-continent directions, qualitative redefinitions of evangelism (salvation for the whole person), and contextualization of theology not only in traditional cultural terms but against explosive socioeconomic conditions.

But earlier hopes have been frustrated to a large measure, leading to a *second stage* of the currently emerging missiological consciousness. Development has failed as much as an ideology as it has as a program. Partnership and equality in fully cross-cultural terms have not been achieved. Dependency—political, economic, cultural, and even theological—remains a bitter fact describing the relationship between the rich and the poor.

Hence the dependency situation has led to the emergence of a new consciousness of what mission with integrity means for our day. The key word has come to be *liberation*—a freeing of both the dominated and dominating. Arne Sovik has written that "liberation is the poor man's definition of salvation. It is the cry of the powerless, the prayer of the oppressed."[7] It is also the need of the dominant to be released from their captivity to ultimately self-destructive and community-destroying patterns of consumption and exploitative use of power.

This does not mean that liberation captures the whole of the biblical witness for salvation, nor that it adequately expresses for all times the single focus for mission. There are some, indeed, who fear that liberation is not a proper direction for Christian evangelism and service.[8] Yet *liberation* is a word of power for our day because it has uncovered a fresh biblical language which describes God's saving actions as putting down the mighty from their thrones and exalting those of low degree (Luke 1:51), or as release to the captives (Luke 4:18)—both passages significantly quotations from the Old Testament used to interpret Jesus' own mission. That language is applied to the point of hurt and wrong in our present world, thus moving from biblical witness to contextual understanding.

We may also hesitate to use liberation theology as a catchall for defining our response to the dependency situation for another reason. It has become an "in" theology, subject to the temptations of sloganeering instead of hard thought. Yet like most "in" things, it captures something authentic about our time. It is under the various banners of liberation theology that the most penetrating and consistent critiques have been brought to bear on contemporary mission theology and practice. The enormous literature of liberation theology shows that it is a movement as diverse as it is extensive. Rosemary Ruether has remarked that Latin America, out of which so much of the focus on "captivity theology" has arisen, stands potentially as "the key interpreter of the identity of Christian faith and revolutionary struggle." There, unlike in Asia and Africa where Christianity inevitably became identified with colonialism, Latin America's Constantinian tradition pits its discovery of the liberating dynamic of the Christian faith against its own inherited tradition and society in an agonizing way.[9] Despite its diversity— one cannot generalize about liberation theologians—there are at least six motifs which point toward authentic directions for mission in the context of dependency.

1. Mission as liberation is to affirm that to undertake theology one must begin with the *concrete human situation.* The movement takes its clue from the Bible itself which it reads as the story of God's grace for the poor and outsider,[10] as a word of new creation enacted within particular historical moments. The Bible is seen to embody a wide diversity of language and images appropriate to the time, place, and context addressed, a clue important in defining a method of theological reflection appropriate for today.

2. Mission as liberation also believes in the possibility of responsible Christian action as a sign of the kingdom in an imperfect world. This is not at all the same as "liberal social action." There is a general rejection by liberation theologians of such simple activism not because such activism is wrong, but because it is unfocused.[11]

3. There is also a rejection of *simple utopianism,* but an affirmative of the possibility of the church now living as a model for free persons, a sign of the kingdom within history.[12]

4. As a fourth theme, liberation theologians generally recognize a *"Christian presence" in wider historical movements* promising justice and liberation, and thus may more readily find appropriate the analytical tools of Marxist social analysis.[13] A liberation perspective thus calls for cooperation with humanitarian movements wherever they appear among other religions or ideologies as a proper form of Christian partnership. This, of course, does not mean a denial of the prophetic and salvic word of the gospel, but rather heightens the kerygmatic task.

5. Thus Christian identity is affirmed in the recognition there can be no possibility of liberation without the *originating and sustaining action of God* if liberation is to be faithful to its biblical roots. Babel of Genesis 11 and Babylon of Revelation 18 remain as meaningful commentaries upon the futility of attempts to renew life while denying the fundamental and given reality of the world's common humanity and vocation as persons created in the image of God.

6. It is also clear that one *cannot escape the risk of conflict* today if one is to proclaim liberation in the name of Jesus Christ. To say no to idols and yes to mission cannot mean otherwise. Emilio Castro, the executive secretary of the Division of World Mission and Evangelism

of the World Council of Churches, has pointed out that today the issues that divide the churches are no longer mainly those of polity or doctrine. Polarization appears today increasingly at the point of commitment to liberation as a focus for mission.

The Struggle for Understanding: An American Dilemma

Dependency and domination—two sides of the same reality—thus form the wider context against which mission today needs to be understood. The new vocabulary of mission, rooted here, faces the churches of North America with a growing dilemma. On the one hand, few North-American Christians remain unaware of the human realities signaled by the new language of mission. Urban decay, the emergence of minority-consciousness movements as a call to faithful mission, American affluence amid a world of want—these are plainly observable facts which form the basis of much of the ferment about the shape of mission to some extent on both congregational and national church levels. And yet the fundamental realities behind these facts are hidden to most North-American Lutherans because few experience in their own lives and communities the oppressive force of poverty, hunger, and domination.[14] Hence, the dilemma. *How can mission be reshaped along the lines of the new vocabulary, or how even can the meaning of the new language be communicated and tested, if no common experience exists to provide a shared vision to rich and poor, powerful and powerless?* Lacking a common starting point out of which a theology of mission is to grow, how can there be achieved authentic partnership and interdependence for the worldwide unfinished task of proclaiming Christ?

The following profile may serve to illustrate the dilemma. Recently I visited a middle-sized Lutheran congregation in a small midwestern town. The church is about a century old, having grown from an immigrant group of German-speaking Americans into an established, English-speaking community. It is not untypical perhaps of the larger number of American Lutheran congregations. Over the years the congregation has sent at least ten men and one woman into full-time ministry, the latter into a life missionary service abroad. Other men and women from the congregation have migrated to urban areas across the country, where many of them, with others of similar background, have helped form the steady, faithful core of dozens of "home mission" churches. The art and stained-glass windows of the church, the posters hanging about the basement walls, the published preaching themes and study series, these all demonstrate an abiding and genuine concern for mission. If articulated, this concern would be expressed in terms of a number of certainties: the validity of the Great Commission; the authority of the word; the affirmation of Jesus Christ as the way, truth, and life; responsibility for regular worship and instruction; and the rightness of helping those in need through humanitarian programs, both church and secular based. Undoubtedly there are serious deficiencies to be discerned in that congregation's total grasp of mission—intrusions of culture-faith; lack of sympathy for, or understanding of, racial and urban issues; and limited knowledge of the complexities of global problems. But the congregation is committed to, and generous in support of, mission as it understands it. It came into existence itself as the result of the missionary efforts of immigrant pioneers. It is now moving toward the mark of contributing 50 percent of its budget to the national church and hence to mission beyond its parish borders. The congregation responded to the United Mission Appeal of the American Lutheran Church by pledging an amount almost equal to one year's local budget. This church, and thousands like it, provide the continuing base of financial support which makes possible North American contributions to the Lutheran World Federation and its program, the World Council of Churches, as well as cooperative structures in the United States—a fact not always appreciated by international churchmen overcome (perhaps rightly) by their own rhetoric concerning North Atlantic ethnocentricity and oppression. Whatever the shortcomings of the congregation here described, it affirms its biblical and confessional identity (however imperfectly). That affirmation, theologically and not merely sociologically based, sustains its continuing commitment to mission.

And yet, having noted all this, there is little in the experience of the congregation to enable it as a whole to understand the new vocabulary of mission—"salvation as liberation," "dependency," "moratorium," "conscientizing," "justice-not-aid," "reparations," "North Atlantic domination and oppression." Individual persons within the congregation are not unaware of global hunger, over-population, under-development. The question is, How may one address the question of integrity in mission for today without appearing to scold, raising frustration levels to intolerable heights without concrete solutions, or being insensitive to their established evangelical missionary certainties based on circumscribed local and global experience?

THE TESTING OF OUR AUTHENTIC
BUT INADEQUATE HERITAGE

Is it possible to address this dilemma by testing our missionary heritage against the valid claims of the new vocabulary of mission now emerging?

To speak of mission as essential to the being of the church is not new. The "sending" motif is rooted deeply within the biblical and confessional resources of the Lutheran churches of America.[15] Those resources have produced explicit fruit in the form of a rich variety of missionary movements in the past, both "home" and "foreign." This heritage, to be honest, is a mixture of both good and bad, strength and weakness, achievement and failure. Our task is to examine what is authentic in the past, while identifying its ambiguities in the light of the present challenge to mission. That is a difficult assignment for responsible American Christians who care about their tradition and know about their past, but for whom simpleminded, uncritical loyalty to the familiar is inadequate.

What thus needs to be determined is how liberation challenges Lutherans to discover a new shape for mission today. I shall examine our missionary heritage by choosing three themes which have determined to a large extent how our churches responded in the past. Each may be seen to have taken its clue for defining integrity in mission from one of the articles of the Apostles' Creed, though of course there is overlap because the whole of faith is viewed from the perspective of the person of Jesus Christ. All three motifs are based on honest biblical perceptions and have generated authentic missionary responses appropriate to their own times. Each provides a point of integration for the identity and work of mission. But we shall also see that a storm of debate about the nature of mission for our day has gathered precisely at the points of these three determinative themes, as Lutheran missionary theology is challenged by liberation motifs.

Mission as Witness: Second Article Foundations

The heart of the Christian gospel is the announcement that in the life, death and resurrection of Jesus, God has acted to save the world. Mission is therefore the communication of God's message of salvation by grace through faith to the end that persons may respond and be saved. As M. M. Thomas has remarked, "we shall only confuse the discussion of the theology of mission if we give any other definition of mission which takes away this cutting edge."[16]

1. *Heritage: God's new humanity as a sign of the kingdom.* Mission is first of all witness. From the perspective of the Second Article, mission is to be seen as the proclamation of the lordship of Jesus Christ in the world, creating by grace a new people whose individual and corporate lives are to be signs of God's new age.[17] Such proclamation lay at the core of the apostolic preaching and lies at the center of what American Lutherans have understood about mission. No doubt other less worthy motivations of mission have been expressed in Lutheran and American missionary history—ideas of manifest destiny, democraticizing or civilizing errands, even anticommunism. But these ideas remained secondary, not primary. A reading of mission theology of the American past does not support the notion that such ideas ever seriously guided the North American missionary enterprise.. This is not to suggest that these ideas have not distorted mission as expressions of cultural religion on a popular level. But it is to insist there is strong evidence that the major motivation to mission, both home and abroad, has been theologically understood by the confessional norm of God's justifying act in Jesus Christ. The heritage of American Lutheranism with respect to the purpose of mission is not untypically summarized in the following statement by Edward Pfeiffer, a statement which stood through four editions of Pfeiffer's book issued between 1912 and 1931:

> The real aim of missions is salvation from sin and death. . . . This is an old-fashioned doctrine that seems out of date when compared with the pretentious aims and claims of some treatises on modern "Christian Socialism" and sociology. But we prefer to live and die by "the preaching of the cross," as we are firmly convinced that the missionary enterprise will live and thrive upon it, while it will perish without it.[18]

But was the Second Article understood well enough? While Pfeiffer's view does root mission firmly within the Second Article, he narrows that witness in two ways typical of his generation. He mounts a clear polemic against the "social gospel," while at the same time he understands salvation in a largely futurist eschatological framework in commending "the more tremendous and enduring issues that hinge upon the reality of death and a judgment to come" over service to the oppressed whose needs he believes will be best served indirectly as the fruits of a more "spiritual" proclamation.

The crucial question is thus not whether the missionary witness of the American churches has remained faithful to the Second Article, but whether our confession of the uniqueness and finality of Jesus Christ as Savior of the world today adequately has caught the fullest dimensions of that confession.

Before pressing the answer to this last question, we need to define further the meaning of mission as witness to the lordship of Christ.

We may ask first what is the *content and quality* of that lordship? The lordship of Jesus means nothing less than an invitation into his servanthood. Jesus was known, strangely, as Lord precisely in and through his life of service and his dying as the way to the risen life. That certainly is the understanding of the early church as both the Synoptic and Johannine witness agrees (Mark 10:35–45; Matt. 20:20–28; Luke 22:24–27; cf. John 12:20–26). The lordship of Jesus testifies to ministry for others, not to lord it over the other. So we are baptized into the lordship of Christ precisely to die to sin, self, and idolatry in order to be servants of all.

We must also ask, What are the effects of the proclamation of the lordship of Christ? In a variety of images the New Testament speaks of the reality of the *new being* created by God in Christ, the new reality of a redeemed community from which flows the response of witness and service. Baptism is perhaps the most comprehensive sign of the new creation.[19] It is the decisive act in the missionary situation signifying that the believer has by grace died to the old self and has been reborn into a new community, and thus committed out of this new identity to live redemptively for the neighbor. But is the change from the old to the new a "real" change? Some have said that the change involved brings a new understanding of human existence (including self) but is not actual change to be observed in historical (ontological) process toward, for example, a more just society, or in a personal transformation. Others have insisted that a new creation does imply a qualitative, visible, and moral change for those reborn into the new community.[20] The latter position would indeed seem to best represent the sense of the New Testament, if salvation is to be understood as the making of new beings who are on the way, a community of the Lord energized to live as a sign of God's presence in the

world. The new creation thus has an eschatological dimension with
historical consequences. The gift of the kingdom is a present possession, with the church called to live as "first fruits" and the "down pay-
ment" of the new age.[21]

A Lutheran missionary statesman has also stressed the primary purpose of mission as witness to salvation in Jesus: "Let God, in Christ, be
known to men that they may receive forgiveness of sins and live in his
fellowship." But Rolf Syrdal, reflecting the kerygmatic theology of the
immediate postwar period, also explores the wider dimensions of salvation in writing of the eschatological tension inherent in mission:

> Salvation is not only other-worldly and for the hereafter. The eternal
> fellowship with God is to begin here and bear its fruits now. The
> consciousness that we are living "between the times" of Christ's first
> and second coming—between the establishment and the fulfillment of
> his Kingdom—has given an eschatological finality to the message of
> salvation and life with God in "the Now," and the assurance of the
> coming fulfillment. It complements the humanitarian view that works
> merely for the betterment of conditions in this world and does not
> limit the kingdom to other-worldly future.[22]

It is at this point that the dilemma of the Second Article perspective
begins to emerge: how "real" are the signs of the kingdom, and how is
salvation to be related dynamically to hopes for justice and peace? On
the one side, the coming of God's new age as a sign of his ultimate
future cannot simply be envisioned as a secularized version of utopian
hope. To live as God's new beings is to live with the realism of the
sinful and ambiguous nature of all human life and structures.[23] On
the other side, Christians cannot be content with a form of witness in
the name of the Redeemer of the world which fails to embody even
imperfectly and to limited extent the reality of the new community as
a sign of hope for the future.[24]

To state the matter clearly: the missionary hope of the Second Article lies in the formation of new people, committed to God and neighbor in ways redemptive for the world. What is asked is not whether
Christians have created places of coercive morality, *Righteous Empires*
(to use the title of Martin Marty's book). Rather, we ask whether the
church lives as a visible if imperfect sign of God's new humanity in
the midst of the specific political, economic, and social realities of our
day.

A fair look at the data may indeed suggest that Christians have affirmed the discipline of faith at moments in the past, however incompletely. Communities of Christians at home and abroad have functioned as leaven and salt in history. Proclaiming Christ has not led to sheer irresponsible individualism alone, however much the tendency was there. In India, for example, there is evidence of Christian influence on Hindu reform movements. In the United States, Christian opinion did finally solidify with effect in the early years of the civil rights struggle and the Vietnam disaster. In Indonesia, the positive Christian response in setting up chaplaincies and organizations of care following the post-Sukarno massacres in 1965 for the benefit of largely non-Christian victims provided powerful witness to Christian concern for justice in a volatile and polarized situation. The Second Article proclamation of the lordship of Jesus Christ as redeemer of the world has powerfully informed the missionary understandings of our American Lutheran churches. They have undertaken mission to make Jesus' name known, have called people to repentance and faith, through baptism have announced the new life, and gathered people at home and abroad into new communities. That these new communities have lived as salt and leaven in the world cannot be ignored. If American history is partly the story of the failure of the Puritan ideal to create a "new heaven and new earth," and if abroad the churches have not created new societies (wrong expectations from the start), yet the church has lived as a sign of the coming kingdom in the sense that the "radical consequences" of faith for human existence and structures have been at least partly in evidence. It is an exaggeration to suggest the effect of missionary piety has been totally individualistic and otherworldly.

2. *Testing: The humanization debate.* And yet where are our churches today? Does mission place us in the midst of the struggle for justice and human liberation, those wider issues of salvation, as a direct consequence of the gospel? Or is there a hesitation in accepting the political consequences of faith within the context of dependency and domination which today cry out for exploring anew the true freedom of the gospel? It is my view that Lutherans in the United States by and large have failed adequately to understand or live out the relationship between justification in its personal and vertical dimensions and justification in its social and horizontal dimensions. There

are two reasons for this failure. On the one side, a misunderstanding of the Lutheran theology of the two kingdoms has let us down, allowing Lutherans to privatize faith. On the other side, American Lutherans have been trapped by the cumulative effects of Protestant culture faith. Hence we are victims ourselves—captives in need of liberation like the layperson described by F. Dean Lueking who had been "taught a semi-heretical form of Christian belief, highly individualistic, law-oriented, other-worldly, and virtually without any sense of the horizontal dimension of the reconciling power of the gospel."[25] As a result, Lutherans of North America are not at present making any serious contributions to the current missiological debate—liberation theology and its motifs are either ignored in the main or so heavily qualified that they have lost their agitating force. If the Second Article has indeed been foundational in the past for mission, one fears that today among Lutherans Second Article witness has become domesticated by theological and institutional self-interests.

How can we grope beyond our theological and practical ambiguities toward a more faithful form of Second Article missionary witness today? We may make two suggestions:

First, we can learn from others, particularly the suffering poor of the present world, to view humanization not only as an effect but legitimately central to the gospel. M. M. Thomas has stated the matter succinctly: "The crucial question raised in the theology of mission . . . today is that of the relation between the gospel of salvation and the struggles of men everywhere for their humanity, constituting as this does the contemporary context of the world in which the gospel has to be communicated."[26] Again, M. M. Thomas, in his usual perceptive fashion has put the dilemma in perspective in his address in 1973 to the World Conference on Salvation Today, organized by the Commission on World Mission and Evangelism of the World Council of Churches, in Bangkok. He asked the question: "Will the creative process and the liberation movements in history ever be redeemed from idolatrous structures of meaning and saved by Christ to the extent that we can hope for a relatively high degree of human emancipation this side of the eschatological hope of the final salvation?" He went on to say,

> The answer to this depends upon the depth of the response of faith. . . . I have no doubt necessities of sinful nature play their part in all

power struggles and must be reckoned with by those concerned with politics of liberation. I am not so utopian as to deny the inevitability of accumulated sin and social history. But I do not think the message of divine forgiveness and the *koinonia* in Christ created by it can be relegated to a realm "beyond" or "after" politics. Just as in the case of individuals, in the case of classes, nations and races also, divine forgiveness and the community of forgiveness can and must break through sinful necessities, transform them and make the struggle more human.[27]

Philip A. Potter has written of how the sentence from Luke 19:9 spoken to Zacchaeus, "Today salvation has come to this house . . ." has haunted him from childhood.

What captured my young mind and has grown on me with the years is the fact that Jesus, at a critical point in his ministry, took the risk of inviting himself to the home of this hated rich man who was an economic pirate, a traitor to his people who were struggling against Roman colonial rule. Above all, the face to face encounter with Christ had an explosive, radical and revolutionary effect on Zacchaeus. The impossible happened. A rich man was saved, liberated from himself and from all he stood for and did, and not only he but those who were related to him, his house. In this experience of liberation which was expressed in his action of justice and compassion, he recovered his identity as a son of Abraham, and therefore, his community with his own people. He found himself and his people, in fact, all peoples.[28]

What these two voices—both of Third-World persons—claim is that the gospel itself has within it radical consequences. Salvation is viewed as both individual and corporate in its decisive intention. Liberation— for evangelical reasons—is placed at the center of the good news because liberation as a biblical way of understanding God's grace is also a word for our special time of captivity and tyranny.

The humanization debate has emerged as a rather tedious discussion between those who sense the wider dimensions of salvation as liberation and those who want so to sense, but who feel either vaguely or explicitly unfaithful to inherited mission theology if they concede too much about the horizontal dimensions of faith. Consequently, the humanization debate has raised a storm of controversy, much of it like the unfortunate tempest in the American Lutheran Church a few years ago over the much-misunderstood study of the youth department, *Called to be Human.* Conditioned as most Lutherans are by four hundred years of confessional emphasis on divine initiative, the title of that study alone was enough to provoke among many Lutheran clergy and laity a widespread feeling of uneasiness. But of course the world remains a terribly dehumanized sort of place, not only for the poor and oppressed (with whom most of us have little to do) but also for a generation of affluent disciples whose deepest inner urge is to mangle the computer card. Once salvation is put back into an incarnational context, in which real history and actual human beings replace the usual notional scholastic images, then humanization cannot be escaped. Once the Bible is read for what it is, the story of God acting for the outsider and despised in quite concrete situations and recalling them to a new identity and vocation, we can no longer quite so easily spiritualize, privatize, and duck the plain meaning of the wider dimensions of salvation.

Humanization as a missionary concern is not the sellout to the secularist and apostasy from the gospel many otherwise sensible Christians claim. The question, as M. M. Thomas and others see it, is that of "true" humanism, a declaration of solidarity with the diversity of the human family in its concrete needs because of an underlying reality having to do with Christians living as new beings in the image of God. There is no secret about what Christians understand. Our witness is nothing less than the audacious claim that all life roots in the redeeming and creating work of God through his Son, and apart from him nothing hangs together—neither well-meant horizontal plans for human good nor the equally well-planned escape routes to the future of disengaged religious freaks. The integrity of Christian mission affirms both the necessity to be founded in the unique given of biblical faith, and to be rooted in the realities of political, social, economic, and cultural life. M. M. Thomas views true humanism as follows: in dialogue with modern secularism the discussion "could be described as a reappraisal of the relations between *secularity* and *transcendence* in the being and becoming of man. In Christian theological categories, it is the relationship of salvation to humanization or the relevance of the *ultimate eschatological* dimension to the *relative historical.*"[29] To use J. M. Lochmann's phrase, witness to the reality of the new being in Christ for the world is to hold on to "radical secularity and radical grace."[30]

Liberation is not a moralistic tag-on to Christian witness, but central to the reality of the new being in Christ and his task, what Emilio Castro has called a "ministry of liberating reconciliation" in the world.

How else might we better come to grips with what is authentic in our Lutheran heritage and yet lacking in our grasp of mission for our day?

Second, we might take another crack at understanding our complex heritage of the two kingdoms. The question at issue: What form might responsible Christian witness take as a sign of the kingdom in the world? Karl Hertz has surveyed the choices from the standpoint of the Lutheran distinction between law and gospel, between the two kingdoms.[31] The options, he writes, are few. The choice of "some kind of evangelical coalition politics," a theocratic ordering of the world under "the mandates of God," holds no option because "such an order could only be imposed from the outside; it would not grow out of the community in a natural way." Nor can we choose the "liberal 'way out'" and work only through alliances with secular humanism, because that option no longer proceeds from the base of Christian identity. "Then the question remains whether anything legitimates religious demand for social justice," leaving the Christian mission for humanization stuck on the level of privatized faith.

Hertz suggests a third option, one which holds in tension the specificity of Christian identity and action in and through the political realm: "One approach to this dilemma is to suggest a new metaphor. Grace and nature do not define two realms of human activity, but two dimensions of a single unity: human existence. They represent different ways in which we are related, not different places in which we stand." Again, if I understand Hertz's suggestions correctly, his metaphor offers a more constructive way of understanding humanization in the light of the lordship of Christ over church and world by uniting identity and service in one reality. Philip Hefner has elsewhere spoken of the dilemma of how the kingdom as an eschatological promise is to be actualized in the world. Hefner too locates the positive responsibility for the world at the point of unity between redemption (identity) and creation (service). "We can be passionate about the things of the earth because we know that in our involvement in those things, our very redeemed humanity, a gift of God the Creator, is being fulfilled."[32] And he goes on to insist that Christian business in the world is not simply functional—there is no separation of the reality of the new being in Christ and the Christian works in the secular realm:

"We do our works in the world, not simply because we are so sensitive to our neighbor, but because we are sensitive to what is necessary to our humanity under God."

Humanization, what we have called a liberating ministry of reconciliation, can thus be seen as a proper goal of mission in two senses. One is the *eschatological.* God in Christ through grace has formed a new community in his image to live in the world as the sign of his shalom. Neither the church nor society can escape the ambiguities of sin. We live as imperfect "first fruits" awaiting the time when God will renew all things in himself. But humanization is also a call for *love in action now,* imperfect, but at work at the points of need. Liberating action can now be a sign of God's creative-redemptive work. As William Lazareth has written, the task is not to "Christianize" the secular realm but to "humanize" it.[33] Liberation, as a mark of the church, does not mean to bring all the world to the level of the kingdom, but to live concretely as a sign of the kingdom through forming new models of liberation under the sign of the cross. In this, we believe, lies the wholeness of witness.

Mission as Service: First Article Roots

North American understanding of mission has also been significantly shaped by the First Article in terms of mission as service to the neighbor in need.

While Lutherans have recognized that God accomplishes his saving work specifically in and through the proclamation of the gospel (the kingdom on the right), they have also confessed that God as Lord of all and Creator of the world works his gracious way in the world through his creating and preserving acts for all people in and through human institutions (the kingdom on the left). To appeal to the First Article as a basis of mission is thus not to substitute nature for grace. In both the confessions and the biblical tradition the work of the Creator is always viewed from the perspective of redemption. The redemptive acts of God for his people are announced as the basis of faith in both the Old Testament (the exodus)[34] and the New Testament (the cross and resurrection), thus justifying Christian concentration upon the work of God the Creator primarily as the work of a gracious and powerful God acting in mercy to bring all things into being and preserve them, and as the work of the merciful God who has the power to form and bring to consummation his new community in Christ.

There may be passages in the biblical tradition which reflect an alternative proclamation appealing to mission independently on the basis of God's creating and sustaining presence in nature. Jonah 1:9 may be one such passage, in which that reluctant missionary's ironic confession read: "I fear the Lord, the God of heaven, who made the sea and the dry land." This passage, like others (Isa. 40:28, for example) may less indicate a separation of creation from redemption than suggest an appeal rooted in the perspectives of "creative-redemption" or "redemptive-creation."[35]   An independent creation motif may however underlie Acts 14:15–17 and 17:22–31, where Luke portrays Paul as speaking of a God who appears to be known and witnessed to by nature,[36] or in Romans 1:20 where Paul himself affirms that the eternal deity and power of God is plain to all nations "ever since the creation of the world."[37]

1. *Heritage: Care for the earth and its people.* But whether viewed soteriologically as a sign of God's gracious work, or independently as a sign of his presence in nature and history, the confession of God as Creator has been of enormous significance in defining mission. The implications of the doctrine of creation for mission are at least threefold.

First, it provides a place of meeting for Christians and non-Christians at the point of their common humanity. Bishop Stephen Neill has spoken of the doctrine of creation in the Bible not as a philosophical or cosmological theory, but as the background to the human story, "God's love story with the human race." He writes:

> If the God of Israel really is the Creator of the whole universe, if he carries all the nations in his hand, then the unity of the world of nature and of men is guaranteed, and it seems to follow, as part of the divine purpose, that sooner or later all men should find their way to the God who has made them.[38]

A second implication of the doctrine of creation may be seen in the picture of the good God who affirms his creation and makes people in his image to care for the earth (Gen. 1:27–28). The framework of the Priestly account of creation in Genesis 1 is that of responsible vocation, with the law presupposed as a sign of God's covenant (redemptive) love. Persons made in the image of God, as Paulo Freire has stated so forcibly, no matter how unschooled or illiterate, have the critical capacity to grasp their own history, and in the process of realizing their "ontological vocation" can be subjects who act upon and transform the world.[39] The doctrine of creation thus speaks of care of the earth both in terms of responsibility for persons (social change) and for its resources (nonexploitative and distributed with justice) as a response to God's grace experienced redemptively in creation.[40]

Third, the Christian understanding of creation also views that doctrine as a basis for responsible caring for those in need. This motif for mission too is interpenetrated by a Second Article perspective—as, for example, in the new commandment of John 13:34 (cf. 15:12): "love one another; even as I have loved you." But the creative sovereignty of God also stands as one factor undergirding the "kingdom on the left" impulse behind the mixture of aid and charity programs so dominant in the West during the past decades, providing responses that were immediate in the face of need and at least partially positive in their effects. This understanding of mission has built hospitals, schools, and institutions of social service (not cynically to snare converts but to live out Jesus' word in Matthew 25:35–36).[41] Mission as service to neighbor has thrust Lutherans into the world through participation in ecumenical and secular agencies for relief and development, and provided a strategy of concrete action for more affluent people of goodwill to act at points of need. The idea of mission as service has thus served to define the Christian responsibility to the poor while, at the same time, offering an apparently helpful and practical route to service. There were no mysteries about what seemed to be needed: give, share, sacrifice, volunteer. The vision of caring service may be indicated by a statement in a 1952 *Lutheran Standard* article: "We Lutherans built a bridge across the ocean. Across that bridge we are sending our Christian love to Europe, Africa, the Orient, and South America in order to help, encourage, and strengthen those in misery"[42] Such is surely no mean vision, though it is quite clear which direction traffic is thought to flow across the bridge.

2. *Testing: the development debate.* And yet the new vocabulary of mission focuses some of its sharpest attacks precisely at the point of how service to neighbor has been understood and enacted. *The*

*critical question today is whether our structures for service are suffi-
ciently penetrating to get at the deeper problems of poverty and need
in an unbalanced world.* Our inherited theology of service, whether
domestic or global, as our secular programs of foreign aid, appear less
to have been proved wrong than inadequate. The gap between the
rich and the poor has grown larger, not smaller, in the past decade
(once so hopefully designated by the United Nations as the "development decade"). Western-sponsored models for development have
worsened, not improved, the situation. Economic domination by the
rich has increased.

To understand what has happened requires knowledge of the problem of economic imbalance on two levels. *The first is the simple level
of factual awareness.* Few people are unaware of the gap between
the rich and the poor nations, though most do not realize the full extent
of its dimensions. There is perhaps no need to do more here than to
outline briefly some the depressing statistics of world poverty. With
regard to distribution of the resources, the twenty or so developed
countries (one-quarter of the world's population) controls 90 percent
of the world's income, 90 percent of its gold reserves, 95 percent of its
scientific capacity. In food, the developed world consumes 70 percent
of the world's meat and 80 percent of its protein. In wealth, the per
capita income of the United States is approaching $5,000 annually; the
comparable figure in Nigeria is $80, for India $30, and overall, half
the world's population exists on a per capita income of less than $100
per year. With respect to illiteracy, more than half the world's population over ten has never been to school. There are 100 million more
illiterates in the world today than in 1940—nearly 850 million. With
respect to health care, the developed countries have 80 percent of the
world's medical doctors with a ratio of one doctor to every 500–750
persons, while the ratio in Africa is one doctor to 7,500 persons.
United Nations Children's Fund statistics for the mid-1960s reveal that
over half the world's population is without facilities for medical care,
and such diseases as malaria, cholera, trachoma, leprosy, malnutrition,
and filariasis (now largely unknown in the developed world) remain
endemic among large numbers of people.[43]

What has been cited above are only the outside facts. What is
required is to press toward a *second level of awareness,* to probe the
reason for this global imbalance. Is poverty the result of the popu-

lation explosion? No, poverty is more likely its cause, provoking a vicious circle in which poverty and population growth feed each other.⁴⁴ Nor is poverty due to lack of hard work and ability among the poorer nations—few Americans could stand the hardworking pace of Indian or Indonesian peasants, nor can we culturally match the staying power and adapability of their ancient societies. *The deeper and more radical fact is that world poverty is perpetuated by the structures of dependency over which the poor have little or no control.* The following "modern parable," though overdrawn, carries the point:

> There was once a factory which employed thousands of people. Its production line was a miracle of modern engineering, turning out thousands of machines every day. The factory had a high accident rate. The complicated machinery of the production line took little account of human error, forgetfulness, or ignorance. Day after day, men came out of the factory with squashed fingers, cuts, bruises. Sometimes, a man would lose an arm or a leg. Occasionally, someone was electrocuted or crushed to death.
>
> Enlightened people began to see that something needed to be done. First on the scene were the Churches. An enterprising minister organized a small first-aid tent outside the factory gate. Soon, with the backing of the Council of Churches, it grew into a properly built clinic, able to give first-aid to quite serious cases, and to treat minor injuries. The town council became interested, together with local bodies like the Chamber of Trade and the Rotary Club. The clinic grew into a small hospital, with modern equipment, an operating theatre, and a full-time staff of doctors and nurses. Several lives were saved. Finally, the factory management, seeing the good that was being done and wishing to prove itself enlightened, gave the hospital its official backing, with unrestricted access to the factory, a small annual grant, and an ambulance to speed serious cases from workshop to hospital ward.
>
> But, year by year, as production increased, the accident rate continued to rise. More and more men were hurt and maimed. And, in spite of everything, the hospital could do, more and more people died from the injuries they received.
>
> Only then did some people begin to ask if it was enough to treat peoples' injuries while leaving untouched the machinery that caused them.⁴⁵

This is not an easy state of affairs for North Americans to understand. Many of us have grown up with the idea that foreign aid and capital investment would solve the problem of poverty among underdeveloped countries. We thought that they too could develop if they adopted modern economic goals, and if their efforts were supplemented with generous aid and transfers of technology. The ideal was that the poorer countries one by one would reach the "take-off point" toward prosperity and slowly achieve parity with the richer Western nations. But the ideal has utterly failed. During the "development decade" (1960–70) declared by the United Nations, the gap between the rich countries and the poor has actually grown larger in both absolute and relative terms. Why has the development ideal failed? Though counterarguments may be cited, several factors seem to be responsible:[46] (1) The rich nations control and operate the non-communist international economic system for their own benefit. The poorer nations can never catch up as things now stand because neo-colonial patterns of exploitative trade still persist, with the effect that the developed countries are profiting most from the aid given, as well as gaining advantage from the world trade system. For example, for every dollar of aid given to Latin America in the past decade, it is estimated that more than four dollars of profits have been repatriated to North America. The net gain lies by far in favor of the donor. (2) *The "catch-up" theory is a fallacy.* There are limitations to the world's resources making it impossible for the poorer nations to achieve the standard of living of the developed world. It is a logistical fact that if the whole world consumed at the levels of the United States, the earth's resources of iron ore, tin, timber, aluminum and oil would be gone in less than six years. Thus the problem lies as much with overdevelopment in the West as with underdevelopment in the rest of the world, leading one Third-World person to remark: "The American way of life is not only unfit for export, but unfit for domestic consumption." (3) *Again, the West in any case it not giving enough aid to make a decisive difference.* Not only does the United States declare its priorities in what it spends—$160 billion annually for military defense and less than $5 billion annually for all forms of foreign assistance—but it has drastically cut what it does give in aid. In 1961 the USA share for foreign aid (including military assistance) was .056 percent of its Gross National Product. In 1976 the figure is .022 of the GNP. (4) Most serious, by making *economic growth and not justice the basic criteria for development,* priority is given to commodities rather than people, quantity rather than quality. James Lamb, the Director for the Center for the Study of Development and Social

Change, has written critically of such recent studies as the Pearson and Peterson reports on development. These reports, he writes,

> examine the problems of underdevelopment as if there were no causal connection between the predicament of the deprived nations and the "development" of the dominant nations. The authors of these reports do not question the worldwide market and military system which is essentially a system of control over the dominated nations. They propose either changes that are relatively trivial and do not threaten the governing system, or else more basic ones without any serious mechanisms for their implementation . . . By failing to make justice the basic guideline they deprive the word *development* of all moral significance.[47]

The development debate has thus moved discussion about the problem of global economic imbalance away from a too-exclusive fascination with economic growth to a discussion of liberation and humanization. The older (and still present) approach of *developmentism* is rejected because it has both proved to be disfunctional and left unattended the question of change in the overdeveloped world. By approaching world economic imbalance from the standpoint of *liberation,* attention is thereby focused on justice, not aid. It is proposed that change will come primarily through the initiating and even revolutionary efforts of the poor themselves as they become aware of their critical vocation to change their own situation.[48]

What then might integrity in mission mean from the standpoint of the development debate?

First, the authentic basis for mission as service to neighbor remains, namely, its roots in the creative and redemptive care of God for all his people. The Christian identity summons individuals and the church no less to work for a new economic order of justice than it summons them to a ministry as care for the earth and its people provides an explosive base for human concern.

But let us locate this explosive base more precisely, if we can. Donald Ziemke has shown how Luther's concept of love for the neighbor came to be based in terms of the nature of society, not only as an expression of faith. "He [Luther] speaks of society as he came to see it in his radical Christological concept of the body of Christ. He regards Christ as the agent of creation, placed over creation, and as the concretion of the will of God, now the pattern for the life of society."[49] What Ziemke seems to suggest, if I am interpreting him correctly, is the possibility of Christian liberating action in the world which remains rooted in the saving acts of God as Redeemer-Creator, an action based in understanding the law as an expression of the gospel, precisely as the covenant provides the "gospel" framework for law in the Old Testament—and yet which action takes its clue for responsible service from an analysis of the concrete forms of injustice and oppression as we discern them in the world today. If the lordship of Christ is set in its First Article framework, then his lordship not only has implications for *why* Christians work for the renewal of economic and political orders. Christ's lordship then also opens Christians to discerning the *how* of responsible service in the world. In short, care for the earth and its people cannot be defined apart from disciplined, disturbing effort in an attempt to face squarely the reasons for the failure of the development ideal. In this regard, it is not inappropriate for Christians to learn from the Marxist socioeconomic analyses which are at least a serious attempt to lay bare the reasons for dependency and oppression.

Second, by taking with utmost theological seriousness what the Christian tradition affirms about human sinfulness, Christians ought not be surprised by the radical analysis of the oppressive nature of the Western economic order in the world. Reasons of comfort and order have never been satisfactory excuses for Christians to accept meekly the reality of sinful structures, or to pretend they do not exist. Confessional integrity demands realism. Such realism, if allowed to surface, ought to allow Christians to understand the oppressive results of economic dependency, to own historical responsibility as Westerners,[50] and to work for change as a response to Christ who is lord of the church and of the world. One of Carl Braaten's criticisms of the Lutheran doctrine of the two kingdoms is that it taught "Christians merely to *uphold* the secular orders, not to *change* them. . . . The problem with the two-kingdom doctrine is that the revolutionary dynamic discharged by the kingdom on the right hand did not set off any explosions in the kingdom on the left hand."[51] He suggests that what empowers mission is the eschatological dynamic—"the vision of the radically new is what links revolutionary action with eschatological hope." If what we have understood of mission as service to neighbor called for individuals to respond with acts of sacrifice, giving, and caring, all as a response to concrete needs as preceived, the global situation of widespread dependency calls today not only for that. It may call for more radical response, even revolutionary change, if our vision of the lordship of Jesus Christ in the church and the world is to have integrity.

Mission as Fellowship: Third Article Perspectives

We look last at the third motif determinative for North American understanding of mission. Mission in ecclesiological terms has been understood as gathering the nations under the guidance of the Spirit. Under the impact of this image, mission has been viewed as a steady if not always triumphant process of cross-cultural movement.

1. *Heritage: geographic expansion.* What are the biblical roots of this motif? They are not to be found in the Old Testament. Movement was important for God's people though not in the sense of a missionary sending of Israel to other nations.[52] Israel's vocation was not to mission but to realize its vocation through worship and service, to live as "a light to the nations."[53] Jerusalem remained the geographic center. All movement was intended to flow from the periphery of the Gentile world toward the land of promise. Covenant history is full of movement, but always movement toward the center: Abram is called to go up to the land of promise for the blessing of the nations (Gen. 12:1–3); Joseph's deportation was viewed as a necessary movement away from the land to preserve the family (Gen. 37–50), but the Exodus meant liberation back to the center (Exod. 3:8), as did the second deliverance (Isa. 40:1–11) and the reestablishment of the house of the Lord in Jerusalem (Isa. 61:1–7; 2 Chron. 36:22–23; Ezra 1:1–4). It is not accurate to speak of Israel's "failure" of mission—her vocation was fulfilled as she became the faithful people among whom the Messiah was born.[54] Within an Old-Testament framework there could be no mission in the sense of a fully pluralistic movement across geographical boundaries in which one faith found expression in a diversity of cultural settings.[55] Jerusalem remained both the geographical and religious center for Israel's faith, even though that faith came to be understood as a light of all nations.[56]

The New Testament brings what has been described as a totally new perspective to mission: "The commission to proclamation to the nations, to mission in the centrifugal sense."[57] Though there continues a long discussion over the authenticity of Jesus' "great commission"

(Matt. 28:19–20) and over the question of his own attitude toward mission to the Gentiles, it has become minimally clear that "Jesus' message and works in Israel became a witness among the Gentiles," and as the eschatological event he proclaimed began to be realized, "salvation came within reach of the Gentiles."[58]   Thus the post-resurrection mission of the early church to the Gentiles may be said to be rooted authentically in Jesus' own proclamation of the kingdom.

It is primarily the writings of Luke which have shaped the view of mission as movement across geographical frontiers.   In the first place Luke (according to Hans Conzelmann) was among the first early Christians to develop a theology of history, enabling the church to settle into history for the long haul and to think through its mission.[59] Equally important is his schema of mission.   Luke and Acts taken together perceive mission as geographical expansion (from Galilee to Jerusalem in the Gospel and from Jerusalem to end of the earth—Rome, in Acts) in ways which have set their stamp upon missionary thinking down to the present.   Luke has also set the theological tone for mission through his emphasis on the power of the Holy Spirit as the church in mission (Acts 1:8; chap. 2; 10:44, and throughout).

But one qualification must be made about Luke's theology of mission.   To some extent, at least, Jerusalem remained central for Luke, and emphasis which may be seen in his tendency to reconcile Jewish and Hellenistic Christian communities and to preserve their unity on the basis of the authority of the Twelve in Jerusalem.[60]   Though mission as sending to the Gentiles is clearly articulated in the Lucan writings, his theology by itself does not appear to be a fully adequate basis for a genuinely cross-cultural diversity.   It was Paul more than any other New Testament theologian who developed the dynamic tension between the confession of Jesus Christ as the one lord and the reality of diversity in freedom, thus laying the theological basis of fully cross-cultural Christian mission (below, Section 3, p. 225).

It was this understanding of mission as movement across geographical frontiers that we have sketched which since has tended to guide at least the western church's idea of mission.   The church for the world was preceived as expansion: from Jerusalem to Rome in the initial instance—and to Ethiopia and India, to southern Europe and western Asia, to Ireland and back to Britain and northern Europe, across to the Americas.   Mission as expansion was not always a dominant motif in the consciousness of the Western churches.[61] But in the last two centuries, often as the result of the work of mission societies and rather than churches, the missionary ideal as geographical expansion once more exploded from largely European and North American centers into every continent. The Lutheran churches of America have played their role in this expansion and establishment of the churches, particularly in the late nineteenth and twentieth centuries: in East, West, and South Africa and Madagascar; in India (but not much elsewhere in southern Asia), in parts of Latin America; in Sumatra and in more limited areas elsewhere in Southeast Asia; in and out of China but continuing in Hong Kong, Taiwan, Japan; in a small presence in Korea and a large effort in Papua New Guinea (but not elsewhere in the South Pacific). At the same time, Lutherans in North America did more than collect immigrant coreligionists from northern Europe, though some would say not much more. A theology of mission as expansion, growth, and evangelism, along with mission strategies aimed at following immigrant and migrant Lutherans across the country and maintaining the confessional heritage amid the pluralism of North America, has preserved and extended the Lutheran tradition at home.

Let it be emphasized that the motives and results were positive. The church was planted. At home, the pressure of the overseas missionary movement did not allow North American Christians to become or remain parochial. Further, the idea of mission in terms of geographical expansion was appropriate to the times. The late eighteenth through the early twentieth centuries were times of exploration and discovery (from a European point of view), and of migration of Lutherans first from Europe to the Americas and then an inner migration. Growth, extension, missionary pioneering in lands without a Christian presence or witness were all required. The missionary efforts that flowed from this perception of mission represented faithful responses in the context of the contemporary situation.

2. *Testing: the contextualization debate.* And yet today a question— or indeed a series of them—must be placed against the Lukan-based understanding of mission. To what extent in the entire process of geographical expansion and extension has "Jerusalem" remained central? If Paul once struggled to free Gentile Christian from the bondage of Jewish legalism—that is, from the centrality of first-century religious

Jerusalem—today we must inquire whether churches East and West still must face the question of cultural captivity. Such captivity may be found either as a form of particularity which denies unity, or as an uncritical culture-faith which denies specific Christian identity. Whenever in history theology has been vital and engaged, it has spoken and acted concretely. The question is not whether to contextualize faith or not, but whether the process is authentic—true both to the controlling source of faith and true to the situation it seeks to address.

Those questions in variant forms provide the background for what may be called the "contextualization debate." What is at stake is no less than the freedom of the gospel.

In its modern form, the debate first emerged in the Third World in recognition of the close tie historically between Christianity and colonialism. It is not new, of course, to raise the question of Western domination of church life, structures, and theology as a dominant missiological issue. For generations Christians, both nationals and missionaries, have struggled with the demand for what has been called "indigenization." But throughout the colonial period of missions and for some time afterward, the question remained a somewhat low-keyed problem of how to find and adapt cultural forms or language to Christian doctrinal and liturgical patterns.

All that has changed today. More than a subject for academic reflection and church practice, the demand for the contextualization of the gospel is understood in a far more urgent setting. Three factors appear to have brought the question into sharper focus.

First, the more radically politicized situations in Asia, Africa, and Latin America force the issue of whether the national churches can develop an authentic, contextualized church life as expressions of missiological faithfulness. In many non-Western countries the question of national identity has become more acute, despite the widespread achievement of political independence. The continued economic domination of the West, through its control of worldwide trade and its vast lead in technology and affluence, sustains patterns of dependence typical of the colonial period. This fact helps explain the growing appeal of the Chinese model which, partially through a time of self-imposed isolation, regained for China economic and social autonomy and a corresponding national confidence. And yet in the midst of this struggle for national identity, many non-Western churches remain heavily dependent upon Western subsidies. In the eyes of non-Christian nationals, if not indeed their own eyes, these dependent national churches appear to be alien outposts of Western Christianity and culture. In India, for example, Hindus of the Jan Sangh party and others suspect that Indian Christians are not fully "Indian" in their commitment to and participation in national development. In South Africa, the fact that many white Christians are ambiguous toward—if not outright supporters of—the white racist government has deeply and perhaps fatally compromised Western Christianity in the eyes of many black Christians. Similarly in Latin America, dominant North American influences, political, economic, and religious, are viewed as obstacles in the way of social revolution. The key question thus becomes: How can the churches of Asia, Africa, and Latin America overcome not only their Western-oriented theology and structures but, more importantly today, also the social and economic presuppositions of North Atlantic Christianity which accompany them and which too often give uncritical support to what is viewed as continued economic and social imperalism?

Second, there is new direction to the question of contextual theology provoked by the urgent demand for social change. "Indigenization," as usually understood, tended to have a somewhat backward-looking direction, searching ways for non-Western Christians to interpret the gospel within their own traditional cultures. But much more than utilizing traditional music in liturgies or adapting classical terminology to Christian thought is involved. The actual frontiers for social change in many countries of Asia, Africa, and Latin America are marked by drives for political reform or revolution, the uprooting of feudal socio-economic patterns, and the battle for a greater measure of justice for the common man too long held at ransom by wealthy and powerful elites. The hopes for such change often center on the liberating promise of secularism and the controlled application of technology—forward-looking dimensions which stand beside, interact, and sometimes have replaced traditional cultures and faiths as the means of realizing the promise of the future. A truly indigenous theology must relate to a series of overlapping and partially contradictory contexts within any one non-Western country, a mixture of the old and the new. For this reason many now prefer to use the terms *contextualization* or *living theology* rather than *indigenization* to describe today's missiological task precisely because the former terms more clearly have the total context in view, secular as well as traditional.

Third, the need to redefine what is "universal" and what is "particular" in the Christian gospel puts new emphasis on the issue of contextualization. There is widespread consensus today about the necessity of holding the universal and local in tension.[62] From the very beginning Christianity affirmed the one gospel for all men as the basis of mission. At the same time, the Christian faith has struggled to affirm the validity of varieties of particular cultural forms through which the gospel is understood and expressed.[63] That acceptance has made it possible for the gospel to cross cultural frontiers and take root. What is truly universal in the Christian faith is the world in and through Jesus Christ which creates new men and societies. What is authentically local is the particular enactment of the word within living traditions—confessional statements, liturgies, forms of personal piety, and patterns of social action.

But what is sharply contested today in Asia, Africa, and Latin America is the way in which the central, universal gospel has been identified. What the non-Western churches have received—and largely accepted—from the West is not a purely universal gospel. What they have received is the one gospel mediated by North Atlantic Christianity. Anglican liturgicalism, Lutheran and Reformed confessionalism, conservative evangelical biblicism—these and all other forms of Western theologies and ecclesiologies with whatever mixing and overlapping, are in fact contextual theologies which grew out of particular historical and cultural situations and which have been passed on, unconsciously perhaps, as universal theology. The facts that more than 80 percent of all active missionaries in the non-Western world today are from Northern Europe or North America, and that nearly all Asian, African, and Latin American churchmen who have studied abroad have done so in the West, have inevitably reinforced an uncritical acceptance of Western theological forms as standard by which the universal gospel is defined.

Nor is the contextualization debate limited to the Third World. Gone, or at least subdued, are the confident visions of the future of the secular theologians of the past decades. Gone too are the overly optimistic hopes for Christian unity based on the dominant "ecumenical" theology of the North Atlantic churches. Instead grounds for social action and Christian unity are being sought first of all in the encounter of the gospel in the particular and the local, moving from those authentic diversities toward the whole and the global. Martin E. Marty and Dean G. Peerman have identified this way of doing theology as an emerging motif of American theology:

> In any case, it is assumed that the language with which theologians work is developed in particular, not universal, communities; that the experiences on the basis of which they do their extrapolating belong to relatively exclusive groups of people; that identity is found when people come to terms with sub-communities before they take on realities like those condensed in the phrase, "the family of man."[64]

Issues of contextual theology are being pressed in North America especially by black and other minority theologians who find themselves in "Third-World" settings. They are dealing with their particular American experience which they recognize as heavily influenced by dominant forms of white theologies, those theologies themselves being contextualized expressions of the gospel forged out of another set of particularities. Minority groups that have long been the object of missionary welfare efforts are becoming increasingly dissatisfied with help from outside and are looking more to their own leadership to find answers to their problems. At the National Fellowship of Indian Workers Conference in 1974, for example, that group's past president declared the time had come for native Americans to develop their own theological statement. At the same meeting, Vine Deloria, Jr., president of the National Institute of Indian Law and writer on Indian affairs, told representatives of eleven American denominations that "it is too late for Indians to seek change through the church" because the churches are not willing to deal with such problems as the concrete forms of economic, racial, cultural, and ecological oppression—the particularities of native Americans.

Contextualization is important also for the white, Anglo-Saxon, Protestant American minority. For this group—which takes in most North American Lutherans—the challenge of contextualization is twofold. On the one side, it calls into question the syncretism of "religion-in-general," ineffective for mission because its levels of faith and commitment have dipped down out of sight of biblical faith. It is neither informed by the kerygma nor engaged by the real world. On the other side, contextualization also challenges this minority to use its particularity not as an uncritical base for withdrawal or domination, but as a springboard of informed commitment within the wider, legitimate diversity of the whole body.

In short, these three factors which have brought new urgency to the question of contextual theology—the more politicized situations, the more pressing demand for social change, the greater need to redefine the universal and the local in the gospel—all indicate that contextualization cannot be viewed simply as a problem of how to interpret or communicate the gospel in each new situation. It is not only a question of translating or applying what is already known. It must rather be asked, How can the Christian faith cross cultural frontiers without remaining tied to the dominant, culturally-conditioned forms through which today it has been mediated? and How can the one gospel be rediscovered as the word creates new forms in each new situation, and what is the dynamic element in the process?

What should be understood, therefore, is that the contextualization debate raises in new form the question of the freedom of diversity within the unity of one gospel and one world. Inevitably contextualization has to do with liberation. Thus, C. Rene Padilla, known as an evangelical Latin-American theologian, has stated that "the church in Latin America is a church without theology"—or more accurately, a church "with no theological reflection of its own." He writes:

> Does anyone doubt the truth of this statement? Let him notice the quantity of Christian literature translated from the English (and how poor many of these translations are!) and the scarcity of literature we ourselves have produced. Let him notice how much of our preaching is limited to a mere repetition of poorly assimilated doctrinal formulas, with no application to our own historical reality. Let him observe to what extent our churches, without thinking, maintain the theological coloring of the missions that establish them, and consider theological study basically as the study of the doctrinal distinctiveness of the churches to which they grace their origins. Let him examine the faculty and the curriculum of the majority of our seminaries and Bible schools. . . . An examination of all these aspects of our church situation will show him that our "theological dependence" is just as real and as serious as the economic dependence that characterized the countries of the third world.[65]

Thus it should come as no surprise that the moratorium issue has come to the fore in contemporary missiological discussions.[66] Some have seen moratorium as one of the ironies of the 1970s, a contradiction of the ecumenical quest for unity and a denial of interdependence. I do not believe that to be the case. At its deepest level, moratorium raises anew the question of the true unity of the church. It is not unity as such that is questioned, but a form of unity perceived to be based on the particularisms of a dominant variety of Western theologies and not on the liberating unity-within-diversity of the Bible. That problem is not new. The early church, Paul in particular, saw the issue as one of the basic problems to be addressed if Christianity were to become a truly missionary faith.

3. *Another look at Galatians in its missionary setting.* An examination of Paul's missionary theology, especially as it emerged in the Galatian conflict and against the background of the growth of the biblical tradition as a whole, may provide an alternative to Luke's tendency to retain a "Jerusalem-centered" understanding of missionary movement across geographical frontiers. What we are looking for is an evangelical ground for mission by which the hopes for liberating contextualization may be more fully actualized.

The process of contextualization is not new in Christian history. It was a demand of the biblical tradition itself from the beginning. The process is clearly evident in the Old Testament. As Israel moved from one historical situation to another—from the patriarchal period, to the times of Moses and the settlement of the land, through the periods of united and divided monarchies and exile, and into postexilic Judaism— throughout, there was a constant process of not only adaptation but reformation. In the end, the Old Testament writers and redactors looked back to a dominating theme which gave unity to the whole: a theology of grace explicit in God's calling a people to be his own (Exod. 19:3-6) and in his repeated acts of new creation (Ezek. 37). Old Testament laws, traditions, and indeed cultures changed and grew, but always and fundamentally under the impact of one constant: the gracious God who remembered and redeemed his people for mission (Exod. 2:24; Isa. 2:1-4; 55:1-5). We recognize, of course, the presence of several strands of Old Testament faith—royal theology, Zion theology, praise of Abraham. Yet this process of contextualization, recontextualization, and diversity is held together by an understanding of the Torah as revelation and not requirement, as grace and not demand.

The process continued in the New Testament. As the good news moved from Jewish-Palestinian soil in successive stages to the wider Hellenistic world, again a single, dominant theme gave unity to the whole: the new creation promised in Jesus Christ (Mark 1:14–15; John 20:30–31; Rom 3:21–26; Heb. 1:1; 1 Pet. 2:9–10; Rev. 22:17). In the midst of changing geography, language, and culture—as well as differing social and political settings—the biblical tradition itself embodies a continuous and dynamic process of the movement of the one gospel across frontiers of cultural pluralism.

But what was the specific element which both controlled and agitated the process of contextualization? I want to suggest that in the history of Paul's mission to Galatia we can observe how justification by faith provided exactly that condition of freedom which made it possible for the Christian faith to cross cultural frontiers, to become at home in them, and still to maintain a distinctively Christian identity. We can thus read the record of Paul's struggles against the Jewish Christians as a case study in contextualization.

It is important to understand justification by faith against Paul's own missionary situation.[67] Protestants often tend to read Paul through the eyes of Lutheran Scholasticism, thus interpreting Paul's theology of grace against a sixteenth- and seventeenth- instead of a first-century background. The difference is decisive. In the sixteenth and seventeenth centuries the key problem was whether salvation was earned by individual acts of piety (monastic obedience, good works, ethical actions) or whether salvation was indeed by grace. Luther and the Reformers were faithful to their own context. Justification was discovered anew as God's gracious gift of righteousness. While Luther and the Reformers certainly did not interpret justification in purely individualistic terms (though later Lutherans have tended to do so), they did read Paul quite properly but one-sidedly against the dominant religious questions of their own day.

But we must for our day once more read Paul through his own eyes —not through the perspectives of scholastic Lutheranism or even the Lukan perspective. Paul, more than Luke or any other New Testament theologian, provides the radical basis for cross-cultural mission in the true freedom of the gospel.

The framework for Paul's working out of justification in Galatians was wider than the question of individualistic salvation.[68] He understood grace within the context of the missionary situation of the early church. The central question, which was all important for the theology of mission, was this: did the new Christians of the expanding Hellenistic mission need to become religious Jews in order to become Christians? or Did evangelical freedom mean that the laws and traditions of one situation, legalistic forms of Judaism, were not binding as the Christian faith moved into new cultures? Naturally, the personal dimension of justification was involved in the struggle against Jewish and Christian legalism. But the discussion was provoked by and centered upon the question of religious and cultural freedom for the Christian mission.

Paul forged his reply through his struggle against the Jewish-Christian opponents of the Gentile mission. Whether or not these opponents came from Jerusalem,[69] Paul was troubled by Judaizing Christians who mounted a counter-mission in Galatia and elsewhere. These people, as described by Dibelius, "were closer to Judaism than Jesus himself was," and were insisting that the Gentile Christians of Galatia "live like Jews."[70] It was against this challenge that Paul sets forth the major theme of Galatians, the freedom of the gospel which liberates men from the bondage of the law and thus makes possible an authentic new Christian existence as God's eschatological community (Gal. 3:1–5:25). Jewish legalistic tradition is an element of a particular religious culture which need not be transplanted within the new missionary communities. It was precisely justification by faith, the announcement of God's grace in Jesus Christ, which provided the basic condition of freedom by which the Gentile Christians were liberated from the yoke of an alien cultural bondage, the Jewish heritage. The way is thus clear for the Christian faith to come alive in each new culture, to accept it, to transform it, and to challenge it. And at the same time, Paul affirmed the Old Testament understanding of Torah as revelation and grace.

The account in Acts 15 (if indeed it reports the same event and despite the Lukan softening of the solution) confirms the direction of Paul's argument in Galatians 2. After the confrontation in Antioch between Paul and Barnabas and the Jewish Christians, and in its resolution in Jerusalem, the apostolic tradition clearly upheld the principle of religious freedom from cultural bondage. The compromise reported yielded to Paul's major point. By affirming that Gentile Christians need not become Jews in order to be Christians (Acts 15:19), a decision was taken which made it possible for the Christian faith to be missionary.

At the same time, Christian freedom did not mean an absence of norms or imply a divided church. Paul insisted that there was but one gospel (Gal. 1:7) and that it is a freely given gift which creates a new and distinctive Christian identity. The new Christian lifestyle is marked by love and by the fruits of the Spirit which are both realized and anticipated in the fellowship of the people of God "who belong to Jesus Christ" (Gal. 5:13–24). Freedom from one alien culture (Judaism) did not mean license to accept the bondage of another culture (Gal. 5:13). To contextualize the faith in the missionary setting did not lead to an uncritical adaptation to the new environment —to such familiar distortions of grace as antinomianism, gnosticism, the mystery religions and proto-gnostic influences. The controlling and dynamic element again, for Paul, is to be found in his understanding of justification by faith. Freedom in the gospel remains a Spirit-directed freedom in Christ.

In brief, the Galatians account of Paul's mission to the Gentiles illuminates two important points with regard to the process of contextualization: (1) Evangelical freedom provides the dynamic element in the transmission of the Christian faith which enables it to cross cultural frontiers and to become rooted in the new situation. (2) Evangelical freedom, because it is a freedom born in Christ, defines the limits of contextualization by establishing the norm for authentic Christian identity.

Summary

We have identified three theological perspectives which have played a significant role in defining the North American understanding of mission. All are authentically biblical and confessional. Each helped forge a policy of mission against a nineteenth- and early twentieth-century background in which the programmatic implementations of the motifs had contextual integrity. If one is to be critical of where we have arrived in our thinking about mission, we must at least first recognize that we are the heirs of a theology of mission which took the theological identity of the church as the new people of God seriously, and sought in faithfulness to proclaim, serve, and expand the kingdom of God's Son.

But each age brings its own new demands. Today the inherited perceptions about mission are under challenge not because the theology was wrong, but because it needs to be tested afresh by the present. Thus a dynamic and continuing interaction between text and context is required. A recent Church of England report on Christian doctrine states that a dialectical presentation of truth is perhaps the way in which God is best communicated: "The miracle of the Bible is . . . that it is inexhaustible; its creative power goes on stimulating new developments in tune with its own spirit."[71] We need therefore, to explore our revealed *identity* in the light of our actual history to discover anew the gift of God's grace as redeemer, creator, and sanctifier for the new community *today*; and we need to test the shape of our *response* in an unbalanced world by both the confessional norms of the one word and the contextual needs of persons and communities in their present situations. In this way mission indeed becomes the test of integrity for Christians, the integration of *who we are* (and are to become in Christ) and *what we are called to do.*

In examining our missionary heritage we observed three points of disturbance and growth: (1) The *humanization debate* suggests that missionary *witness* to Jesus Christ as Savior of the world explore the fuller dimensions of what it means for God's new people to live as the sign of his kingdom, engaged on evangelical grounds in the struggle for new communities in the world. (2) The *development debate* makes us inquire whether our *service* in his name has adequately penetrated the deeper problems of poverty and injustice, conditions which require first of all our own liberation. (3) The *contextualization debate* tests our ideas of fellowship, asking how church expansion may adequately realize in the power of the Spirit the liberating freedom of the gospel to create its own new cultural forms in each new encounter, thus releasing evangelical potential for true universalism and authentic plurality.

The following chart may help summarize the questions that have been put.

MISSION WITH INTEGRITY

Theological Base	As once defined, authentically but inadequately	As now under challenge: dependency	Shape of Today's Liberation Response
Service (First Article redemptively interpreted)	Mission as care of the neighbor. Vocation of welfare, sharing, aid. Development.	Unbalanced economic order. Development debate shows service not wrong but inadequate.	A creative-redemptive affirmation of critical vocation in and through the secular realm. Service informed by justice.
Witness (Second Article)	Mission as proclaiming lordship in the world. Salvation as creation of a new humanity.	Complicity of the church in oppression. Privatized faith. Where are the signs of the kingdom? Political withdrawal.	Salvation as human-ization under the cross. Church as sign of present and final kingdom.
Fellowship (Third Article)	Mission as geographical movement across frontiers.	Cultural dependency. North Atlantic dominance of theology and culture.	Unity and freedom. Vigorous context-uality as sign of one universal gospel.

INTERDEPENDENCE AND THE FUTURE OF MISSION

We do not now attempt to predict the future shape of mission. That task can only be done as an ongoing process as Christians together around the world struggle forward to reshape locally and ecumenically models of responsible witness and service. What I do offer are hints of the future, especially as evident in forms of critical theological reflection emerging in North America in response to the crisis of dependency. It becomes my special purpose to attempt to define ways in which the dynamic and controlling heritage of justification by faith may provide an authentic resource for Lutherans of North America to discover the particular profile of integrity in mission for our churches.

Signs of Response in American Lutheranism

The hints are genuine clues, not notional projections. An incomplete analysis of the official denominational publications of the Lutheran church press indicates both a sustained concentration upon mission among America's Lutherans and a changing analysis of what mission today needs to become. A table setting out the articles published demonstrates continuity of focus upon mission, though the ennumeration below is only approximate—category definition is difficult because nearly all articles in one way or another could be said to have to do with mission.

| | 1952–55 | | 1972–75 | |
	HOME MISSION	FOREIGN MISSION	HOME MISSION	FOREIGN MISSION
Lutheran Standard (ALC)	57	68	9	31
The Lutheran (LCA)	11	11	3	8
Lutheran Witness (LC-MS)	11	27	4	12

Each denomination, of course, simultaneously published its own overseas missionary magazine or newsletter. It is important to note that in terms of emphasis, the lower number of "home" mission articles between 1972 and 1975 in the denominational press probably reflects the slowdown in the establishment of new congregations, while a concentration upon the overseas mission held about the same (considering the above journals were published less frequently by 1972 than in 1952).

It is of more significance, however, to trace the change in approach to mission, whether home or overseas. In 1952, a much sharper distinction was made between mission at home and abroad. Also, between 1952 and 1955 the emphasis lay on evangelism, growth, sending. Race issues were beginning to boil at home, while colonialism was drawing to its close abroad, events viewed as a time of challenge for white Christians to go and to do. Note the titles of some articles of the period:

"Seizing Neglected Mission Opportunities"
"Mission Begun in Thriving Suburb"
"America's Neglected Millions"
"Steady Growth, Progress Speak Well for Central District"
"ALC Missionaries Are on the Move"
"Transfer of Negro Missions"
"Pittsburgh Plants a Package"
"We Can Have 35,000 Missionaries"

By 1972, in contrast, a series of themes emerged which speak of the mutality of mission. Much attention is given to redefining mission for

the future in the face of poverty, political oppression, black consciousness, violence, and Vietnam. On the whole, the Lutheran church press
has begun to stir with respect to liberation—but it seems to have responded to themes pressed by black and liberation groups, rather than
forcibly initiating the recasting of mission. With respect to two key
issues—Vietnam and the American Indians—the church press, while not
always consistent, appeared to be ahead of the constituency in taking
stands on the liberationist side. Articles on Namibia, Bangladesh,
world hunger, ecology, and American foreign policy (economic and
political) appear to be on the increase in direct attempts to educate
the Lutheran public to the impact of these questions on congregational
mission, often at the risk of appearing to irritate parts of the general
readership as well as some church officials. Two examples show
rather clearly emerging directions as mission at home is linked with
its global dimensions. The first statement, by the late Kent Knutson,
sought a six-continent framework:

> Our concept of mission is expanding. I would like to expand it still
> further. Mission is not just that which we do for others in other
> places. It is also a name for the very purpose of our existence as a
> Christian community. Suddenly our idea is very wide. We exist in
> order to worship God, in order to witness to him to others, in order to
> teach our children, in order to contribute to the well-being of the
> community and the nation in which we live. In short, our purpose is
> not only to reach others but to grow in understanding and effective-
> ness ourselves in order both to proclaim and live the Gospel.[72]

A second statement is incorporated in an article by George Muedeking,
quoting Morris Sorenson, the Executive Director of the ALC Division
of World Mission: "But there has been a significant change in missionary methods," Sorenson observes. "The ALC clearly defines its
mission obedience now in relationship to the local expression of the
body of Christ." That is, the ALC deliberately sets out "to provide
enabling personnel to the national churches. It is no longer 'our field'
or 'our work'," Sorenson adds. "It is rather the mission of the Church—
the responsibility of all of God's people, particularly those who are
God's people in a particular place."[73] In addition to magazines, Lutheran denominations have published a wide variety of handbooks,
study guides, brochures, and booklets aimed at educating the Lutheran
public to such missiological issues as violence, minority consciousness,
world hunger, ecology, and economic justice—though no Lutheran

publishing house has come close to the record of Orbis Books and Eerdmans in range or quality.[74]

These signs, and others like them in the Lutheran church press, stand as signs of hope. The question before the churches remains whether the Lutheran heritage will be able to make its own unique contribution through a more complete involvement in the various liberation and captivity theologies, and thus through a deeper grasp of the resources of its own evangelical tradition.

The Reality of Grace

If there is to emerge a distinctive Lutheran participation in the emerging missiological consciousness generated by liberation theology today, it can only come through a rediscovery of the realism of justification by faith, that uniquely but not exclusively Lutheran formulation of the Christian life. To distinguish between the gospel and the law as the generating center for mission is not to split theological hairs, nor is it to qualify away the cutting edge of commitment to justice as the specific focus and goal for mission today. Grace and its free, disciplined response provide the sole starting point. Grace is God's everlasting response to humanity's injustice and oppression, and the basis of the possibility of free, incisive response to human evil. Moral rigor, for all of its disciplined good intentions, lacks the stamina provided by the daily experience of grace within the baptized life of dying and rising. Nor does grace allow us to turn inward and forget mission. Suffocating attention to "putting myself together"—that near-whine of so much religious activity today—remains another way of privatizing faith and blocking mission.

How do we understand justification as a word of realism today? To emphasize again the basics, grace is alone a realistic route to the formation of a new people equipped for mission.

The late, controversial American Episcopal Bishop, James Pike, was once asked what was the most quoted Bible verse. He replied, "I suppose that it is the golden rule of Matthew 7:12, 'So whatever you wish that men would do to you, do so to them.'" But he went on to say, "I wish it were instead John 3:16, 'For God so loved the world that he gave . . .' because this passage far more expresses the heart of the biblical message." Luther is once supposed to have remarked that if a person was able to distinguish between law and gospel he deserved

then and there to be awarded a doctorate in theology. The confusion
of the two lies at the root of much of our ineffectiveness in mission.
From the beginning God is known as a God who redeems. Both the
Old and New Testaments begin with the gospel—what God has done
as Redeemer and Creator. Law, in the sense of ethical codes and not
as Torah, follows as the response of God's free and forgiven people.
Here, one must believe, lies the realistic power for mission as witness,
service, and fellowship. The tension between freedom and discipline
as response was stated succinctly by Luther:

> A Christian is a perfectly free lord of all, subject to none;
> A Christian is a perfectly dutiful servant of all, subject to all.[75]

If what was said before about Galatians is correct, the task before
the churches may not be to recover the old morality, as many see it.
The problem may lie today at the point of discerning the ambiguities
of sinful existence within the larger racial and economic injustices—
naturally without denying the reality of individual wrong. It could be
argued that one of the chief causes of our churches' seeming ineffectiveness in speaking and acting with evangelical purpose in the present
generation is not primarily due to a loosening of the old morality, but
rather to the dominant legalistic bent of "American religion" and its
failure fully to grasp the implications of life under grace for a world of
tyranny and imbalance. In short, legalism makes mission captive to
the status quo.

Here we might learn from an Indian writer about the nature of legalism. T. K. Thomas has described with penetrating insight the effects
of legalistic Christianity upon one segment of the Indian church—a
description not unfamiliar to those Americans who have read the sociological critics of American Christianity in the 1960s—Marty, Berger,
Winter, Lenski, Wilmore, Littell, and others. Thomas's remarks are
prompted by his reflection upon the Malayalam novel, *Ara Nazhika
Neram* (Half an Hour) by Parappuram, a novelist of Kerala. The
central figure of the book is an old Syrian Christian, proud of his
traditions and community. But, comments Thomas, "in him I recognized myself and my people . . . all caught and held in the besetting
web of *Syrianity*." Syrianity (implies Thomas, referring to the Syrian
Christians of India) is a religion of legalism more akin to the faith of
the Rabbis than to Christianity. Thomas describes the hero of the
novel in telling terms:

> He was a loyal member of his church. The church had its say in the
> hatching and matching of him and later in despatching him as well.
> He knew his Bible and could quote copiously and sonorously from the
> books of the Old Testament. . . . Our friend, in brief, was a typical
> product of Syrian culture and exemplified in his life its peculiar ethos.
> But his understanding of the New Testament was marginal. Neither
> the cross nor the resurrection contributed appreciably to his character.
> He lived under the law, and had not tasted the freedom and joy of
> divine grace.[76]

It is clear from this description, again not far removed from what
could be written of many American Christians, that legalism emerges
on two levels. On the one level, legalism appears as a reduction of
Christianity to a few external moral principles, the ethical content of
which is common to most religions and all people of goodwill. There
can be demonstrated no unique moral content here, whether founded
on the Ten Commandments or the Sermon on the Mount. The distinctiveness of the Christian faith lies not in any of its specific ethical
codes but in its grasp of the gospel as the good news which calls
persons to live under grace. The Christian contribution to liberation,
while to be tactically engaged, does not lie on the level of ethical
codes in any unique sense. We are not calling the shots today even
though we may want to. We have much too much to learn about
what direction into which to fire, particularly as North American
Lutherans. But if we can overcome our depoliticized, privatized, and
at most heretical captivity to justification wrongly understood, and
become engaged as evangelical partners in a mission of liberation,
there is still one other word of realism to be said. Liberation as a
motif for mission risks legalism in its most rigorous form if it loses
either its ability to be self-critical under the knowledge of human
sinfulness or its agitating center. Lutherans, however, can not say such
things smugly or apart from the struggle. Our task is not to sit by and
warn those engaged in liberation in the name of God of the ambiguities
of all human structures. It is a theological point which can only be
made from inside the partnership.

Legalism also appears at another level. Moralistic Christianity leads
quite naturally to the identification of the faith with a particular culture. Thus Christianity becomes Syrianity (to use Thomas's analogy,
or Americanity) or its equivalent form of religion-in-general and other
forms of contemporary tribalism which are neither true to the gracious

roots of faith nor true to what is required in contextual forms of witness and service. Cultural Christianity as a form of legalism is a danger not to be taken lightly. It threatened the covenant faith of Israel and finally reduced it to Pharisaism. It very nearly aborted the mission of early Christianity until Paul made clear the difference between the freedom of the gospel and the cultural legalism of an inherited Jewish past. Many American Christians feel a strong sense of guilt when they face the realities of world poverty as contrasted to general affluence in this country. That sense of guilt is only matched by a feeling of frustration and despair over what can be done.

But grace brings a word of realistic hope to churches turned inward and who want to get out. To begin with grace is not to lift the burden of unease to the point of inaction. But as an answer to helpless guilt, the justified Christian knows two things: (1) there is no need to fear cultural revolution (the loss of our familiar and comforting dominant ethics) because Christ is lord and may be working through others and other social forms; and (2) grace gives the critical perspective necessary to bring our own institutions under the scrutiny of God's judgment and promise of renewal.

Toward Integrity in Mission

How then do we integrate Christian identity as the new community called by God's grace with responsible missionary witness, service, and fellowship? By way of summarizing some of the implications of what has been viewed as the challenge to our established missionary perceptions, I offer three such marks of integrity.

1. *Interdependence with justice.* Integrity in mission requires an exploration of interdependence in its most free and comprehensive dimensions, that is, with both justice and reconciliation as fixed goals. The failure of the development ideal and the consequent growing gap between the rich nations and the poor nations defines the primary area of concern'within international relationships for the years ahead, and forms the background against which our domestic issues must be worked out. World hunger, poverty, and oppression are not the exclusive property of missiologists or of the political left. The test of our own political and economic future is likely to be whether we are able to respond creatively to the challenge of the development debacle. The problems cannot be solved in isolation. Inflation, employment,

the energy shortage, and dwindling natural resources—described in the chapter by Dr. Lee Snook—impinge upon North Americans precisely because our domination of these resources (taken so long as a natural right) is now under challenge. Underdevelopment in the largest part of the world must be seen as the reverse side of overdevelopment in our part of the world. Thus liberation of the economic order becomes squarely a matter of interdependence. As Dr. Samuel Parmar has said, "If salvation of the affluent is seen in freedom from the dominance of too much, that of the poor nations must be seen as freedom from the domination of too little."[77]

The so-called development problem comes to a focus in China. As George Plagenz wrote in a recent Scripps-Howard release, the question is how to account for the widespread practice of virtue and the absence of vices in an antireligious society of many millions, while "religious" nations are sick from overdoses of violence, greed, injustice, selfishness, prejudice, pornography, crime, drugs, and weapons. Or to widen the issue, the question is how to respond to a society which has apparently produced a workable solution to underdevelopment by breaking, as other Third-World nations have not been able to do, centuries of oppressive dependency. Once more, then, in matters of social and economic analysis, the Christian task of justice becomes an interdependent task, even in matters of defining the shape of service in the world. In this matter, but in quite a different context, Ernst Käsemann once remarked, "Contemporary theology is still having to pay for the fact that it is still a victim of the heritage or curse of idealism to a greater degree than it cares to admit. It could have learned as much from Marxism as it did from Kierkegaard and would have then been unable to go on assigning the absolutely decisive role to the individual."[78] (He is of course referring to Western theology, not contemporary Latin American liberation theology.)

Quoting Käsemann at this point perhaps can help lead us to the root of the issue, namely, the question of the doctrine of humanity. Justification, as he notes elsewhere, does not hold a subordinate place in Paul's theology nor can it be understood in simply individualistic terms. Paul witnesses to the reality of the new creation in Jesus Christ, a reality in which he perceives salvation in Jesus Christ to be a word of grace for the whole person in the whole of society, and the basis for Christian service in the world under the cross. "Paul's doctrine of justification means that under the sign of Christ, God becomes Cosmocrator, not merely Lord of the believing individual or the god of a cult. . . ."[79] Salvation itself thus may be seen as grounded in *interdependence*: interdependence among the people of God, whose mission is dependent upon the sending God to act interdependently in the world. Once more identity and service may seem to be interrelated. The question of mission is at root theological and thus also at root social-communal. Churches east and west, north and south, must ask together: Can we appropriate the gift of justification so that our churches and institutions will have the stamina and commitment to present the gospel as the dynamic source for the renewal of individuals and societies?

What specifically may North Americans learn from the Third World about interdependence in mission today? Let me mention just two points among many others that could be named.

First, *we may learn that God may be calling others than Americans or Westerners today as his instruments of salvation.* We are so used to the idea of mission going from "us to them" (a historically understandable fact and indeed a mark of past faithfulness, as we have remarked), that we scarcely think that it may not be possible for our North American ingenuity to solve the problems of the imbalance of wealth between the rich and the poor, or to meaningfully address the revolutionary situations emerging as a result of this increasing imbalance. We may be called upon today to learn of our captivity to our standard of living. Our own culture may not have the resources to provide a model for healthy, reconciling, loving societies. The minority churches of Asia may teach us again about how to care for the community through their concern for family and the church. The growing political might of the Third World, while threatening because of its challenge to our right to consume, may provide a new political milieu to deal realistically with the problem of economic imbalance. North Americans may not be able because of captivity to affluence to reduce their standard of living voluntarily or support justice when it threatens our affluence—"pork barrel" politics are too real and perhaps inevitable.[80] Release from the domination of overabundance may come as a gift— God's gift we may believe—through shifts in global power. Many Americans naturally enough fear such changes. Others, concerned about global poverty, have reached intolerable frustration levels: "But what can we do?" is the question often asked. The answer may be, "There is little you can do. You can await the gift that is coming from outside, and meanwhile try not to get in the way!" Of course, one must not become romantic at this point. The poor and oppressed of the world by themselves are no more or less sanctified than the rich. We all live by grace. But the poor may be grasping new insights into the radical nature of the gospel for today, hidden from those for whom a vision of change for justice is blocked by self-interest. And the historical forces now apparently in motion, while not excusing North Americans from responsible action, may be one way of underscoring that God's salvation in history still comes as under the sign of grace, a witness we may hear by declaring our interdependence. And we may be released from an obsession with our own doing as the ultimate doing. Even in this way, justification by faith may become the dynamic center for mission.

North Americans may learn a second thing from the Third World about interdependence in mission. *It may become clear that God may be using ecumenical realities to bring change.* I do not speak primarily of North American ecumenical realities. Ecumenism in the United States by and large has either been wildly polemical or hopelessly dull. It is otherwise in many Third-World settings. The difference is to be found in the reason for ecumenical sharing. In North America we have dulled the edge of ecumenical realities by a concentration upon limpid fellowship ("let's get together for Thanksgiving service") or on bureaucratic structures. In many Third-World nations ecumenical realities are vital and meaningful because they concentrate on *mission.* Not that the ecumenical bureaucracies are absent in Asia, Africa, and Latin America—they are there, often heavily subsidized and smelling vaguely of nepotism. But when ecumenical encounter arises out of the need for shared witness, service, and fellowship—as it does among the Mizo churches of Northeast India and as it came alive in the program of theological education in Tamilnadu in Southeast India—then mission breathes life into what otherwise may have become over-subsidized dead bones. We have much to learn about dying to self and uniting with others in a common mission of the redeemed. For such integrity, interdependence is indispensable.

One attempt to give focus to interdependence in mission was the 1973 program which brought eight overseas churchmen to the United

States both to reflect critically upon what they saw and to educate American Lutherans to mission on six continents. Sponsored by the USA National Committee of the Lutheran World Federation and the three largest Lutheran denominations, a report of the project was published under the title, *We Declare our Interdependence.* One purpose of the project was summarized in the following sentences: "Another new direction of the past decade has been in the flow of speaking and listening. Church and mission leaders of the traditional *sending* continents were learning that they needed to hear what Christians of the traditional *receiving* lands were saying to them."[81]

2. *Waiting witness.* Integrity in mission means learning to live as waiting witnesses, dependent upon God's grace and thus released for service. Jacques Ellul, perhaps more than most conciliar theologians today, calls the church to a radical waiting upon God. At first glance he presents an extreme position, almost a reactionary reading of political and liberation theologies. At the Uppsala Assembly of the World Council of Churches in 1970, for example, he spoke a strong word against the humanization motif so dominant there. But perhaps his extreme position contains a note of needed warning, though his word cannot be accepted by most Christians as the only final word. In his book, *Hope in Time of Abandonment,* he speaks of the literal silence of God in history and of the church as a bad orchestra playing a poor performance of fine music.[82] Hope does not arise from any certainty of the future nor of concrete signs in history, he writes, and thus "theology of hope" and "political activism" offer no possibilities for faithful witness. He seeks to recall Christians to only three responses: *waiting* (not with expectations of change but in the spirit of Maranatha as an SOS); *prayer* (not because we are to expect a reply, but because God has commanded it); and *realism* (not a balancing of pessimism and optimism, but with the rigor of those who say with Abraham, "Here am I"). Hope, in short, is to be found alone in the radical promise of God.

More can and must be said about mission than what Ellul says, if what we have discerned about the kingdom as a present sign of God's future is to determine our witness and service. And yet that word of radical grace must be heard, and that word of radical realism applied to all our imperfect efforts of humanization and liberation. What might that word of waiting mean for churches in search of integrity in mission today? Let me suggest just two things.

First, perhaps Ellul's somewhat depressing summons to waiting may remind us that *liberation must first of all begin with us, individually and locally*. In the Bible, God's liberation of Israel from Egypt and Babylon is always seen first of all as God's redeeming love for his people. In the New Testament too, liberation is always a liberation from the powers that hold persons in bondage (disease, demons, darkness, wrath, sin, the law, death). In short, God's liberating salvation is a new creation experienced as a necessary *precondition* for liberating service in the world. In Old Israel as in the New this redemptive act of forming an elect community in grace as always *for* the many, but always *through* the community of the redeemed (not only, of course, through individuals). Such language may sound like sheer withdrawal. But it is not. The gifts of the Spirit are first released within the company of those God has called. Not every word of human hope is a word of salvation. If Christians cannot believe that good news or comprehend it, if we cannot first die to self, then any attempt at participation in the larger struggle for the liberation of the poor and oppressed will flounder. The church's role in liberation is first of all to be the church. And it is first of all to be the church where we are, experiencing God's renewing grace in our local congregations and communities. Mission in a global or evangelistic sense will naturally help us learn to know what it means to the church. The dynamic inherent in the tension between inner renewal and outer mission is not a matter of chronological ordering but of evangelical priorities. Neither the Third-World church nor the church of the West can help the other in their interdependent task without each first becoming waiting witnesses.

To wait carries a second obligation, the matter of didache. Franklin Littell has taught the American churches to see themselves as "younger churches," beset with all of the problems of new Christians and thus in need of disciplining and nurture. The teaching and equipping ministry of the churches remains of highest priority, for it will yet be decided whether our American churches achieve a new self-understanding of their identity as the people of God and thus release life and energy for the task of mission or whether as Littell remarks, "sink back to the sullen religion of a declining minority with eyes fixed on the past."[83] The difference between a missiologically impotent culture-faith and critical openness to the new demands of mission with integrity lies at the point of faithfulness in Christian education. There are at least five key elements in our Lutheran heritage which, if appropriated in a disciplined way, promise faithful and redemptive foundations for mission. (1) Justification by grace through faith, not as an otherworldly goal but also as a here-and-now deliverance from self-justification and bondage to the powers of oppression and sin. (2) Baptism as the experience of grace which frees us for repentance, mutual admonition, newness of life, self-criticism, and mission. (3) The Lord's Supper as a sign of the new community of Christ, called and nourished by God, shaped by the sacrifice of Christ, and equipped to be the suffering, crucified community in the world. (4) A mutual ministry which may involve controversy and participation in controversial enterprises, but always within the context of prayer in the name of Jesus which frees us to disagree with each other within the family of humanity, but which also declares our reconciliation in Christ. (5) The eschatological hope of eternal life which means we can trust the Lord of history. We need not run scared. We may be free to risk being wrong.[84]

3. *Invitation to vocation.* Integrity in mission remains an invitation to become makers of history, to become a people among whom the transforming reality of God's reign is to be found in affirmation of our critical vocation as God's new humanity. Denis Goulet, an American, Roman Catholic Christian, trained as a political scientist in Brazil and now applying his critical skills to the study of development theory at the Center for the Study of Development and Social Change in New York, has written of the agonizing tension Christians face in defining mission: "How can they be present in history without abdicating their specific witness to a transcendent absolute beyond history?"[85] That question describes the dilemma of the Christian as he waits in witness and yet is invited to become a participant in human efforts for social change. That, too, is the dilemma we spoke of earlier in terms of the humanization debate. Goulet's analysis confirms the tension we have tried to hold between affirming the priority of grace and yet declaring the necessity of positive strategy of Christian action in the world. What might such concrete evangelical action mean within the future of mission?

To turn to Goulet once more, he discerns the need for three new types of ministry.[86] The first type he calls "prophets of development," Christians known for their actions as well as their theological writings. Among this group he names such persons as Camilo Torres, Dom

Helder Camara, Paulo Freire, Emilio Castro, and Gustavo Gutierrez. Such prophets understand the contextualization of the gospel in terms of its rootedness in present-day socioeconomic realities. Goulet's second type may be seen to be emerging in political leaders whose view of development is linked to Christian faith—such persons as Julius Nyerere, Leopold Senghor, the late Tom Mboya, and others. The third type are *development scholars*—Barbara Ward is one example—who are not preachy moralizers but persons able to combine authentic Christian insight with technical competence in economic and sociological analysis.[87] Goulet himself belongs to this third type, though he is too modest to make the claim for himself. The direction for the future of mission hereby indicated calls for people trained to work across disciplines in teams, and cross-culturally. The Lutheran World Federation's Commission on Studies has formed several teams of this nature. For at least two decades the American churches have mounted efforts at training people for specialized ministries in urban areas and hospitals often utilizing teams of ordained and laypersons If the dependency crisis indeed does define the shape of our human struggle for the future, it would seem to require pioneers to emerge from the Lutheran churches to rise to the challenge of this task, just as in the past others in faithfulness gave their lives to more traditional forms of ministry and missionary service.

What we must struggle to define is a new form of obedience in mission appropriate to our day, fully interdependent and increasingly ecumenical if the needs of mission are to be met. If pioneering in mission once primarily meant crossing geographical frontiers to bring the gospel to a different land, it may still require that today but also three new forms of pilgrimage. Movement in *space* needs to be no longer one-directional but multidirectional. Pilgrimage in *quality* requires new levels of critical theological reflection. And pilgrimage in *time* means to claim the promise of God's future as lord of history. To be radical, literally, is to "go to the roots." It is to the roots of our heritage that American Lutherans may turn as we seek to become responsible to our own time.

Whatever else Lutheran churches in the United States become and achieve, little will be done that is meaningful if not done under the critical review of our biblical and confessional traditions, and through informed concern for the world. There, one must believe, we shall find the resources to affirm anew for our own day the kind of vigorous contextuality that will enable us to become churches of integrity in mission.

NOTES

1. 1 Cor. 5:7–8; Gal. 5:25; and the subjunctive reading of Rom. 5:1 (RSV note, "let us have peace").

2. Told by Peter Ritner, *The Death of Africa* (New York: Macmillan, 1960, pp. vii–viii.

3. Barbara Ward, "Commentary" in Encyclical Letter of His Holiness, Pope Paul VI, *On the Development of People* (New York: Paulist Press, 1967), p. 6.

4. It has been noted frequently by social historians that the concept of white or Aryan supremacy did not arise until the colonial movement was well underway, linked thereby to the growing economic dominance of the colonial powers. Racial conflict as such between the English and Indians, for example, did not exist in the early stages of English encroachment into India. It arose with the opening of the Suez Canal when British wives began to be able to join their entrepreneur husbands, the interest of domestic bliss thus forcing for the first time questions of social status between the Indian and the British. For a contemporary critique see Poikail John George, "Racist Assumptions of the 19th-Century Missionary Movement," *International Review of Mission* 59 (1970): 271–84, who discusses the relationship between colonialism and racism.

5. *Time*, 25 March 1974.

6. Theodore H. White, *The Making of the President, 1972* (New York: Atheneum, 1973). This and the other quotations in the paragraph from pp. xi–xvii.

7. Arne Sovik, *Salvation Today* (Minneapolis: Augsburg Publishing House, 1973), p. 48.

8. Peter Beyerhaus calls the WCC Uppsala statement on humanization as the goal of mission "nothing less than the bankruptcy of responsible missionary theology"; "Mission and Humanization," *International Review of Mission*, 60 (1971): 21. Cf. Peter Beyerhaus, *Missions: Which Way? Humanization or Redemption* (Grand Rapids: Zondervan Publishing House, 1971). Beyerhaus speaks generally for the evangelical conservative movement which has widely endorsed "The Frankfurt Declaration" as a counterstatement to the Uppsala Assembly's focus on humanization. See pp. 107 ff. for the text of the declaration.

9. Rosemary R. Ruether, *Liberation Theology* (New York: Paulist Press, 1972), pp. 180–81.

10. Among Latin American liberation theologians, José Porfirio Miranda has carried out the most searching attempt to understand the Bible as a protest against institutional dehumanization, in *Marx and the Bible: A Critique of the Philosophy of Oppression*, trans. John Eagleson (New York: Orbis Books, 1974).

11. Frederick Herzog, *Liberation Theology* (New York: Seabury Press, 1972). As against the liberal activists, Herzog argues that the "problem with white Christianity is not that it does not do enough . . . but that it does not have power enough to do effectively whatever it does" (p. ix). He believes that *secular Christianity* failed to argue its claims with regard to the poor and oppressed, omitting the "wretched of the earth" (Fanon) as the starting point for its theology.

Similarly, he sees *process theology* as an academic argument about the possibility of transcendence when, again, the proper starting point of theology ought to be the realities of poverty and oppression. My former colleague, Aharon Sapsezian, Associate Director of the TEF, has passed this biting critique of "academic" theology: "Mediocrity is not only the result of too little intellectual labor, but also of exclusive intellectualization."

12. Rubem A. Alves, "Christian Realism: Ideology of the Establishment," *Christianity and Crisis* 33, 17 September 1973, p. 175. Cf. Jürgen Moltmann, "Political Theology," *Theology Today* (April 1971), pp. 6–23.

13. José Miguez Bonino, *Doing Theology in a Revolutionary Situation*, ed. William H. Lazareth, Confrontation Books (Philadelphia: Fortress Press, 1975), pp. 86ff.

14. Michael Harrington more than a decade ago called attention to the irony of hidden poverty in American society in *The Other America: Poverty in the United States* (Baltimore: Penguin Books, 1964). With respect to global poverty, James Lamb has charged, "America is profoundly illiterate" with regard to any critical understanding of third world domination and oppression at the hands of the rich world." In Denis Goulet and Michael Hudson, *The Myth of Aid* (New York: An IDOC Book, 1971), p. 7. In both cases, social realities are hidden not only because of malicious intent but also because they remain hidden on the experiential level to the "illiterate" rich or powerful.

15. This is true with respect to American Protestantism in the United States. As Franklin H. Littell has noted in his *From State Church to Pluralism* (New York: Doubleday Anchor Books, 1962), the idea that the American people were once Christian and have subsequently declined is false. The growth of Protestantism in North America was due to a vigorous mission of evangelism and growth among largely non-churched populations. Hence Littell speaks of the "triumph of home missions" in the nineteenth century: "the most successful century of missions and accession of 'new Christians' anywhere at any time in church history" (p. 98). Later in the same book, Littell describes the "flowering of foreign missions" in the early twentieth century as a time when "world-view and missionary passion were still held in tight span." He depicts the period as a time "before the larger churches lost their discipline and sense of mission" (pp. 130–31). Intermingled with a sense of mission rooted in disciplined Christian identity there also emerged ideas of mission associated with themes in American democratic faith, the idea that America itself has a mission to the world—and eventually such inauthentic culture-faith grounding for "mission" yielded tragic results in Vietnam and other forms of noncritical American expansionism following World War II. Earl H. Brill traces this development in a helpful study booklet *The Future of the American Past* (New York: Seabury Press, 1974), pp. 26–37.

16. M. M. Thomas, *Salvation and Humanization* (Madras: The Christian Literature Society, 1971), p. 2.

17. But under a wide variety of images and language: kingdom of God (Synoptics); life (John); the new being in Christ as a partaker of God's new age now and as a witness to its future (Paul). For an excellent review of biblical eschatologies and contemporary eschatological discussion, see Hans Schwarz, *On the Way to the Future* (Minneapolis: Augsburg Publishing House, 1972).

18. Edward Pfeiffer, *Mission Studies* (Columbus: Lutheran Book Concern, 1931), p. 276.

19. Joachim Jeremias, *The Central Message of the New Testament* (London: SCM, 1965), pp. 57–66.

20. See the discussion in John Reumann, "Creatio, Continua et Nova (Creation, Continuing and New)," in *The Gospel as History*, ed. Vilmos Vajta (Phila-

delphia: Fortress Press, 1975), pp. 97–98. Also, Roy A. Harrisville, "Bultmann's Concept of the Transition from Inauthentic to Authentic Existence," in *Kerygma and History,* ed. Carl E. Braaten and Roy A. Harrisville (New York: Abingdon Press, 1962); and Jeremias, *Central Message,* pp. 61ff.

21. The *aparchē* ("first fruits") of Rom. 8:23 and the *arrabon* ("down-payment" or "pledge" of what is to come) of 2 Cor. 1:22, 5:5 and Eph. 1:14.

22. Rolf Syrdal, *To the End of the Earth* (Minneapolis: Augsburg Publishing House, 1967), pp. 3–4.

23. The helpful comment of Denis Goulet on the question of reforming institutions or converting people: "Making everyone good does not necessarily result in a just society; conversely, adopting good institutions does not guarantee that a society will be just." *A New Moral Order: Development Ethics and Liberation Theology* (New York: Orbis Books, 1974), p. 113.

24. Rubem A. Alves, "Christian Realism: Ideology of the Establishment," p. 175: "Christian utopianism (and I use this expression in a positive sense) is not a belief in the possibility of a perfect society but rather the belief in the nonnecessity of this imperfect order."

25. F. Dean Lueking, "The Local Church," *The Future of the Christian World Mission: Studies in Honor of R. Pierce Beaver,* ed. William J. Danker & Wi Jo Kang (Grand Rapids: Eerdmans, 1971), p. 119.

26. Thomas, *Salvation and Humanization,* p. 2.

27. From selections of an address printed in Sovik, *Salvation Today,* pp. 99–100.

28. Ibid., pp. 5–6.

29. Thomas, *Salvation and Humanization,* pp. 42ff.

30. J. M. Lochmann, "Radical Secularity and Radical Grace," *Christian Century* 87, no. 30 (29 July 1970):911–14.

31. From a selection in Karl H. Hertz, ed., "Problems of Dualism in a Complex Society," *Two Kingdoms and One World: A Sourcebook in Christian Social Ethics* (Minneapolis: Augsburg Publishing House, 1976), pp. 327–28, originally published in Philip Hefner, ed., *The Scope of Grace* (Philadelphia: Fortress, 1964), pp. 221–22.

32. Ibid., p. 344.

33. Ibid., p. 324. Cf. the epigram of Raymond Panikkar in *Worship and Secularization* (New York: Orbis Books, 1973), p. 1: "Only worship can prevent secularization from becoming inhuman, and only secularization can save worship from being meaningless."

34. Reumann, "Creatio, Continua et Nova (Creation, Continuing and New)," pp. 84–91, in an analysis of Old Testament tradition confirms creation never attained the status of an independent doctrine but remained under the formative impact of a covenant-related redemptive perspective.

35. Ibid., p. 91.

36. Ibid., p. 82, where the passages are cited as evidence of an alternative tradition in which creation not salvation may lie at the heart of the missionary appeal reported by Luke.

37. But the appeal to creation in this passage is used by Paul to state that "observation of created life is sufficient (only) to show that creation does not provide the key to its own existence." C. K. Barrett, *A Commentary on the Epistle to the Romans* (London: A. & C. Black, 1967), p. 35.

38. Stephen Neill, *A History of Christian Missions* (London: Penguin Books, 1964), p. 18.

39. Paulo Freire, *Pedagogy of the Oppressed,* trans. Myra Bergman Ramos (New York: Herder & Herder, 1968), esp. pp. 52ff.

40. The biblical roots for noexploitative care of the earth provide a more positive base than the "threat and scare" approach of much of the contemporary popular writings on ecology and global poverty, or the self-interest motif which many Third World people detect in such Western efforts at limiting growth as the Club of Rome reports. Though variously interpreted in differing strands of biblical tradition, there is a consistent story of a good God who claims his creation through his redemptive acts and sets new people in his image to care. The Old Testament framework is largely that of responsible vocation, with the law as the sign of God's covenant (redemptive) love. Grace as prior to the law also informs Jesus' ministry as the bringer of the kingdom and life, grace always the base for ethics. Grace as prior to law and as the dynamic which makes effective responsible service to neighbor centrally informs Paul not only in his major epistles where justification is to the fore (Galatians and Romans), but in his other writings as well. There appears to be an institutionalization of grace which sets in during postapostolic times, reflected in many of the Pastoral and General Epistles. But it can be argued that the emergence of canon, creed, bishop, and liturgy are not simply the first stage of a new legalism, but that these developments emerge as normative responses to the kerygma and thus preserve in the community the inner dynamic of grace and response (identity and service).

41. Cf. Adolf Harnack's comment: "Christianity never lost hold of its innate principle; it was, and it remained a religion for the sick." *The Mission and Expansion of Christianity,* trans. and ed. James Moffatt (New York: Harper Torchbooks, 1961), p. 109. Harnack develops at some length how "love and charity" informed the preaching and service of the early church. He writes from an idealistic position and thus inadequately of the kergymatic dynamic for such service. It is also significant he speaks of mission as "for" and not "of" the poor and sick, a shift in language which liberation theology makes central in its challenge of older, paternalistic forms of Christian service. On this point, see the critique developed below.

42. Quoted from an article titled "We Bridged the Ocean," printed in a special feature insert, "Through Church Windows," p. 3, in *Lutheran Standard,* 110, no. 18 (May 3, 1952), inserted between pp. 8–9.

43. Paul Cavadino, *Get Off Their Backs!* (Oxford: A Haslemere Group and Third World first publication, 1972), pp. 3–4.

44. Peter Adamson, "A Population Policy and a Development Policy are One and the Same Thing," *New Internationalist* no. 15 (May, 1974), pp. 7–9 cites a number of recent studies which show that "the birth rate only falls significantly for the majority of the people." This view is related but not identical to the Marxist ideological assumption that capitalistic exploitation and not overpopulation is the cause of world poverty—a point at least partly justified by the new model of development in China which places a premium on human development at the local level and not upon economic growth as such. In its ideological form, however, one must conclude that the point is unrealistic. India, Sri Lanka, and Bangladesh, for example, badly need increased food production and employment but find gains in these areas erased by population growth. Again both economic-cultural revolution and population limitation need to be seen as two lines on the same vicious circle of cause and effect.

45. Cavadino, *Get Off Their Backs!,* p. 2.

46. For general documentation on the development question see especially the publication of the World Council of Churches, *Towards a Theology of Development* (1970)—an annotated bibliography. For sources critical of developmentism see in particular: Charles Elliott, *The Development Debate* (London: SCM,

1971); Goulet and Hudson, *The Myth of Aid*; Teresa Hayter, *Aid as Imperialism* (London: Penguin Books, 1973); C. I. Itty, "Are We Yet Awake?", *Ecumenical Review*, 26 (1974):6–20; C. T. Kurien, *Poverty and Development* (Madras: CLS, 1974); and B. N. Y. Vaughan, *The Expectation of the Poor* (London: SCM, 1972).

47. Goulet and Hudson, *The Myth of Aid*, p. 8.

48. An approach developed by Paulo Freire and reported especially in his *Pedagogy of the Oppressed*, esp. pp. 52ff.

49. Printed in Hertz, *Two Kingdoms and One World*, pp. 325–26, originally in *Love for the Neighbor in Luther's Theology* (Minneapolis: Augsburg Publishing House, 1963), pp. 69–74.

50. James Lamb charges that "developmentism" as an approach to global imbalance "is nonthreatening and presents no serious problems of guilt or historical responsibility" to the developed nations. In Goulet and Hudson, *The Myth of Aid*, p. 9.

51. Cited in Hertz, *Two Kingdoms and One World*, p. 345, 344–45, originally in *The Future of God* (New York: Harper & Row, 1969), pp. 147–48.

52. J. G. Davies, *Worship and Mission* (London: SCM, 1967), p. 22. On this point Davies also cites H. H. Rowley, *The Missionary Message of the Old Testament* (London: Carey Kingsgate Press Ltd., 1944) and *Israel's Mission to the World* (Toronto: Macmillan, 1939).

53. See Isa. 42:1–12 and especially 49:1–6. Compare in particular the parallel prophetic passage of Isa. 2:2–4 and Mic. 4:1–4, where the emphasis lies on movement toward Jerusalem, "Come, let us go up to the mountain of the Lord."

54. Davies, *Worship and Mission*, p. 25. Compare Robert Martin-Achard, *A Light to the Nations* (Edinburgh: Oliver and Boyd, 1962), p. 75; and J. Blauw, *The Missionary Nature of the Church* (Grand Rapids: Eerdmans, 1974), p. 66.

55. This was true even for the "proselytes" and "God-fearers," those converts to Judaism in the Hellenistic period. Though Hellenistic Judaism did indeed develop differing attitudes to the law than Palestinian Jews, conversion to Judaism always meant assimilation into the culural-religious legal norms of Judaism and not the development of a truly pluralistic (Hellenized or other) community as later developed among Christians. The difference lay in this: for Jewish proselytes Jerusalem and its religious norms remained determinative in both a geographical and cultural sense, thus limiting the emergence of a fully universalistic Jewish movement among the Gentiles.

56. Even the book of Jonah, rightly seen as a caricature of the militant particularism of postexilic Judaism, seems to maintain the geographical centrality of Jerusalem as both 1:9 and the prayer of chapter 2 indicate.

57. Blauw, *The Missionary Nature of the Church*, p. 66; and Davies, *Worship and Mission*, p. 25.

58. Ferdinand Hahn, *Mission in the New Testament*, SBT 47 (London: SCM, 1965), p. 39. See also Joachim Jeremias, *Jesus' Promise to the Nations* SBT 24 (London: SCM, 1968).

59. Hans Conzelmann, *Theology of Saint Luke*, trans. Geoffrey Buswell (London: Faber & Faber, 1960), p. 214: "Before the time of Luke the missionary task was thought of as a universal one (cf. Mark 13:10), but Luke was the first to build up the picture of a systematic progress of events, the plan of which bears witness to the guidance of God." According to Conzelmann, Luke views the history of salvation in three stages: (1) the period of Israel, culminating in John the Baptist; (2) the period of Jesus' ministry, the "center of history"; (3) the period since the ascension, the period of the church, in which Luke (and the Christian) look back to the period of Jesus as the redemptively unique epoch, and

forward to the future fulfillment. We should note one additional feature about the period of the church. Luke further distinguishes between the foundation period of the apostles and eyewitnesses, and his own—and subsequent—time of witness and mission.

60. For Luke, his narrower use of the title "apostle" appears to give emphasis to the authority of the Twelve in Jerusalem as the basis for the church's unity. Outside of Acts 14:4–14 Luke consistently limits the title to the twelve disciples. In his view, apparently, Paul is not an apostle. He is rather commissioned by the church in Antioch for mission (Acts 13:1–3), but that church itself is under the direction of the Twelve in Jerusalem as 15:4 indicates. This is in contrast to Paul's own view. He considers that he was commissioned directly by the risen Lord (Gal. 1:1, cf. 1 Cor. 15:8 and 2 Cor. 5:20), freely calls himself an apostle and so names James (1 Cor. 15:7). Other evidences of the continuing centrality of Jerusalem and the Twelve in Luke's view may be noted: (1) In Luke's account of the dispute over freedom for Hellenistic Christians he stresses the unity with Jerusalem by reporting much more of a compromise over the solution (Acts 15:19–20, vs. Gal. 2:10). (2) In Luke's presentation of the pattern of Paul's missionary "journeys," he gives an impression that Paul kept checking back with the Twelve in Jerusalem (Acts 9:26, 15:4, 18:22 and 21:15), whereas Paul insists on independence from Jerusalem on the basis of evangelical freedom (Gal. 1–2), while expressing unity based on common kerygmatic tradition (1 Cor. 15:1ff.) and concern for the welfare of the poor in Jerusalem (2 Cor. 8–9, cf. Gal. 2:10, Rom. 15:25).

61. It was not a major emphasis among the churches of the German and Scandinavian Reformation until the eighteenth century, nor among the Dutch and English until about the same time. Rolf Syrdal, *To the End of the Earth*, pp. 106–11, lists four reasons often cited by church historians for the lack of mission beyond the borders of the nations of the European Reformation during this period: (1) political infighting among the Protestants and with Roman Catholics until the Peace of Westphalia in 1648 drained Protestant energies and made sheer survival the chief issue; (2) Protestants had no possibility of physical contact outside Europe until the defeat of the Spanish Armada (1588) and the subsequent rise of trade and colonial enterprises among non-Hispanic (and thus non-Roman Catholic) nations; (3) the emergence of theocratic states on the principle of *cujus regio, eius religio* ("he who rules determines the religion") undercut the idea of mission beyond one realm to another governed by a ruler of a different religious faith, while at the same time (4) this slogan later promoted the principle that the colonial rulers had the right to insist upon their faith as the official faith (as in Indonesia, where the first Roman Catholic Christians, converted by the Portuguese, were forced to become Dutch Reformed Christians by their later colonial rulers, or as in India, where the Portuguese at one stage in the sixteenth century forced the ancient Syrian Christians to submit to Rome). There also existed a curious exegesis of Matthew 28, rather common among Lutherans and other Reformation theologians of the sixteenth century, which interpreted the Great Commission as having been completed by the original apostles, all peoples now having had their chance to believe. Syrdal, however, quotes Luther as rejecting this exegesis of Matthew 28. The reasons together indicate how closely missionary expansion was tied to colonial penetration. Samuel Eliot Morrison, *The Oxford History of the American People*, vol. 1 (New York: Mentor Books, 1972), confirms this interpretation by frequently noting how the Spanish and French consistently prohibited any non-Roman Catholic layperson, let alone a Protestant missionary, from residing in their colonial possessions.

62. There is a debate, to be sure, reaching back to the first century, over the nature of God's revelation. To what extent is the gospel God's unique word, a

word which comes from beyond, and to what extent is the gracious work of God known or reflected in human cultures and religions? Lutherans have taken up the question within the categories of the two realms, while others have spoken of special and general revelation. More recently the question has centered on the question of the possibility of what Karl Rahner has termed *anonymous Christianity* within other religions—but even in this concept it is the Christian understanding of grace which is thought to be discerned in those other religions, thus retaining the idea of uniqueness in a way in which, for example, William Ernest Hocking's *Re-Thinking Missions* report of forty-two years ago did not. For a review of Rahner's position see Prudencio Damboriena, S. J., "Aspects of the Missionary Crisis in Roman Catholicism," *The Future of the Christian World Mission*, ed. William J. Danker and Wi Jo Kang (Grand Rapids: Eerdmans, 1971), pp. 73–88. See also Paul Tillich, "Missions and World History," *The Theology of Christian Mission* (New York: McGraw-Hill, 1961), pp. 281–89.

63. The failure to recognize the necessity of contextualization and the historically-conditioned character of Christian confessions leads inevitably to a rigid confessional fundamentalism, the reverse side of culture-faith. Various formulas have been used to express the tension between the universal and particular: unity and diversity, kerygma and didache, gospel and law, the traditions and the Tradition.

64. Martin E. Marty and Dean G. Peerman, "Peoplehood and Particularism," *New Theology No. 9: Theology in the Context of the New Particularisms* (New York: Macmillan, 1972), p. 9.

65. *Theological News Monographs No. 5*, October, 1972 (published by the Theological Assistance Program, Union Biblical Seminary, Yeotmal, Maharashtra, India).

66. See several articles reprinted in *Mission Trends No. 1: Crucial Issues in Mission Today*, ed. Gerald H. Anderson and Thomas F. Stransky, (New York: Paulist Press, 1974). See also *International Review of Mission* vol. 64, no. 254 (April, 1975) for an issue largely devoted to the moratorium question.

67. The contextual character of Paul's writings is sometimes forgotten because of the Protestant tendency to filter Paul through the Confessions, thus leading to a far too heavily doctrinal interpretation of Paul. His letters must be read as writings addressing particular and concrete questions which arose in specific situations.

68. "The Pauline doctrine of justification never took its bearings from the individual, although hardly anyone now realizes this." Ernst Käsemann, *Perspectives on Paul*, trans. Margaret Kohl (Philadelphia: Fortress, 1971), p. 74.

69. Critical opinion remains divided about the question. Most commentators believe the opponents of Paul in Galatia had some connection with Jewish Christians in Jerusalem, perhaps to be identified with those who came from James to Antioch (Gal. 2:12; Acts 15:1), but not as representatives of the Twelve. Johannes Munck contested this view. He argued that Paul's opponents in both Galatia and Corinth were local Gentile or Jewish Christians who distorted the gospel by insisting that the law—Jewish legal tradition, more precisely, as separated from its covenant framework—remained essential. *Paul and the Salvation of Mankind* (London: SCM, 1959). Whatever the case, the main point of Paul's argument is clear. He asserted against these opponents in Galatia that Christians do not need to become Jews in order to become Christians.

70. In Gal. 2:14 Paul is referring to the counter-mission which came to Antioch, a situation probably also described in Acts 15:1. In Antioch as in Galatia the issue was the same and the apostolic reply was consistent: the freedom of the gospel liberates Christians from an alien culture and makes it possible for the Christian faith to be expressed in a variety of cultural forms.

71. *Christian Believing*, Report of the Church of England Doctrine Commission (London: SPCK, 1976).

72. Kent Knutson, "The Mission of the Church," *Lutheran Standard*, 12, 1 (January 4, 1972), p. 13.

73. George Muedeking, "Partnership in Mission," *Lutheran Standard*, 12, 8 (April 18, 1972), p. 17.

74. Two examples of Lutheran publications: José Miguez Bonino, *Doing Theology in a Revolutionary Situation*; Loren E. Halvorson, *Peace on Earth Handbook* (Minneapolis: Augsburg Publishing House, 1976).

75. Martin Luther, *A Treatise on Christian Liberty*, printed in *Works of Martin Luther*, Philadelphia Edition, vol. 2 (Philadelphia: Muhlenberg Press, 1943), p. 312.

76. T. K. Thomas, "A Meeting, A Novel and a Moral," *The Guardian* (India), Sept. 3, 1970, pp. 282–83. Cited also in James A. Bergquist, *The Ten Commandments and Responsible Freedom* (Madras: CLS-ISPCK, 1971), p. 6.

77. Samuel L. Parmar, "The Limits-to-Growth Debate in Asian Perspective," *The Ecumenical Review*, 26 (1974), p. 43.

78. Käseman, *Perspectives*, p. 11.

79. Ibid., p. 75.

80. A pointed illustration of the way American domestic politics undercut wider issues of racial justice internationally may be seen in Republican reaction to Henry Kissinger's call for black majority rule in southern Africa only four days prior to the Texas primary election. *Time Magazine*, 107 (17 May 1976), p. 19 reported: " 'The s.o.b. cost us 100,000 votes,' complained one (presidential) aide. Said another: 'The timing of the Kissinger trip was bad enough. So why did Henry have to be quite so outspoken and provocative in reading the riot act to the Rhodesians?' " Such domestic handling of international issues is not limited to just one of the major American parties, of course.

81. *We Declare Our Interdependence: Report of the Mission on Six Continents Consultation*, USA National Committee of the Lutheran World Federation (October 1973).

82. Jacques Ellul, *Hope in Time of Abandonment*, trans. C. Edward Hopkin (New York: Seabury Press, 1973).

83. Littell, *From State Church to Pluralism*, p. xx.

84. From an unpublished paper by Walter Bouman, Lutheran Theological Seminary, Columbus, Ohio.

85. Goulet, *A New Moral Order*, p. 110.

86. Ibid., pp. 79–108.

87. Ibid., pp. 109ff.

EPILOGUE:
REFLECTIONS ON THE CHURCH EMERGING,
SERVING IN THE WORLD

Satis est. "It is sufficient," Lutherans have always said, "for the true unity of the Christian church that the gospel be preached in conformity with a pure understanding of it and that the sacraments be administered in accordance with the divine word" (Augsburg Confession, Article VII).[1] That simple, ecumenically open definition has kept Lutherans centered on the gospel when treating and doing ecclesiology. It is the gospel of God which identifies, defines, and empowers the church, not organizational form (ancient or modern), types of piety, or even manner of worship.

Satis non est, the world replies today. Such things are "not sufficient" anymore. It is not simply that Lutherans are being asked to define more clearly what "the gospel" is or a "pure understanding of it," and to spell out the forms in preaching and other sacramental manifestations in which it is set forth "in accordance with the divine word." It is rather that a time of great change, with many problems (of which our ancestors never dreamed), is threatening old identities and is telling Lutherans and all Christendom, that the church which exists in all sorts of societies, nations, all sorts of human and natural conditions, must redefine itself anew. It dare not retreat into concepts of an "invisible" church which is the "true" form; it must be measured by its impact and vision for the world and humankind—or prove irrelevant. Churches cannot help but be measured by the human and world situations in which they exist. They are identified today situationally and relationally, as well as by their own "eternal verities."

The four essays in this volume, and the entire LWF ecclesiology study, with its case methodology in forty-six countries worldwide, are

1. Notes appear at the end of the Epilogue.

an attempt to speak in this identity crisis and to the demands for a fuller self-understanding by Christians of that divine-human mission called the ecclesia—whether specifically the ALC, or the Evangelical Lutheran Church in Tanzania, or the LCMS (which, without a hyphen, stands for the Lutheran Church in Malaysia and Singapore).

The fact that theology is here being done so contextually does not mean these Lutherans take their heritage of the centuries lightly, whether since the Reformation in the sixteenth century or since the first Pentecost in Jerusalem and the founding of the universal church. They prize more than ever the confession of the ancient creeds that the body of Christ on earth is "one, holy, catholic, and apostolic." They take seriously the best insights of Christians over the centuries, and especially in recent decades the truth and experience that the church of Jesus Christ must be a servant church, witnessing and suffering. They regard as authoritative the New Testament parameters and central identity of what the ecclesia is according to Scripture, even though they may read the biblical books with greater awareness of the historical settings of those documents and with fuller appreciation of biblical diversity than their ancestors did. They remain committed to what Lutheran forebearers professed, and indeed bring forth for our reexamination what our heritage has insisted on. Thus, for example, Dr. Hefner's essay reminds us about the marks of the church set forth in the "Washington Declaration" of 1920: "every group of professing Christians" which calls itself a church "will seek to express in its own life the attributes of the one, holy, catholic and apostolic church . . .

1. By professing faith in Jesus Christ. . . .
2. By preaching the Word and administering the sacraments. . . .
3. By works of serving love. . . .
4. By the attempt to secure universal acceptance of the truth which it holds and confesses. . . .
5. To accomplish these purposes . . . every such group will maintain the office of the ministry, commanded and instituted by Christ."[2]

Of course, since its inception, the church has been about those tasks and has, in the process, been "coming to identity" constantly. Professor C. F. D. Moule, of Cambridge, has given us an intriguing picture of the followers of Jesus, in the New Testament period, developing through "stages of self-awareness." He portrays the church "explaining itself" as, in light of Jesus himself, worship, use of Scripture, and the experienced perception of the reign of Christ, it becomes God's people emerging—a "new race," yet "Israel" with a world mission.[3] Those early Christians were confronted, on one hand, at times with an anti-Semitic tendency in Christianity which threatened to cut away the "Israel-consciousness of Jesus," as well as, on the other hand, a Judaism (also then emerging in a new pattern) which was anti-Christian, against which, among other things, Christianity had to define itself. For Christians in that situation, writes Professor Moule, "one branch of the stream of identity flows out to cut off those who try to bypass the spiritual heritage of Israel on the way to salvation," while from that stream of identity "its other branch . . . is directed against the anti-Christian Jew who denies that the Church is Israelite at all, or against the extreme Judaizing Christian who will only allow that it is Israelite if it is marked by a rigorous observation of circumcision" (as in Galatia).[4] Further, just as in our day, early Christians too had to develop an identity in the face of political circumstances and economic-social facts. As an illustration of the former, Moule notes "the disastrous war of A.D. 66–70" in Palestine—and some would see the fall of Jerusalem as a formative factor in Christianity second only to Jesus himself and his resurrection[5]—and, in the social realm, what might be called the "middle-classness" of the early church.[6] The point, without arguing it further, is that from the outset Christianity has been "emerging," developing, coming to self-awareness and identity, in the face of the world in which it lives.

SUMMARY

What message for us ecclesiologically do these four essays give in 1977 and beyond? Clearly and overwhelmingly that our understanding of the church, of what we are and do as Christians—and ought to be and do—is being impacted upon by the ecological crisis, the movements stressing human identity (above all, for women), the concreteness of our historical and sociological setting as institutions, and the changing perceptions—yes, demands—in what has been the church's imperative since the Great Commission, namely the mission task.

Ecologically, the world setting, with its catastrophic potential in undifferentiated growth, calls on us not simply to "change our habits a bit" but to reexamine our whole orientation toward "nature" and reality, our image of human identity, and our very way of thinking and talking about God, metaphysically. It is not merely that the "United Wasters of America are a threat to the world population," or that one American consumes the life necessities of fifty persons in India, or "the U.S.A. . . . uses 40% of the world's non-renewable resources,"[7] and our churches are part of this American scene. It is rather, in Dr. Snook's analysis, that only a new view of things, including our Christian view of God, such as is offered by process theology, will suffice to help our dilemmas. The immense questions of "God" and of the cosmos are thus raised.

Humanly speaking, and in theological conversation, the talk nowadays is more and more about "coming to true identity," as a person or in groups, for blacks, Hispanics, and women, among others long downtrodden. Donald Luck's test case, the American woman's movement, confronts us not only with the stark fact of sexism in society generally but in the churches in particular. It is not enough to let women vote at church meetings or be ordained. In the opinion of some theologians in the woman's movement, the situation is so grave that changes must be made which strike at the very fabric of Christianity—ideas of God, revelation, language, sin—while other women thinkers are content to let the experience of liberation they are undergoing serve as a key hermeneutically to the Bible as a book of liberations by God. Professor Luck presses on us the need to take seriously these voices and even to reconsider that "androgynous identity" implied in Genesis 1 and Galatians 3:28. But he also is critical of aspects in the theology from this movement. His own call is for the church to witness "to the manifestation of the genuinely human in the eschatological event of Jesus the Christ" and allow "that witness to find its own redemptive way in human history." His essay thus sets (1) a christological criterion but (2) counsels openness about tomorrow's accents in God's word to us.

In very concrete ways a case study of a U.S. church reminds us of the importance of history and sociological setting. Who we are, derives from the route whence we have come historically and from the placement we have in society, as well as from the gospel and our confessional stance. A good hard look at the Lutheran Church in America jars us away from the vagaries of universal ecclesiology. It makes us take seriously the facts of being the church "in this time and in this place." In Professor Hefner's hands such a study also becomes a meditation on that church's destiny. He sees the LCA as a particular concatenation of unity and pluralism. Its self-understanding, past history, and the very geographical and social location of its members open the LCA to modern currents of knowledge, ecumenism, and American life in a way that no other American church is opened up. "Middle-class-ness" characterizes the LCA and modulates its ministry, structure, and worship, in ways both good and bad. Yet Dr. Hefner is optimistic enough to believe the LCA is not so much a victim of its history and social setting as that there is opportunity to express its basic catholic, Christ-centered faith by reaching out into God's world, following the Spirit, to actualize divine grace. To be "a signal community" embodying the gospel, to and through the middle class (indeed, transcending social placement), is the dream of LCA destiny. Lest this sound too pretentious, like a "theology of glory," one must keep in mind the motifs of "cross" and "kingdom" in its theological resources, which point the church to service, inclusivity, and self-critique. How important is the response of this segment of American Christianity? "Our age is the epoch in which . . . the fate of the world may rest on the middle class's ability and willingness to lay down its life for the world."[8]

Missiologically, too, there is hope, and expectation. Dr. Bergquist's essay certainly makes clear that there are dilemmas and problems with mission. *"Foreign* missions" are gone; indeed, the singular term *mission* must be used, holistically and including us at home. We live in a time of world-interrelatedness (compare the ecological scene), where "dependency" is the watchword. "Development," of nations and churches, which was the aim from roughly 1950 until 1970 in many parts of the world, has been replaced by "liberation" as a theme. Some of the characteristics of liberation theology should especially be compared with notes struck in other essays, including (as liberation does) the following ideas: (1) "one must begin with the concrete human situation"; (2) there is "the possibility of responsible Christian action as a sign of the kingdom in an imperfect world"; (3) the church can be "a model for free persons, a sign of the kingdom within history"; (4) one notes "a 'Christian presence' in wider historical movements promising justice"; and even if (5) it's God's action which originates and sustains, (6) church people must risk conflict for liberation in Christ's name. Indeed churches are divided today not by "polity or doctrine" so much as over "commitment to liberation as a focus for mission." One is tempted to suggest that the old canard is no longer so, that

"Doctrine divides, service unites"; in recent years it has been "service" that divides, at least when it is service to political-social-economic freedom rather than merely to "spiritual liberty." In this new situation—where the saints and members of Old First Church on Main Street, U.S.A., no longer understand what is at stake for the church or humanity in Namibia racially, in Chile or China politically, or with multinational corporations economically—our sense of mission is unclear in a changing world. Dr. Bergquist's own answer is, however, clear: to reexamine, against this agitating background, the full depths of the church's trinitarian faith. Mission with integrity will take the shape of liberation as:

Service	Development and interdependence, in secular realms, with justice	First Article, interpreted redemptively
Witness	Humanization, under the cross; the church = a sign of the kingdom	Second Article
Fellowship	Contextualization; freedom yet unity in the one gospel	Third Article

For each of these elements of mission there is appeal to the biblical basis of the Christian heritage, specifically to the doctrine of "redemptive creation," the christological kerygma in Acts and its implications, and the way the theme of justification crosses cultural frontiers in the Epistle to the Galatians.[9] The Bergquist essay sees signs of hopeful response among American Lutherans as their future witness emerges.

All four essays agree, whether they approach ecclesiology from the standpoint of ecology, human identity, a denomination's historical-social placement, or the universal mission task, that: (1) Our view of the church must be concrete, rooted in our own situation, today. For all the normativeness of Scripture and past confessions, the church must be biblically shaped and confessional *in the scene and context* where God has given its people the task of ministering. (2) The context of the church is *in God's world*—man's world, woman's world, the first, second, and third worlds, the whole gamut of national, natural, and human problems. (3) The role of the church in this world is to be a *servant* church, serving, like its lord. *Synkatabasis*, "coming down together with," "descent," "accommodating oneself to" others—in Latin, *con-de-scensio(n)*—was one of the great words in patristic theology.

In Christ, God came down to man, he who "was in the form of God" taking on "the form of a servant" and emptying himself (*kenosis,* in Greek; Phil. 2:6–7). Such "coming down together with" the world and its problems, all agree, must also mark the church. The list of identifying features for Lutherans compiled by the Strasbourg Institute speaks of "condescension" or "kenotic love which stoops to serve";[10] such an attitude, such actions ought to be characteristic of the church in days to come.

Recognition of the kind of world in which we live is made by each essayist as he (4) underscores *change.* There is change for the worse in the resources of nature known to be still available, and we must change habits and attitudes. There are changes in interpersonal relationships and lifestyles nowadays. Change marks U.S. churches. The LCA is applauded for being "open to change." Mission work has been and is changing, and will continue to. Yet it is striking that all four essayists view these changes not with alarm or despair, but as *opportunity.* Chalk it up to a characteristic of the American psyche, to a commonsense attitude of adaptation to the times, or to a deep and true reflection of the Christian faith—the agitating action in the mechanism of the world moves these observers to view further changes with hope and to hope for further change. God's will is not static and fixed. Even God, it has been suggested, is with the forces of change and freedom, if not himself in the process of change. Finally (5) each essay, in one way or another, asserts a *core identity* for Lutheranism and the church. For all these changes, there are constants to which to hold fast. Most frequently our essayists express this central identity as "the gospel" or (Lutheran shorthand) "justification by grace through faith" or (at least) "love." The essay on mission selects "five key elements in our Lutheran heritage" with which the other writers would seem to agree: (a) justification, (b) baptism, (c) Lord's Supper, (d) ministry, and (e) hope. The propria from the Strasbourg statement should also be compared.[11]

Our essayists are also agreed, I think, that it is not structure, nor even liturgy, which shapes Lutheran identity (however much Lutherans stress worship and prize forms for worship). All four see belief and actions as both important and related, and assess who we are not only by the relation to Christ, "in Christ," but also by what the church does in the social setting where it is.

It could, in summary, be said that these four essays challenge ecclesiology in terms of process, people, prospects, and purpose. *Process—*
not simply of a brand of contemporary philosophy/theology but in
seeing the church and ourselves in and with the world of nature and
God. What does the kind of thinking here proposed say to us? Is it
a vision of the church, like that in the Epistle to the Ephesians, growing in Christ, filling all in all, a temple structure developing according
to God's pervasive power and plan? *People—*the "coming of age" by
women, and of minorities, and of humanity in general, challenges
church identity to make good on the relation of this phenomenon of
the seventies to the "new humanity" envisioned in verses like Galatians 3:26–28 ("in Christ . . . neither male nor female; for you are
all one").

*Prospects—*the destiny of the LCA is sketched with daring and even,
some may feel, a certain chutzpah. But, given the hardnosed analysis
at times in this essay, often unflattering, is there not a kind of Christian
boldness here, like that of the early believers in Acts with their *parrēsia*
("fearlessness," Acts 4:13, 31), or like those who insisted "We have a
destiny," with God in Christ. *Purpose—*the Great Commission of
Matthew 28:16–20 has always shaped church identity, "to go, baptize,
teach, 'disciplize'. . . ." The Matthean imperatives do not specifically
include all items which traditional missionary work has included, and
a modern list may go far beyond. But that Gospel which is the only
one to use the word *church* (Matt. 16:18; 18:17) is also the only one
to enjoin *mission* so directly and climactically. Perhaps there is also a
note of comfort for us who are so slow to embrace the mission task in
the word Matthew often uses for disciples: *persons of little faith.* We
have faith—but not enough. We are like the eleven on the mountain-
top in Galilee: they "worshiped and they doubted" (28:17).[12] We
who worship, but have our doubts and suffer from weak faith, are being
asked to be the church afresh, with mission purpose and dazzling prospects from God, for peoples throughout the world—a church emerging.

CRITIQUE

The call to such an ecclesiology from these four essays is not without its problems, however. To each essay, questions of one sort or
another can be addressed. The Advisory Committee on Studies of the
USA National Committee, LWF, which set up the study process lead-

ing to this volume, devoted a special meeting on April 9–10, 1976, to a critique of the materials being developed. Concerns of Committee members sometimes led to revisions in a further draft, and in other cases to comments which at their request are included here, to round out the study process called for in the Committee's resolution.

"Ecology" as a topic has led to new insights for the church. One reads the analysis on "The Politics of Resources and Development" (above, pp. 40–54), drawing as it does on the reports to the Club of Rome and other research, with excitement—and alarm. The next part of Dr. Snook's essay about the widening gap between humanity and nature (employing the work of younger theologians like the American Lutheran, H. Paul Santmire), carries the argument further along. Then comes the proposal of process theology as that alternative way of thinking which can help us out of our dilemma. The obvious criticism to such an approach is that the first part has "no theology or Bible" in it, and "the gospel" enters only at the end of the whole essay. A bridge from data to reflection seems missing, and what emerges in conclusion could be mistaken as just a response to the alarmist predictions of the Club of Rome (sometimes corrected in later reports). The "facts" about a crisis in resources are never placed within the framework of a "biblical understanding," nor does theology have a critical function in looking at the data.

A deeper level of concerns about the first essay, however, has to do with biblical theology, gospel, (Lutheran) church, and "revelation" and "God" in connection with "process theology." (1) Are a few quotes from articles by Langdon Gilkey and James Barr sufficient to unseat Scripture and so set aside biblical theology that a totally new metaphysics of reality is needed? Is the Bible's vision of God as Creator otherwise "unintelligible" today? (2) When *gospel* is invoked at the end, what is meant by the term? Obviously, "love," and that is especially associated with the cross, but traditional propria like justification are missing. (3) While the ecological crisis as thus sketched has a lot to say about how we humans need react and think about the world, what are the immediate and direct implications for the church—specifically for Lutheran churches in the U.S.A.? In dealing with global problems, and ultimately with "God," the treatment has not touched base with the concrete and specific ecclesiologically. There are few imperatives. (4) Fear was voiced that such Christian categories as "revelation," "sin," "judgment," and even the distinction between the Creator and his creation (cf. Romans 1:18–32, which labels their identification as idolatry) have been lost in the application of process thought. Process, indeed, is so big an issue as to require special attention below.

The essay on "Human and Church Identity," as originally envisioned, planned to take in far too much material. Its outline dealt with "identity" as a cultural question, an ecclesiastical and a theological one, and then (especially with attention to Lutheran thought) examined church identity "in light of mission to the whole human person." The final version, as written for this volume—while aware of these broader topics and reflecting cultural, psychological, and theological concerns in the opening sections—came to concentrate on the "woman's movement" in America. Even that subject is so multifaceted and—in the hands of its varied proponents—has taken so many turns, that Geneva's emphasis on "empircial data," on studies which are concrete and specific where we live, had to be underscored. Philosophies may need to be treated, but contemporary specifics are to inform the study. While spreading its nets widely in current thought and experiences, this essay did seek to speak in a self-consciously theological and Lutheran way; this the Committee viewed as positive. "Liberation" as a central theme was also always implicit in it, though not uncriticized.

The thesis advanced in this essay is thus that the woman's movement does deserve theological interpretation, church support, but also (at points) correcting, or even opposition, because some proposals within it are a serious challenge to the theological enterprise. The paper seeks participation in the ongoing struggle to discern more clearly "the 'dynamic catholicity' of the christological criterion of both human and church identity." The church is to participate, knowing it is "not the sole locus of God's redemption" or "the exclusive agency of redemption in the world," its witness never final, never absolute. At this point, those who found difficulty from a classical point of view in theology with the position in the first essay would likewise be troubled here: to say the church "can only struggle to speak a faithful word" (p. 127) is not much different than to say that in the process "the church's task is to be faithful to the ministry of the gospel" (p. 75). It is the vision of reality assumed that differs, and use of traditional propria seems more reassuring than a Whiteheadian metaphysic. Exactly how "manifestation of the genuinely human in the eschatological event of Jesus Christ" (p. 127) functions is the needed link not yet spelled out.[13]

As might be expected, the case study in Essay III on the LCA raised problems for the Advisory Committee. Its desire was for a similar treatment concerning other U.S. Lutheran bodies, at least the ALC, but the limitation to one U.S. member church in the LWF had to be accepted pragmatically. The method is on target in terms of what Geneva sought: data are empirical, the case is specific and concrete, conclusions are drawn which could be instructive for other churches. But *is* the method clear? Has it drawn too much on constitutions and related documents and on one recent history of Lutherans in America?[14] History is never simple; so one must ask, Has enough justice been done to its complexities in arriving at the final product? Thus, for example, pietism might be cited as contributing to "openness to American life," and pietism is no monopoly of LCA Lutherans and their predecessor groups. (One may note the number of Norwegian-American Lutherans who have gone into politics. But then the Norwegian strand does not emerge in the LCA-analysis.) Historians would also be tempted to point to the role of a series of able church presidents since Frederick Knubel who have shaped what is today the LCA. And pragmatically, as well as historically, for the ULCA (and still in the LCA) the role of synods (which make up the national church) should not be ignored. Their lifestyles differ, and they are the ones who give life to the national church.

The Advisory Committee also had certain difficulties with the term *middle class* and its applications. The word means different things in different parts of the country and different parts of the world, and must be measured by local standards, whether in Chicago suburbs, rural Kansas, or Puerto Rico. More truly, perhaps, the LCA has middle-class *leadership*, it was suggested, but more *working*-class members, perhaps far more below any theoretical "middle-class" parameters than above it as "wealthy." Question was raised whether this essay in "religious socio-theology" might not be "Defining the LCA—from Illinois," while the picture may look different from South Carolina, South Dakota, or elsewhere—if, indeed, it captures the pluralism even in Illinois. The method runs the danger of descriptive vulnerability, generalizations beyond the data, and difficulty for others to apply conclusions. Above all, is the LCA profile too bright and untarnished, for example, in its picture of inner-city activities? LCA churches are there partly by default: that is where Germans and Scandinavians *once* lived, and there are far more failures than success stories in making Sankt Johannes Kirche serve blacks or Hispanics. Finally, what precisely is meant by that phrase which other essays also invoke, the " 'catholic' tradition"?

The final essay, on "mission," introduced a term, *integrity*, which could have run through all four treatments. *Integrity* is defined in terms of identity and response, when "outer actions and responses reflect the truth of inner lives," and thus action is consistent with identity. Having said that, Dr. Bergquist goes on to deal with the inner being of the church to which its outer actions and responses in witness and service must correspond. The Advisory Committee welcomes the way in which church identity was kept to the fore and how (in a churchly, pastoral way) great themes in Lutheran theology (like grace and law) come alive, all the while there being no diminution of how great the changes are and how prominent the new emphases on liberation. The broad, balanced outline of the argument is anchored in the specifics of mission praxis in the United States and throughout the world. The attention to biblical symbols was particularly applauded.

However, it must be acknowledged that even the use of the Epistle to the Galatians in its missionary setting to illustrate "the contextualization debate" today is not without its problems. For one thing, much as Lutherans resonate to that Epistle as the place "for Paul's working out of justification . . . within the missionary situation of the early church," one must be conscious of the fact that justification was not Paul's only way of enunciating the Gospel, and of the charge that in Galatians "justification" is brought front and center by local conditions in a way which is not true in other letters.[15] One must ask what the study in contextualization would be like if 1 and 2 Corinthians were the documents studied. Even in Galatia, were the problems caused solely by "Jewish-Christian opponents of the Gentile mission," or were Jews involved, or "over-converted Gentiles" who took Paul's sacred books (the Hebrew Scriptures) differently than he? Indeed, some suspect, Paul was fighting on *two* fronts: against "Judaizers" (legalists) but also against "Gnosticizers" (antinomians). Paul's troubles in Galatia may have come from opponents from "headquarters" in Jerusalem, or also from those in Galatia with their own religious-cultural heritage.

To what extent was syncretism involved? Agreed (Dr. Bergquist's two chief points, p. 228), the gospel must cross cultural frontiers, but also freedom *in Christ* will set limits for contextualization. The New Testament experiences in Galatia and elsewhere thus set patterns for coming to identity, but leave many questions unanswered with which we today still wrestle, as to when and where the limits are.

With all four essays in view, question must also be raised—as the Advisory Committee did—about how they fit together. Overall, it was judged, there is complementarity: one is stronger on Lutheran tradition, another on setting in the world today. The order in which the essays are arranged reflects a judgment by the committee as to how they balance each other. Nonetheless, there are remarks in passing and salient trends in one essay which do not fit easily with the others. For instance, the advice that Christians respond to the world today with "waiting, prayer, and realism" (Ellul, p. 240) is out of line with the emphasis on action elsewhere, unless one uses it to underscore Dr. Bergquist's point that liberation must begin with *us* and God's grace precedes our activity. There is, more seriously, a difference of opinion over the role of liberation theology. Those dealing with human identity and mission plainly approve it in one form or another. The essay on ecology, some felt, too cavalierly rejects it (p. 52) or, more accurately, makes it *one* emphasis alongside "development" which American Christians need. The LCA case study while not taking up liberation directly, could give the impression that, for all alleged "openness," the "middle-class outlook" precludes much involvement here.

At two places discussion within the Advisory Committee was most intense, as it is likely to be by those who study these essays—on process theology as a tool, and on the type of analysis of the LCA in the case study.

Process theology seems not to leave many people neutral. While Dr. Snook recommends it merely as "an *alternative* way of *thinking* about reality," his put-down, seemingly, of all classical theology, especially biblical, is too easy. Further, all other options are ignored. Liberation theologians are particularly stung by rejection of their interests in favor of process, which they regard as "an academic argument about the possibility of transcendence when . . . the proper starting point . . . ought to be the realities of poverty and oppression."[16]

What is right about it is the attempt of process to come to terms with modern ways of thinking and the general view of reality today, especially in the sciences. The alternative being rejected is really the Aristotelian world view and metaphysics. Lutherans have scarcely had great affection for Aristotelianism and have little reason to defend it. Biblical theologians are put on the spot by the fact that they usually operate without any metaphysics whatsoever, and recognize, generally, that the biblical view of the world and God, which their documents assume, does not comport much with the view of reality with which they themselves and our contemporaries operate. In recent years many biblical scholars have found it congenial to follow the Bultmannian route of laying the christological kerygma in the bed of (early) Heidegerian existentialism, so as to make the gospel "meaningful for me." If the Bultmann School was trying to state the gospel existentially, *pro me*, with a borrowed philosophy, the process school can claim it is seeking to restate the gospel, or as much of the Bible and Christian tradition as is compatible, cosmologically within the framework of a philosophy borrowed from Whitehead and modern sciences and mathematics. As some biblical scholars have been doing, it is worth the attempt to explore the degree to which the "tradition-history" approach and "trajectories" so prominent in contemporary New Testament studies have "process" written all over them as they trace the development of biblical passages (and often thereby relativize them). To this extent it can be argued process is a current option, some would say *the* one, beginning to do in our day what Aquinas did with Aristotle's philosophy in the Middle Ages.

At the same time, this process approach raises all sorts of questions about its implications. In addition to those already noted, the questions of "beginnings" and "endings" (protology and eschatology) loom large. The relation of God to world is seemingly reversed in process from what the Bible says. And when, with apparent approval, the idea is quoted (p. 72) of "the world as 'the body of God,'" we are back with a position which New Testament Christianity seemingly rejected. For there are exegetes who feel the original reference intended in Colossians 1:18a to "the body" was to the world. Stoicism knew of the cosmos as "the body of Zeus." It is likely that Christians, in doxologically singing of Christ's role in creation, made him not only "firstborn of all creation" but also "the head of the body," the world. It is the position of these exegetes that the author of Colossians corrected this idea, where it occurred in an early Christian hymn, by approximating it to the Pauline view that "the body of Christ" is the church, not the world. That is how the passage now reads. Ironically, this verse and the view implied about the world and revelation played a part in U.S. discussion for the 1970 LWF Assembly.[17] Process raises it again. Is the world, or the church, Christ's body? Do God and world so relate that the latter is his body? Does the Creator stand over against the world, or infuse the world and evolve with it?

A specific problem is how process theology treats the resurrection and life after death. Dr. Snook's approach we need not guess at, for an article of his appeared in 1976 in an issue of *Dialog* dedicated to "Life Beyond Death," and it stirred up no small controversy.[18] Claimed Snook: "Christian hope does not require us to believe in 'life after death' as that is generally construed in ordinary speech," at least for individuals, but rather in "God's faithfulness and everlastingness," in light of which we minister to those who are dying or who survive. As in the essay in this volume, there is an onslaught against biblical theology, against the sharp contrast Oscar Cullmann made in 1955 between the Greek idea of immortality and the biblical one of resurrection. Again Barr and Gilkey are enlisted to prove the demise of biblical theology. The church fathers are invoked to show that both immortality and resurrection were considered distinctly Christian, but what both express is a Christian hope which must be squared with a view of reality. In contrast to "a theistic world view," the "different tack" of process is proposed. The upshot is an argument "against eternal life conceived individually"—it is sin and idolatry to want to be like God. Christian hope here should point us "to the One who alone lives," but "not to another life" for us. In this way a process view, where individuals die, having presumably made their contributions to the kingdom, is said to be "a radical theology of the cross" applied to us and our pretensions.

The columns of *Dialog* were filled with vigorous responses for the next two issues. Under the heading "Contra Process Eschatology," George Forrell chalked up to "theological menopause" this "brazen attempt to make . . . personal debility normative for the entire Christian movement"; Leigh Jordahl found process theology so dominated the gospel in the article that the final position "is simply incompatible with the faith of the Christian tradition"; and in a longer analysis,

James H. Burtness, a colleague of Dr. Snook at Luther Seminary and a member of the Advisory Committee for our study on ecclesiology, opposed a way of thinking which makes Whitehead's metaphysics normative, over the Bible as final norm.[19] Yet an issue later one pastor protested these attacks, and Philip Hefner spoke a word in favor of Lee Snook as "one of a breed that is attempting to speak Lutheran theology in a new tongue" that "calls into question the old categories."[20] Hefner endorsed Snook's analysis of "the current theological situation" and urged him to offer more detailed explanations of controverted points. His own guess is that we have here "a 'Christology of exemplification,' namely, that Jesus Christ is not unique, but that he is the exemplification of all that God is about and is in this sense revelation, redemption, etc."; to which it is added, in process-thought style, "no single event of history is in any sense one of finality," of course, for "every act shares in a very real power and love of God." At this point we are back to the issue of whether process can preserve that uniqueness and definitiveness of Jesus Christ which historical Christianity has claimed. Or is every man "a Christ" and revelation of God?

The type of analysis in the case study of the LCA is the other main area of discussion which these essays are likely to stir up. Allusion has already been made to the debate over the Hefner-Benne volume, *Defining America*.[21] Reference to the present essay as "Defining the LCA —from Illinois" suggests a parallel in approach which some see. The volume on the U.S.A. finds a linkage (*not* identification) of American "civil religion" and Christian faith. While many deplore "Americanism" as a religious substitute, or dwell only on the "dark side" and failures of the American dream, Benne and Hefner celebrate this dream as "still the major opening to transcendence for most Americans and for the society as a whole" and call for "reformation of the civil religion" and its symbols as a concern of Christianity.[22] In this way the U.S. churches participate in "nation-building," just as churches do in Third-World countries. The ecclesiology essay, on the blending of the LCA with its middle-class environment, offers so obvious a parallel as to require no elaboration. But with all this could come a suspicion, especially on the part of Christians in other lands, that American Lutherans have embraced their cultural captivity. Dr. Hefner having made his own case in the book, articles, and this essay, let it simply be noted that other U.S. Lutherans, LCA-ones included, question alliances with civil religion, and see the gospel and confessional strength of Lutheranism at odds with much in the American dream (or illusion) or prefer the tension of the Two-Kingdoms doctrine between church and state. Indeed, civil religion with its covenants and trappings was severely criticized in the bicentennial study book on Christian Social Responsibility prepared for the 1976 LCA convention.[23]

Whether one agrees with the analysis and prognostication about the LCA by Dr. Hefner or not, the ultimate question is whether this is a proper way of doing "ecclesiology." That is the matter surely stirred up by the approach developed by the Geneva Department of Studies of LWF in the last seven years.

WHICH WAY ECCLESIOLOGY?

These pages have sought constantly to explain the interdisciplinary, international, but regional and local approach to ecclesiology developed by the LWF since the shakeup of its Department of Theology in 1970. Has the new methodology worked?

Dr. Ulrich Duchrow, in his report as director of the Studies program, in November, 1976, hailed the self-studies in over forty churches for their extent, depth, and mastery of new materials and methods, yoking theology with other areas of life and study. Commission Chairman Karl Hertz pointed to rapid change in the member churches, "the understanding of what God has done for us," and a "vision of the church as one, holy, catholic, and apostolic" as impelling forces, and "more mature, more committed, more competent" churches with increased awareness of responsibilities, as a result.

In the report Director Duchrow lashed out at attempts to "repress questions concerning the future that had been raised in the 1960s . . . or to treat them in a rhetorical way only." He saw parallels between the way rich Western countries dominate the rest of the world economically and the way rich Northern churches try to dominate theologically. Some specific recommendations growing out of the studies have already been noted (pp. 9–10). The goal has been to "help the churches in their reflections on their life and work in the midst of the complex socio-political, economic changes of these years, to help the churches in ways by which they may come to know more fully who they are and to do their work with greater competence and maturity." Is this "ecclesiology"?

The undertaking here described has not been without its costs, not merely in time and budget but in suspicions that "theology proper" has been set aside. Duchrow's final report in 1976 admitted the Studies Department had come under heavy criticism, heavier than for any other LWF Commission, in the past six years, particularly through "the call for more 'classical theology,'" raised, he said, exclusively "by some European theologians and church leaders."[24] His own answer was that "the LWF as a *world* federation should offer passionate resistance, if the call for more classical theology were to go hand in hand with a call for returning to the predominance of Western and, in particular, European theology. Today, universal theology cannot be done merely on a European basis but only through a common listening by all traditions to the word of God in history and the present."

It will remain for the next Assembly and new staff to set future directions. Likely the broader way of working since 1970 will continue, but with more emphasis on theology per se and concerns neglected in the last six years. Clearly the approach practiced by Geneva since 1970 is receiving endorsement in many quarters—for example the conference on liberation theology in Detroit in 1975[25] and the "ecumenical encounter of Third-World theologians" in Dar es Salaam in August, 1976.[26] Just as in other disciplines, so in theology, new times evoke new methodologies.[27] Yet the interdisciplinary approach, or an emphasis on sociology or economics, may not be any less "Western" or "Northern" than the theological ideology they seek to replace. Indeed, one suspects that "classical theology" may flourish in many Third-World churches, with their great loyalty to Scripture, and they may regard the new interdisciplinary "worldly" approach as another Western (Northern) imposition, from a tired theology which has lost its heart and will to believe.

What surely all desire is splendidly encapsuled in a phrase by Kosuke Koyama, the Japanese theologian who has been a missionary in Thailand and a theological educator in Singapore: "theology *in contact*," in contact with the world and life and reality, and therefore affected by where it is spoken and done.[28] This is the choice, rather than "theology intact," which is delivered in toto "as is," whether spoken in Geneva, Rome, Canterbury, or even Jerusalem and then supposedly delivered intact to audiences everywhere. Contact with environment does not mean "syncretism," as if the Apostles' Creed could be merged with the Four Noble Truths of Buddhism, so as to say, "We believe . . . 'in Jesus Christ, the Buddha, that is, the Enlightened One, Only Son our Lord, . . . was crucified; thus he completed the Noble Truth of the fading away and extinction of all kinds of cravings. The third day he rose again as the Detached One. . . .' "[29]

Rather it means "accommodation" (*synkatabasis*, condescension, in the etymological sense), coming down to terms with the situation at its level and needs, as when God came down to us, incarnate in Christ, or when the church forsakes any supposed superiority in order to serve in love. It may involve even the way we translate Scripture, Koyama suggests, as in the Thai version of John 1:1, "In the beginning was *tamma'* (*dharma*) . . . ," that verse which describes how God "experiences history."[30] Or it means people being open to change, or an institution actually changing to meet new needs. In any case, theologians can't provide a book of convenient answers, like the Singapore Telephone Directory. "The word of God cannot be put in the form of a telephone directory. It is living. It is moving. It is speaking. We must find out what the commandment says to *our own situation*."[31]

Ecclesiology—in contact—with where we are, and whither we and God's world are moving.

Few will agree with every analysis or prescription given in the pages above. Yet all will appreciate afresh the problems in gaining identity as the church of Jesus Christ in today's world, amid the insistent questions addressed to us by the ecological crisis, the woman's movement, our American scene, and the changing mission task, to say nothing of minorities' demands and the experience of our fellow-Christians in other churches: are we willing to take these critiques seriously enough to change—ourselves and our institutions? to let a reformation into what our church has been? to be open to new things under God?

"The church is aptly compared with a boat," notes Bishop Helmut Frenz, Lutheran pastor in Chile until his expulsion by the Pinochet government. "When we join the church, we go aboard a boat where Christ is already present and in command. His will is to move the boat away from the shore, out to the turbulent sea. But we are afraid to cast off the moorings that hold us in the safe harbor of our well-established and prosperous society. The church accumulates so much capital, so many privileges, so many special interests that it almost ceases to be the Church of Christ."[32]   But it's always easier to see that in Chile than in our own country.   To all of us, the question is, Are we willing to "launch out into the deep"?   That would be revolutionary.

Revolutionary involvement comes hard for modern-day Americans, even in a bicentennial period.   It seems, traditionally, to some almost "un-Christian."   Hence one reads with surprise, as I did, many of the documents from the 1760s and '70s on display in 1976 at the Historical Society of Pennsylvania during an exhibit entitled "A Rising People: The Founding of the United States, 1765–1789."   From the time of the Stamp Act on, those early Americans made their appeal for liberation with the use of a host of Bible passages and through overtones of biblical symbols.   "For freedom Christ has set us free" (Gal. 5:1) was a text invoked frequently, in the manner of the most ardent liberation theologies today.   The serpent in Genesis 3 was readily identified with King George III and oppression, in a manner some of the most fervent liberationists of today might not use and which many church people would find alarming.   Change is part of a forgotten heritage for Americans, nationally.   And ecclesiologically, *semper reformanda!*

One does not conclude a book on ecclesiology with a peroration. God's people and his church are always emerging—from Acts chapter 2 onwards, in Luther's day, in 1977, and beyond.   Even though there is good reason for seeing a special identity crisis today, the church has been and ever will be in a process of change and developing—yesterday, today, and on into God's future.   Hence there is no final summary or everlasting directive, except the gospel.   As Christopher Evans once wrote, "Eloquent perorations are reserved either for those who believe optimistically that they have the answers, or for those who believe cynically that there are no answers to have; perorations are debarred to those for whom God's act is the last word."[33]

Christians can only ask for God's guidance, correction, and blessing— for his world and for the fellowship of which they are a part, the church emerging. . . .

NOTES

1. Even more succinctly in the Latin form: "For the true unity of the church it is enough to agree concerning the teaching of the gospel and the administration of the sacraments."

2. Adopted by the United Lutheran Church in convention at Washington, D.C., in 1920. Reprinted in Richard C. Wolf, ed., *Documents of Lutheran Unity in America* (Philadelphia: Fortress, 1966), pp. 348–49. The statement on which it rests, "The Essentials of the Catholic Spirit in the Church" (Wolf, *Documents,* pp. 293–312), was drafted in 1919 by the President of the then recently formed ULCA, Frederick H. Knubel, and Professor C. M. Jacobs, of the Philadelphia Seminary; it phrases the fourth attribute (five in the list above), "By the creation of an organization for these purposes" (*Documents,* pp. 303–5). To be precise, only "Word and sacraments' are called "marks of the church"; the rest are "attributes." The "Knubel—Jacobs statement" was created because ULCA leaders felt the position in the "Chicago Theses" of 1919 (by representatives of a number of bodies in the National Lutheran Council; *Documents,* pp. 298–301) "was not sufficiently dynamic." The ULCA was a predecessor body of the LCA, and all the documents in question were concerned with the formation of the "National Lutheran Council," a predecessor to the USA National Committee of LWF.

3. *The Birth of the New Testament* (Black's/Harper's New Testament Commentaries, Companion Volume 1; New York: Harper & Row, 1962), especially Chapter III.

4. Ibid., p. 36.

5. See especially S. G. F. Brandon, *The Fall of Jerusalem and the Christian Church* (London: SPCK, 1951).

6. Moule, *Birth,* pp. 44 and 159; there is little evidence Christianity in this period attracted many of the affluent, nor did it reach "the lowest of the low," such as slaves in labor gangs on estates or in the mines. That New Testament Christianity was more "middle class" that we often suppose, ought to be explored.

7. *From Here to Where? Technology, faith and the future of man: Report on an exploratory conference, Geneva, June 28–July 4, 1970,* ed. David M. Gill (Geneva: World Council of Churches, 1970), p. 26, as quoted by Kosuke Koyama, *Theology in Contact: Six reflections on God's Word and man's life in God's World,* "The Word for the World Series No. 4" (Madras: Christian Literature Society, 1975), p. 83. He scores other developed countries too, including his native Japan. Four million inhabitants of Norway are said to be using more natural resources than 40 million people in developing countries of the world.

8. See above, p. 178.

9. The interpretation of biblical motifs is always subject to exegetical debates. Thus the position espoused above on creation and redemption in the Old Testament and New is the one thing in the essay cited in notes 34–36 which is *not* found convincing by Norman Young in his recent book, *Creator, Creation and Faith* (London: Collins, 1976). In any case, it is not so much that creation passages like Acts 14:15–17 or 17:22–31 reflect "an alternative tradition in which creation *not* salvation may lie at the heart of the missionary appeal reported by Luke" (note 36, italics added) as that they represent the Old Testament assertions about God as Creator being added to supplement the christological kerygma and in some situations being made the starting point for proclamation about Jesus and salvation; cf. Reumann, "Creatio . . .," *The Gospel as History,* pp. 82, 91.

10. See above, pp. 1–27.

11. See above, pp. 1–26 & 27.

12. While the verse is usually rendered "they worshiped; but some doubted," the text indicates no other persons to be present besides the eleven disciples (v. 16). Nor is there any suggestion that two, four, or five of the eleven worshipers doubted. The phrase conventionally translated "*some* doubted" can just as well mean "they (who worshiped) doubted," an interpretation which fits well with

Matthew's designation of disciples as "little faiths" (6:30, 8:26, 14:31, 16:8). Cf. Benjamin Jerome Hubbard, *The Matthean Redaction of a Primitive Apostolic Commissioning: An Exegesis of Matthew 28:16–20*, SBL Dissertation Series, 19 (Missoula, Montana: SBL & Scholars' Press, 1974), pp. 75–77.

13. At this point one senses we are back in the debate in the literature for the 1970 LWF Assembly on "The Lordship of Christ and the Quest for true humanity," save that now the question of "true humanity" *for women* has come to the fore.

14. See p. 000, note 4. Would the later volume by E. Clifford Nelson et al, *The Lutherans in North America* (Philadelphia: Fortress, 1975), have given any different slant?

15. Albert Schweitzer called justification "a subsidiary crater" alongside the "mystical relationship 'in Christ' "—an extreme view. Justification is Paul's central theme in Romans as well as in Galatians, but not equally, everywhere else, or his only theme in the rest of the epistles. Cf. J. Reumann and William Lazareth, *Righteousness and Society: Ecumenical Dialog in a Revoluitonary Age* (Philadelphia: Fortress, 1967), pp. 36–55, especially 40.

16. See above, p. 000, note 11, citing F. Herzog.

17. *Christ and Humanity*, pp. 87–109.

18. Lee E. Snook, "Death and Hope—An Essay in Process Theology," *Dialog* 15, no. 2 (Spring 1976):123–30.

19. *Dialog* 15, no. 3 (Summer 1976):214–17.

20. *Dialog* 15, no. 4 (Autumn 1976), Mark C. Thompson, "Contra the Statements: 'Contra Process Eschatology,' " pp. 305–6, and (Hefner), 303–5, cf. 246.

21. Cf. above, p. 000.

22. Robert Benne and Philip Hefner, "The Challenge of American Religion," *Currents in Theology and Mission* 3, no. 4 (August, 1976), p. 208.

23. *Equality and Justice for All: Christian Calling in an Age of Interdependence* (New York: LCA Division for Mission in North America, 1976), especially pp. 25–34. The booklet was prepared by the LCA's Consulting Committee on the Bicentenary of the United States, but it is not an official statement of the LCA or DMNA. Hefner's downgrading of the Two-Kingdoms theme is also at odds with the emphasis put on it in the writings of Ulrich Duchrow and much of the approach of the Studies Department in Geneva in recent years (cf. above, Introduction, note 10).

24. The reference is, in part, to an article in a German church paper by Dr. Kurt Schmidt-Clausen, a former general-secretary of LWF, who deplored the lack of emphasis on biblical and theological work, stewardship, religious education, and worship. The sentiment is not exclusively German but would be shared by many in the U.S.A.

25. Compare Sergio Torres and John Eagleson, eds., *Theology in the Americas* (Marynoll, N.Y.: Orbis Books, 1976). "The dominant task . . . was to raise the question of a fresh theology from our U.S. experience."

26. The twenty-two Protestant, Roman Catholic, and Orthodox theologians agreed that economic, political, cultural, racial, and religious realities of each country should be the starting point for theological reflection.

27. Is there an analogy in historical studies over the last century and a half? Just as the nineteenth century von Ranke brought about a revolution in the study of history (leading to the aim of discovering *wie es eigentlich gewesen*, history "as it actually was," instead of demanding that historians also play the role of philosopher or judge), so, in the opinion of some, Fernand Braudel has introduced a new way of doing history in his two-volume study published in 1949, Eng.

trans. by Siân Reynolds, *The Mediterranean and the Mediterranean World in the Age of Philip II* (New York: Harper & Row, 1972–73). Braudel's endless files of data on climate, landscape, diet, trade, finance, and daily life among the common people yield treatments on environment, "collective destinies and general trends," and "events, politics and people," or as he terms it, "man in his relationship to the environment," "social history," and the "history of individual men." His account of the Mediterranean world in the second half of the sixteenth century thus developed from a conventional dissertation in diplomatic history (the Mediterranean policy of Philip II) into a "history of the sea" in its full context and with amplifications which stretch across most of the world. The second edition (1966) was revised to give further attention to connections with northern Europe and new sources which begin to make possible a glimpse of the Turkish world from inside the Ottomen empire. Similarly, the LWF ecclesiology study, while not overlooking traditional components in the history and doctrine of the church, has opened itself to seemingly irrelevant studies of economic-social development in Tanzania, the place of women in India or Ethiopia, the relation of the church to society and culture in Sweden and Indonesia, the political impact of events in China and Chile, and attention to broad trends in the U.S.A., so as to arrive, via the "new ecclesiology" and broadened methodologies, at a fuller understanding of the church and its identity.

28. *Theology in Contact,* pp. v, 63–64. Cf. also Koyama's earlier volume, *Water-Buffalo Theology* (Marynoll, N.Y.: Orbis Books, 1974).

29. Ibid., p. 55.

30. Ibid., p. 60: *"tamma'* in Buddhist Thailand is as rich as *logos* in the Hellenistic world of the New Testament times."

31. Ibid., p. 83.

32. As quoted in *World Dateline,* Nov., 1976, (no. 2), p. 4, a supplement to *World Encounter,* the magazine of the LCA Division for World Mission and Ecumenism.

33. C. F. Evans, "I will Go Before You into Galilee," *Journal of Theological Studies,* n.s. 5 (1954):17–18, as cited in *What About the New Testament? Essays in Honour of Christopher Evans,* ed. Morna Hooker and Colin Hickling (London: SCM, 1975), p. vii. In the same festschrift volume, Sophie Laws, "Can Apocalyptic be Relevant?", pp. 90–91, sums up an article by Carl Braaten, "The Significance of Apocalypticism for Systematic Theology," *Interpretation* 25 (1971):480–99, as follows: "Its dualism . . . may provide support for a real theology of liberation . . . and for a hope of freedom expanded to cosmic dimensions. Its vision of a new heaven and earth may awaken a much-needed theology of nature in the present ecological crisis; its picture of world history moving forward into the future may revive the ideal of mission. . . ." Apocalyptic is thus made to relate to a remarkable number of themes touched upon in this volume of essays. But note also Ms. Laws's critique, pp. 92–93.